Who Killed Albus Dumbledore?

**What really happened in HARRY POTTER
AND THE HALF-BLOOD PRINCE?**

**Six expert Harry Potter detectives
examine the evidence**

John Granger, editor

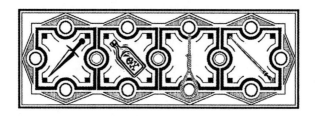

WHO KILLED ALBUS DUMBLEDORE?
Copyright © 2006 Zossima Press
Wayne, Pensylvania

Zossima Press titles may be purchased for business or promotional use or special sales.

Cover illustration and design by Red Hen Productions

ISBN 0-9723221-1-6
Printed in the United States of America

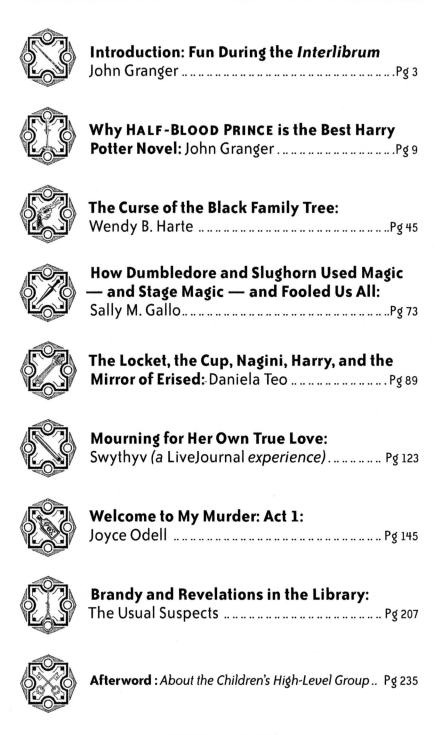

Introduction: Fun During the *Interlibrum*

A FAVORITE WORD that I rarely see outside of histories of the English civil war or of the Papacy is *interregnum*. It means literally "between kingdom" and is used to describe a time period between two rules of government. The most famous *interregnum* was the decade plus in the seventeenth century between the decapitation of Charles I in England and the restoration of Charles II.

I'd like to coin a new word to describe the months we're living in between the publication of HARRY POTTER AND THE HALF-BLOOD PRINCE, the sixth book in the series of HARRY POTTER novels, and the release of the seventh and final book, the title of which at this writing has not been made known. The word I'm hoping will catch on is *interlibrum*, meaning 'the time period between books,' a curious and fascinating time with qualities all its own.

The *interlibrum* we're enduring now, for example, while we await the arrival of the ultimate novel in the series, is a time of both suspended activity and frantic speculation. The universities are offering courses that include HARRY POTTER in the curriculum but the dons in the ivory tower have not yet started writing dissertations on its meaning (except for several essay collections dissecting the Potter-mania phenomenon as a "culture studies" lab specimen). They are waiting on the last word before publishing their insights lest the last book reveal their folly.

In the maelstrom of Fandom, however, the literally millions of readers who have read the six books repeatedly and are personally invested in the stories, the *interlibrum* is anything but the refreshing pause before the frenzied analysis that will follow publication of the last book. Fandom has never been more alive and fascinating a place to visit than it is now.

Because, for the most part, Fandom is not about analysis and interpretation of the finished novel. The concerns of these thousands of intelligent writers with a border-line memorized grasp of HARRY POTTER who post on the thousands of HARRY POTTER web sites, forums, and Live Journals is in discerning what will happen or what happened beneath the surface story of HALF-BLOOD PRINCE. To a remarkable degree, the name of the game in this cultural hot-spot is speculation and revelation. "What *really* happened in HALF-BLOOD PRINCE?" "What will happen in the last book? Will Harry die?"

These aren't just the concerns of a bizarre ghetto of American young men and women with too much time on their hands. When Ms. Rowling, the author of these books, gives her bi-monthly interview (timed no doubt to keep interest alive and white hot during the *interlibrum*), it is front page news in daily newspapers everywhere and something worthy of mention on the Nightly News teevee broadcasts.

She "let slip" (ho!) in a June, 2006, interview that she had "given a reprieve" to a character she thought would die, but that two other characters had not been so lucky. As a so-called "HARRY POTTER expert" ("as seen on CNN!"), my e-mail box was filled with questions from media the next day with requests for interviews and the conversation threads on my private boards for lit geeks at www.HogwartsProfessor.com pretty much shut down until everyone had had their say about who would live and die.

Fandom is not teenagers and life-deprived adolescents in their forties. HARRY POTTER EDUCATION FANON, INC. (HPEF) sponsors academic and fan gatherings every year in the US and UK. Exhaustive resources exist on the Internet for serious and casual readers alike; if you don't believe me, search for the HARRY POTTER LEXICON, MADAME SCOOP'S INDEX to J. K. Rowling's interviews, and the QUICK-QUOTE-QUILL that also has every interview she has given to newspapers, magazines, radio, and television.

THE LEAKY CAULDRON and MUGGLENET publish daily news updates on all things POTTER, especially the movies, with forums and essay pages for readers to peruse and correct at their leisure with halo box responses. Not to mention the whole worlds of speculation and fan fiction to be found at HARRY POTTER FOR GROWN-UPS, HARRY POTTER FOR SEEKERS, and the thousands of HARRY POTTER "Live Journal" sites and semi-private and public discussion boards.

The collection you are holding is a grab-bag of unique voices with engaging insights into the POTTER books and, specifically, about what we missed in HALF-BLOOD PRINCE. Let me tell you how it came into being and what delights are in the pages that follow.

I guess you should know right off that, if I am a BNF ("Big Name Fandom-er"), it is not because I spend a lot of time speculating about the outcome of the HARRY POTTER novels online. I don't have a reputation to speak of on Fandom web sites because of my ability to guess the answer to the pressing questions, "what happened that I missed in HALF-BLOOD PRINCE?" and "what has to happen?"

The reason I am a HPEF certified "HARRY POTTER expert" is that four years ago I tried to answer a very different question in a common sense fashion which had unforeseen results. The question that holds my interest is "Why are these books both so popular and so controversial?" My consistent approach has been to read the books as books rather than as a culture-war touchstone or as an artifact of popular culture akin to advertising and iPods.

The unforeseen consequence of this approach was the revelation that Ms. Rowling was writing edifying Christian fiction in the tradition of English literature, an almost exclusively Christian tradition. My book, HIDDEN KEY TO HARRY POTTER (Zossima

Press, 2003; much revised and reissued by Tyndale House in 2005 as LOOKING FOR GOD IN HARRY POTTER), argued that the symbols, structures, and themes of these novels were all uniformly and thoroughly traditional Christian story telling elements.

This threw a wet blanket on the culture warrior movement that had branded the books as "dangerous" and "contrary to scripture" because of their positive portrayal of magic. The incantational magic of the POTTER books, when looked at from the perspective of historical usage *and* theology, turn out to be anything but "dangerous," as the declining numbers of occult groups despite HARRY'S universal popularity seems to support.

Anyway, the reason I'm the *last* person you'd think would be editing a collection of Fandom speculation is because I don't have a dog in this fight. My interest, by and large, is about the conventional academic interpretation game, not with figuring out where the stories are headed.

On the other hand, I *am* as curious as the next serious HARRY POTTER reader, of course, about the plot subtleties I may have missed and how the stories will end. Though, as a rule I avoid Fandom sites, I have included in every book or article I've written or talk I've given about the literary elements of these books a few predictions about the endgame. If my interpretation is good, I figure, it should reveal patterns about what is coming. And I've had a few big hits that these patterns pointed to (Ron-Hermione as a couple and Dumbledore's death, for example, were guesses I made because of traditional literary alchemy that Ms. Rowling uses).

I have a side interest in speculation, then, and have gained quite a few friends from the speculative side of things who have a like interest in interpretations from the literature side of things. Maline Freden, a very popular essayist at MuggleNet.com (THE NORTH TOWER), championed literary alchemy on one of her posts — and she referred me to Joyce Odell's collection of speculative essays at Red Hen Publications.com. Ms. Odell and I began corresponding to compare reflections from our different sides of the fence. She dropped in regularly at my private boards to share her insights.

The Red Hen is a cartographer/graphics designer with the City of Los Angeles and her not-so-private joy is designing books. When she shared with me some of her favorite Fandom postings, the thought occurred to me, "If I'm enjoying reading these speculative essays *this* much, why not make a book out of them?" Ms. Odell agreed to do the designing and to contribute one of her best postings from the Red Hen collection — and the rest, as they say, is history.

What you are holding is a *representative* collection of various types of speculation from a broad cross section of HARRY POTTER web sites and Live Journals, expanded and edited for this edition. It isn't an *exhaustive* collection, by any means, with respect to topic, genre, or original location but what is represented here is both challenging and edifying to the serious reader engaged in speculation about the ending of the world's best selling books.

My contribution, for example, 'Why HALF-BLOOD PRINCE is the Best HARRY POTTER Novel,' is an *interpretative* effort that explains the key concept of "narrative misdirection" with a few speculative ideas as illustrations (which later articles expose as half-baked theories). It was adapted from posts I made at my HALF-BLOOD PRINCE class at Barnes and Noble University.com in July and August, 2005.

Sally Gallo's essay that originally appeared in THE LEAKY CAULDRON's 'Scribbulus' forum in December, 2005, is speculation based on her *historical* researches into stage magic and on characters in the novels based on these real world magicians, Horace Goldin and the Great Albini. It may seem dated now (how appropriate for a history paper!) because of Ms. Rowling's revelation at Radio City Music Hall that Dumbledore is definitely dead, but if Dumbledore died before the Astronomy Tower melodrama, Ms. Gallo will be remembered as a prophet.

In addition to the historical and interpretative, you will also find here a printed version of what a dynamic 'Live Journal' internet posting is like, especially when thoughtful people disagree online. Swythyv's qwirky voice and keen insights consequent to her remarkable grasp of canon will make you scratch your head as you ponder what at first seems a perfectly impossible plot twist.

Dr. Daniela Teo from MuggleNet's TWO WAY MIRROR and LJ maven "Professor Mum" Wendy B. Harte have expanded several of their posts to show us what quality backstory detective work looks like. If you're like me, their insights about Horcruxes will make you re-examine your list of favorite objects for Harry to locate and disarm (ouch — "disarm" is an unfortunate choice of words for Horcrux defusing).

And the anchor and jewel of the set is the Red Hen's "Welcome to My Murder: Act 1," a classic in the Fandom genre of logical and deductive work both because of its comprehensiveness and its implicit challenge to readers to do better. No one reading the Red Hen's take on the Astronomy Tower scenes and the Severus/Albus back story will ever think about the books the same way again.

Along the way, you'll learn about:

☞ "Stoppered Death" or why Dumbledore trusts Snape without reservation;

☞ "Regulus Redux" or what motivated R.A.B. to do what he did, when he did, and why the Black family is Voldemort's bane;

☞ "Horace the Magnificent" or how Horace Slughorn pulled off the performance of his life on the Astronomy Tower;

☞ "Horcruxes Roulette" or why the Mirror of Erised is not a bad guess for a Voldemort Horcrux;

☞ "Tonks's Folly" or how the man the Metamorphmagus thought was a wolf turned out to be a rat; and

☞ "Dumbledore's Deadly Dinner-Theater" or how Dumbledore hijacked Malfoy's mission and used it to cast, star in, and direct his own murder.

And, at the end, just to show we're not cowards, we all turn from our speculations about what we missed in HALF-BLOOD PRINCE to go out on a limb on the tree in the Public Square to say what we think *must happen* (ho!) in the series finale.

Is this the best possible collection of speculation about what really happened in HALF-BLOOD PRINCE? No, I know it isn't. My best thoughts, for example, on what the books are about, the patterns of literary alchemy and postmodern realism, are in UNLOCKING HARRY POTTER: FIVE KEYS FOR THE SERIOUS READER (Zossima, 2006). The other writers here could say the same thing and, of course, there are sites and genres we could not represent in a single volume collection.

What we do have, though, is a coherent and exciting sample of some of the best voices and thinking going on in HARRY POTTER Fandom, gathered in one place for your delight and for you to try and refute or better during the remainder of the *interlibrum*.

I hope you enjoy this who-dunit themed speculative romp through the neglected part of HALF-BLOOD PRINCE even half as much as I enjoyed working with Joyce Odell, Sally Gallo, Wendy B. Harte, Dr. Teo, and Swythyv. Expanding and editing the articles, sending corrections well after Joyce had finished creating pdf files in the beautiful format she designed, and harping at each other playfully about our LJ posts and butcherous, barbarous predictions ("John, you cannot kill ALL the Weasleys…") has made this a blast.

I hope, too, that you will join in the fun after reading through our pooled ideas by writing me at john@Zossima·com with your comments and concerns, your shock and awe, and your corrections and criticisms. Feel free, too, to tell us what essays and articles you think we should have included. If the *interlibrum* continues longer than its expected two years (the anticipated 7/7/07 release date), we may put together another collection. Where, oh where, is the playful EVIL!Snape article we couldn't find?

Thank you again for joining us and thanks in advance for letting us know what you think when you're done.

Gratefully,

John Granger

John@Zossima·com
Editor, Zossima Press

John Granger

John Granger, a Latin and English teacher at Valley Forge Military Academy in Wayne, PA, is the author of THE HIDDEN KEY TO HARRY POTTER (Zossima Press, 2002) and LOOKING FOR GOD IN HARRY POTTER (Tyndale House, 2005). Granger has taught Harry Potter courses at Barnes and Noble University (BNU) online since 2004 to students around the world. He is a frequent guest on radio and television programs on which he speaks in defense of reading Ms. Rowling's books against culture warriors and Harry Haters who think the books are dangerous.

One of the leading authorities on the Harry Potter books as read in the context of English literature, his special interests are the postmodern qualities of the Potter novels and the traditional literary alchemy Ms. Rowling employs both as symbols and for thematic structure. His UNLOCKING HARRY POTTER: FIVE KEYS FOR THE SERIOUS READER (Zossima Press, 2006) demonstrates the importance of these two patterns in understanding the popularity of these novels and why both academics and "true believers" despise them.

Granger has taught Latin using HARRIUS POTTER ET PHILOSOPHI LAPIS (Bloomsbury, 2003) and is teaching a survey of Literature course using the Harry Potter novels, Austen's EMMA, Shakespeare's 'Romeo and Juliet,' and Swift's GULLIVER TRAVELS. His HARRY MEETS HAMLET AND SCROOGE his text for these classes will be published early in 2007. John's book on understanding great literature through reading Harry Potter plus a collection of his essays on the controversies and Christian content of the Harry Potter novels will be published in 2007.

Granger's speaking dates, book publications, and internet classes can all be tracked at his web site, www.Zossima.com. The following essay was taken from one of his BNU lectures online about the importance of narrative misdirection in understanding HALF-BLOOD PRINCE. We include it here to set the stage for the speculation in depth that follows about how deceived we were in PRINCE.

Why Half-Blood Prince is the Best Harry Potter Novel:

Stoppered Death, EVIL Slughorn, and What Really Happened

*S*INCE THE MIDNIGHT PUBLICATION of the sixth and penultimate Harry Potter novel, HARRY POTTER AND THE HALF-BLOOD PRINCE, I have received on average five e-mails of some length every day from readers asking me what I think of it. [Note to authors not wanting this kind of contact from thoughtful and not so thoughtful readers of their books: don't put your e-mail address in your book's introduction as I did.] I usually refer them to articles I've posted on the internet or pieces I've written in answer to questions at the Discussion Room I often lead at http://www.BarnesandNobleUniversity.com (which free class I urge them to join). If I am just asked if I liked the new book or not, I write to say that I think it is easily the best book of the series.

I don't recommend this answer to you, again, unless you want a Howler in response and more mail than you can answer if you didn't have a life or a job bigger than your MS Outlook in box. Most fans, indeed almost everyone I have spoken and corresponded with about HALF-BLOOD PRINCE likes the book. Almost no one considers it their favorite. Why not? They tell me it's one of the least satisfying books as a stand-alone novel, in effect that it feels like the preamble to part seven more than a book that can be loved on its own.

I think these readers have their answer right but to the wrong question. The reason HALF-BLOOD PRINCE is far and away the best book is the remarkable degree to which Ms. Rowling has succeeded in writing a stand alone novel that still invites us to the ultimate adventure to follow. Some appreciation of the challenges she has overcome masterfully with HALF-BLOOD PRINCE, I think, helps in understanding what a wonderful book this is. It also serves an excellent introduction to the essays of this collection, all of which focus on *what really happened* in HALF-BLOOD PRINCE

Ms. Rowling's writing is a "dull" story

In an interview given to a gaggle of teen reporters on the night after HALF-

BLOOD PRINCE was published, Ms. Rowling was asked what advice she would give to an aspiring writer. She responded, as she has many times to this question, that budding authors should read *everything* they can and that they should plan their work very carefully. She thinks planning is crucial:

> **Alexandra Le Couteur Williamson** for the SOUTH AUSTRALIAN ADVERTISER: *When you start do you do a complete plan before writing, or do you just have an idea from the start and then just keep writing?*
>
> **JK Rowling:** I do a plan. I plan, I really plan quite meticulously. I know some-times it is quite boring because when people say to me, "I write stories at school and what advice would you give me to make my stories better?" And I always say and people's face often fall when I say "You have to plan," and they say "Oh, I prefer just writing and seeing where it takes me." Sometimes writing and seeing where it takes you will lead you to some really good ideas but I would say nearly always it won't be as good as if you sat down first and thought, "Where do I want to go, what end am I working toward, what would be good, a good start." Sorry, very dull. [CBBC interview, pg. 7]

This is hardly the magical answer that her fans want but it points to an impor-tant point. Ms. Rowling is not a publishing miracle that has fallen *ex machina* in our midst. In many ways she is a conventional artisan of a craft. She plans her books in tremendous detail, so much so that she says she has boxes of notebooks filled with back-story for her sub-creation. Popular legend has it that she planned the seven story series for as many years before she finished writing the first novel.

Ms. Rowling, too, is conventional in her artistry in her adherence to a working formula and in her obedience to the "rules" or conventions of the various genres in which she works. Every Harry Potter novel, as I explain in detail in my book, LOOKING FOR GOD IN HARRY POTTER (Tyndale, 2004), adheres to the structures, plot formulas, themes, and symbols that she used in the previous years' adven-tures. She deepens and expands on the themes and is never mechanical in her "working a formula" so this repetition is almost invisible to her readers, but she is a "formula writer" nonetheless.

Ms. Rowling also obeys the "rules" much more carefully than do her youthful wizard friends. In her rambling interview with two fan web site representatives also the day after HALF-BLOOD PRINCE'S release, she mentions these rules specifically:

> [Having been asked if Dumbledore's death was inevitable:]
>
> **JKR:** Yeah, well, if you take a step back, in the genre of writing that I'm work-ing in, almost always the hero must go on alone. That's the way it is, we all

know that, so the question is when and how, isn't it, if you know anything about the construction of that kind of plot.

ES: *The wise old wizard with the beard always dies.*

JKR: Well, that's basically what I'm saying, yes. (MN/TLC 1, pg..5)

[In answer to a question about the romances in HALF-BLOOD PRINCE:]

JKR: There's a theory — this applies to detective novels, and then Harry, which is not really a detective novel, but it feels like one sometimes — that you should not have romantic intrigue in a detective book. Dorothy L. Sayers, who is queen of the genre, said — and then broke her own rule, but said — that there is no place for romance in a detective story except that it can be useful to camouflage other people's motives. That's true; it is a very useful trick. I've used that on Percy and I've used that to a degree on Tonks in this book, as a red herring. But having said that, I disagree inasmuch as mine are very character-driven books, and it's so important, therefore, that we see these characters fall in love, which is a necessary part of life. (MN/TLC 2, pg.. 13)

Ms. Rowling in these comments points to several important things to remember about her as a writer. She is aware of the rules of the various genres in which she writes and she obeys the rules as best as she can, given as the rules of one genre may conflict with others. She knows, too, that one of the peculiarities of her work is that she has been "rowling" various genres into one story, simultaneously and seamlessly. You'll have to forgive me here for using her name as a clue to her secret. I am writing a book to explain the various types of writing she includes in her Harry Potter novels and how each contributes to the story. She mentions fantasy, mystery, and romance fiction in these interviews — believe it or not, there are seven other genres in her winning recipe.

{An aside: though she denies that Harry is "really a detective novel, but it feels like one sometimes," Ms. Rowling mentions Tonks as one character she has used in the way Dorothy Sayers says a romantic character can be used in a mystery. Not much of a surprise there, if I am right in guessing that Tonks' surname is a tip of the hat to Ngaio Marsh, celebrated British writer of detective fiction, whose DEATH ON THE AIR features a character with this name.}

No less a writer than Stephen King, I'm told, has discussed Ms. Rowling as being principally a writer of detective fiction. While I disagree with this assessment if it is true, there's no denying that each year's mystery is part of the mix of genres — and a critical one. Professor Philip Nel of Kansas State University, in his talk "What makes a Professor Behave like Snape? Literature, Marketing, and the Critical Backlash against Harry Potter," says that Ms. Rowling's stories, in contrast with the historical narrative of the LORD OF THE RINGS, has its narrative drive from the detective story and mystery Harry, Ron, and Hermione are trying to solve each year. This is no small thing!

The Challenges of a "Next-to-Last" Book

If you want to know the rules of writing a great mystery, here are the "Ten Commandments" of detective fiction first written by Fr. Ronald Knox in 1928.

1. The criminal must be someone mentioned in the early part of the story, but must not be anyone whose thoughts the reader has been allowed to follow.

2. All supernatural or preternatural agencies are ruled out as a matter of course.

3. Not more than one secret room or passage is allowable.

4. No hitherto undiscovered poisons may be used, nor any appliance which will need a long scientific explanation at the end.

5. No Chinaman must figure in the story.

6. No accident must ever help the detective, nor must he ever have an unaccountable intuition which proves to be right.

7. The detective must not himself commit the crime.

8. The detective must not light on any clues which are not instantly produced for the inspection of the reader.

9. The stupid friend of the detective, the Watson, must not conceal any thoughts which pass through his mind; his intelligence must be slightly, but very slightly, below that of the average reader.

10. Twin brothers, and doubles generally, must not appear unless we have been duly prepared for them.

More expansive lists of these rules can be found on the Internet, if they are all, by and large, echoes of Fr. Knox's choices (excepting the rule against "Chinamen"). These "Ten Commandments" and all others can be reduced to two rules, of course, just like the real Ten Commandments.

The simple version is [1] be fair to the discerning readers by giving them all the clues they need to solve the mystery alongside the detective — but [2] be artful enough about these revelations that the mystery is not easily solved (i.e., keep it exciting to the last page). Detective fiction, like every other literary genre in the English tradition, is about "instructing while delighting" as Spencer put it, and the chief virtue of mysteries is their cultivating the virtue of "penetration" in their readers. Reading Sayers, Christie, or even a Nancy Drew story, the attentive reader is trying to solve the crime before Lord Peter, Miss Marple, or Nancy.

There is more than one challenge in writing a sixth novel in a seven novel series largely defined by several unsolved questions (e.g., Snape's allegiance, Harry's relationship to Lord Voldemort, etc.) that are not resolved in the mystery the heroes work out each year. The next-to-last book, if fair to the discerning reader, must reveal or at least suggest however obliquely the answers to the over-arching mystery while not "giving it away" by any means. No small trick while writing a novel that has to "stand on its own" as a mystery, romance, fantasy, satire, alchemical drama, hero journey, etc., etc.

The first challenge is that of any novel. It needs to be interesting in itself with drama, engagement with the story-line, and some changes in the main character that make the story's resolution meaningful to the reader who identifies (or refuses to identify) with the hero/anti-hero.

A novel in a series with a defined end, as the Harry Potter novels have at seven books, faces the extra challenge of advancing significantly the characters' qualities as they age (an important concern of Ms. Rowling she has said repeatedly) as well as the over-arching mysteries, story-lines, and themes of the series to maintain interest in the larger story's meaning and outcome. This becomes especially important — and difficult — in the next-to-last adventure in the series.

It is important because we're almost home — and, if we're playing by the rules, the clues have to be pretty much all on the table for the discerning readers to sift through. Anything less would be tantamount to learning Harry has a twin or Voldemort dated Aunt Petunia's mom halfway through the last book. Readers would find this both disappointing and cause for riot, I fear.

The difficulty, of course, is putting out all the clues but being sure in the display that none of the mysteries or "big questions" that we expect from experience in the previous books to discover only at the finale have been revealed prematurely. So, we want [1] a satisfying story that [2] gives us all the information we need to solve the mysteries we have struggled to solve or understand through the previous years' adventures but [3] a story that gives the necessary information in such a way that we cannot be sure one way or the other.

Quite a burden for one story!

If I have this right, then, HALF-BLOOD PRINCE is obliged to be a novel that is a good read in itself, that gives us plenty of clues about the ending, but which does not answer the major questions. How did she do?

Of course, I cannot tell if Ms. Rowling has given us all the clues we need until I've read the last book. My strong suspicion is that she has given us almost everything we needed to know because of her regard for the rules and because

HALF-BLOOD PRINCE was both a wonderful read and gave us no sure or undeniable answers to the larger questions.

HALF-BLOOD PRINCE standing alone: fun *and* no answers

Maybe you didn't enjoy the story as much as you should have because you were distracted by Dumbledore's death — and by your confusion about whether or not Snape killed him in obedience to instructions or because he is indeed as evil as Harry (and now everyone in the Wizarding world) believes. That distraction and confusion would be too bad, if very understandable, because HALF-BLOOD PRINCE is as good as any of the other novels standing alone.

The mystery-to-be-solved in PRINCE is about Draco's mission from Lord Voldemort and who is sending cursed objects and poisoned mead into Hogwarts castle. We also learn about the Horcruxes after Harry (and Felix) figure out how to relieve Professor Slughorn of the essential memory. The story features, too, the tortured stories of teen romance — will Ron and Hermione ever get together? Will Harry be able to choose between his "best mate" and, well, his "hoped-for mate"? The ending is a page from too many Shakespeare comedies and almost every Austen novel. Not to mention the action with the Inferi in the dark cavern lake and the climax on the Astronomy Tower! Really, this is a wonderful book with something for everyone...

But, hey, there really are not any hard and fast answers here to the questions you came in with (unless it was a 'shipping question...). We don't know the Voldemort-Harry connection any better than we did after HARRY POTTER AND THE ORDER OF THE PHOENIX (Lord Thingy is off-stage, in the present time at least, for all of HALF-BLOOD PRINCE). Snape seems to be a very bad guy under orders to the Dark Lord at story's end - but is he really? Believe me, drop into any chat-room of the several thousand Harry Potter fan sites on the Internet and you'll see how Snape's position as a Death Eater *and* as a "Dumbledore man, through and through" can be argued persuasively (and passionately). We also have no idea how Harry will be able to find and destroy four Horcruxes and if he will then be able to fulfill the Prophecy and vanquish Voldemort with "the power he knows not."

So, great story and one that protects the ultimate mysteries... What about the clues?

Clues and the Beginning of Doubt in the Narrative: Twenty Questions

Oh, yeah, we have plenty of clues. None, certainly, that are transparent or indisputable. If you doubt this, try, as I have, to float a theory about what has *really* happened in HALF-BLOOD PRINCE. What you will find, if your experience is like mine, is that serious readers will explain to you that you are wrong either by explaining how you have missed a critical piece of information ("Abigail Bones cannot be R.A.B. because her middle name is Jane; we learned that in PHOENIX") — which is humiliating — or by telling you how what you think is a clue is really explained very well, thank you, by the explanation in the narrative ("Slughorn is just a despicable climber; there's nothing necessarily evil about him"). Which last is really annoying. Ms. Rowling isn't giving us clues or information that can be understood like a red light at an intersection! Of course the clues are not obvious…

There are enough clues, however, to begin trying to answer the questions left unanswered about what Happened in HALF-BLOOD PRINCE by story's end. If you can answer most of these (or all of them!), you have a theory worth extending to the last book in the series. A theory able to cover all the bases is something like the elusive "Unified Field Theory" of physics in being a "Theory of Everything" or T.O.E. — "a means of tying together all known phenomena to explain" the Harry Potter saga and solve its open questions.

Here is my list of "Twenty Questions" left hanging at the end of HALF-BLOOD PRINCE. To give a demonstration of the rules that have to be followed for a T.O.E. to guess about the last book, I'll construct a sample T.O.E. from several theories about HALF-BLOOD PRINCE and what happened in that story below the radar of most readers (i.e., beneath the narrative story-line). This is a lot of fun for me, if I'd have a better chance of hitting the Lottery than of getting guesses correct. This, as you'll see in the questions, is a carefully guarded story ending! I hope my T.O.E will illustrate, however, both how many clues and red herrings Ms. Rowling has dropped in HALF-BLOOD PRINCE as well as the constraints within which she wrote this penultimate thriller.

20 Questions not answered in HARRY POTTER AND THE HALF-BLOOD PRINCE:

1 **How do you make a Horcrux, that is, what is the spellwork procedure, and what are the four remaining Horcruxes?** We learn a lot about what a Horcrux is in HALF-BLOOD PRINCE but not about how one is made or what the four Horcruxes remaining are. Until we know this, it is impossible to speculate meaningfully about what can and cannot be a Horcrux…

2 **What is the nature of Harry's scar?** Harry's scar in HALF-BLOOD PRINCE went from constant reminder in the previous story of his psychic link with the Dark Lord to not a twinge in HALF-BLOOD PRINCE (a change that allows for Harry-Dumbledore contact but with the thin excuse that the broken link was because Voldemort didn't want Harry to know what he was thinking). We don't know still if the wound is an echo of Frodo's knife wound from the Dark Rider on Weathertop or a Horcrux or a "curse scar acting like an alarm bell" or what...

3 **How did Dumbledore learn about the Cave Horcrux (which is to say, why didn't he think it was a trap)?** We don't know from whom the Headmaster learned the location of the Cave, when he was told or given the information that allowed him to deduce the location, and how much he learned about it before the trip versus how much he was learning with Harry in the dark, if, in fact, he hadn't been there before...

4 **Why did Dumbledore give Snape the cursed D.A.D.A. position?** We learn in HALF-BLOOD PRINCE that the doomed "wise old wizard with a beard" believed Voldemort had cursed the Defense Against the Dark Arts teaching position when he did not get the post. Why, then, would Dumbledore appoint Snape to this position, effectively terminating him as a Hogwarts teacher (albeit with a year to put his things in order)?

5 **What happened on the Astronomy Tower?** We know that Dumbledore or someone very much like him fell from the Astronomy Tower and that Snape seemed to have killed him — but was the Headmaster pleading with Snape to spare him or to kill him? Are the "GOOD Snape" partisans simply in denial for their insistence that Snape could have done another curse non-verbally and only *appeared* to have murdered his mentor and the leader of the Order of the Phoenix?

6 **Who helped Draco Malfoy?** Could he fix the Vanishing Cabinet in the Room of Requirement, Imperius curse Rosemerta, and brew the potions he needed on his own? All we know of Draco makes us look for someone helping him in these difficult tasks, help, that is, from an accomplished wizard. Draco tells us much in his whispered conversation with Snape on the night of the Christmas party when he says that he has help on the inside from "better people" than Crabbe or Goyle...

7 **Who threatened Draco Malfoy with death for failure on his mission?** Malfoy is terrified and near hysterics through much of the year because the Dark Lord or an agent ("he" in Draco's talk about it with Moaning Myrtle) will kill him and his family if he doesn't figure out how to kill Dumbledore. Is this threat a memory of Lord Thingy's words when he gave the assignment — or something that someone who is also on assignment from Lord Voldemort inside the castle has been reinforcing with painful regularity?

8 **Why did Voldemort assume with no little surety that the Potters'**

child was the subject of the Prophecy? HALF-BLOOD PRINCE gave us no more information on this question, if we do learn that Snape certainly didn't anticipate this choice (i.e., Voldemort's reason was not common knowledge among the Death Eaters)…

9 What happened to Dumbledore's hand? We believe that the wound was a consequence of Dumbledore's attempt to destroy the ring Horcrux and that Snape saved his life but we don't know what happened to make such a horrific wound (unusual in being incurable and unmaskable) and how Snape saved him, not to mention how this wounded arm performs so well.

10 Why did Dumbledore trust Snape? Why couldn't he tell anyone? The Headmaster doesn't even try to explain until Harry learns that it was Snape who told Voldemort about the Prophecy. Only then does Dumbledore tell Harry that it was the shame and anguish that Snape felt consequent to Voldemort's attack on the Potters that caused him to become a double-agent. Harry thinks Dumbledore was suckered — and Lupin, a man without Harry's "age-old" prejudice against Snape, agrees Dumbledore's explanation is unbelievable. Is there another better reason to have trusted Snape without reservation? Why didn't he tell anyone what it was?

11 Where has Fawkes gone? And why was he AWOL on the Astronomy Tower? Granted, Fawkes the Phoenix, the signature of the adult Dumbledore's Army, is no ordinary pet. But where was he when Dumby needed him? Are we now to believe he has flown to the Land of the Undying never to be seen again? And did the flood of tears he wept over his master's corpse or stand-in have any effect on the old man? Is Fawkes the only character whose judgment every one in the Order can accept?

12 What was the Snape/Evans relationship and/or debt? Professor Slughorn tells Harry and the world at every opportunity that Lily Evans was the most gifted potions student he'd taught. We know, too, that Professor Snape was in Lily Evans' year at Hogwarts, and, if the notes in the N.E.W.T level Potions Text are his, that he was a stellar Potions student as well. Was their relationship in class one of rivalry, respect, egad, even romance? Dumbledore believed that Snape's regret for his part in the death of the Potters caused his repentance from service to the Dark Lord; was this because of his relationship with Evans or a Potions debt he owed to the Queen of Cauldrons and Liquid Magic?

13 Why did Snape choose the Half-Blood Prince name? We have

Hermione's answer (that he was Half Muggle, Half Pure Blood, and that his mother's maiden name was Prince) but it is not especially satisfying. Wanting to call oneself a "Prince," of course, is understandable, but why point to one's "impurity" if a Slytherin? The name is something like "Mulatto Duke" in the American South of the 1940's or "Half Juden Baron" in Nazi Germany. Does it point to a relationship with Evans the Muggle Born, more word play, or both?

14 **What was Voldemort doing during action of Half-Blood Prince?** The Dark Lord is off-stage in the present time of HALF-BLOOD PRINCE though his presence is felt because of the biographical scenes we visit in the Pensieve and Draco's terror. It is not credible that he is sitting on his hands waiting for Draco's suicide mission to pan out. Does he have another plan to kill Dumbledore of which Draco's part is only a small piece? Does he trust Snape? Does he have a Death Eater at Hogwarts watching over Draco, checking up on Snape, and furthering the final solution to the Dumbledore problem? Has he gone into the Dementor breeding business for a reason?

15 **Why did Snape make the Unbreakable Vow?** Severus claims to know Draco's mission at Hogwarts in his meeting with Narcissa and Bellatrix. Did he really or was this bluster to get them to confide the details with him? If he did know Draco's mission, how could he take the Unbreakable Vow to kill Dumbledore if Draco failed? Could he have known that he would not have to kill Dumbledore, because, as Dumbledore told Draco, they cannot kill you if you are already dead? Or could he and Dumbledore have already planned a staged death?

16 **Why does Slughorn come to Hogwarts? Why does Dumbledore invite him?** The reason in the story line for bringing Horace to Hogwarts is the need for a Potions teacher because Severus is moving up to Defense against the Dark Arts. We learn later that Professor Slughorn also has a memory that is a big piece of the Horcrux puzzle (riddle?). Are these the only reasons why Dumbledore invites him in? More important, why does Slughorn agree to come? We are told (by suggestion) that it is because he wants to "collect" Harry, the Chosen One. Could Dumbledore's ring Horcrux that he wears to the interview have affected Slughorn's decision? Could his desire to collect Harry be to sell him to a higher bidder as he does Acromantula venom and unicorn hair?

17 **Why does Snape object to Harry calling him a coward?** After Severus appears to blast the Headmaster from the Astronomy Tower, he escapes with Draco to Hogsmeade to Disapparate to points unknown. He saves Harry from the Cruciatus curse before leaving, though, and gives him a quick lecture with demonstration on what he must do to prepare for a battle with the Dark Lord (i.e., learn Occlumency and to cast nonverbal spells). He also does some kind of brain lashing or surgery on Harry's scar before Buckbeak drives him away, with a white light reminiscent of the light behind the door in the Department of Mysteries.

For an enraged man, he seems to be doing Harry a lot of favors. Severus also tips his hand by losing his treasured bearing when Harry calls him a coward. Does a cold-blooded murderer have such a sensitive conscience that calling him a coward undoes him? Or is this precisely Severus' greatest failing, a la Wormtail, and his most sensitive point? Or just the opposite? Could it be *Harry* calling him this that unwinds him? Why?

18 **Who or what is R.A.B.?** Readers are clearly cued to accept that R.A.B. is Regulus Arcturus or Alphard Black, the only character with Death Eater status we know of with these initials. Regulus ("Prince") also has a link to the locket in Grimmauld Place. Whether this is a clue or a McGuffin, why does R.A.B. want the Dark Lord to know s/he figured out the Horcrux riddle? Why does s/he (they?) have a sacrificial fondness for the Dark Lord, being willing to sacrifice themselves (sic) to make him mortal for his meeting with the Vanquisher? How does s/he (they) know they are going to die before he discovers the switch? Could this be another Voldemort trap, this one to discover the location of Grimmauld Place or sucker Harry into a Death Keeper dark alley?

19 **Who has been given sanctuary and new identities by the Order of the Phoenix?** Albus the Late offers Draco and his family the promise of Phoenix "witness protection" in his discussion on the Astronomy Tower. To and for whom has this been done previously that Dumbledore is so sure it can be done? Mr. Olivander? The Candy Man? Regulus Black? Snape's parents?

20 **What was Albus's relationship with brother Aberforth? With Petunia?** There are quite a few strings left dangling at Dumbledore's demise and not just leadership issues within the Order (which, lacking written direction or a plan of succession, should prove quite the headache in the series finale). The Headmaster had peripheral, undisclosed relations with the Centaurs, the MerPeople and quite a few individuals, most notably, Petunia Dursley and Aberforth Dumbledore. Petunia didn't make it to the funeral, alas, but I'm eager to see her response to the news of his death.

No doubt you asked yourself many of these questions as you were reading the book. If you didn't, I hope seeing all these questions together will cause you to stop and scratch your head. How can an intelligent reader get through HALF-BLOOD PRINCE and not notice that the narrative is raising more questions than it is answering? This is the great trick of Ms. Rowling's careful planning, and, quite frankly, she is the reigning master of this particular literary device.

I need to pull a chapter from my works in progress here because Ms. Rowling didn't invent the method by which she fools her readers (and she fools every one, truth be told). She gets it from Jane Austen, whom she always mentions as her favorite author and whose EMMA she cites without fail as her single favorite book (cf., Karin Westman's WHEN HARRY MET JANE: THE LEGACY OF AUSTEN IN HARRY POTTER, an abstract read at HPEF's "Nimbus — 2003" convention).

In my own project there is, as you'd expect, an entire chapter on Austen and her influence on Rowling. Ms. Rowling's manners-and-morals fiction focusing on relationships, her critique of prejudice and the Hume inspired empiricism that values "first impressions" (the original title of Austen's PRIDE AND PREJUDICE), and her below-the-radar satire and social criticism are all evidence of her close study of Austen's novels. The point of influence that is most important for a discussion of the genius of HALF-BLOOD PRINCE, though, is the perspective in which the Harry Potter novels are told and how this perspective lulls the passive reader into traveling down the erring path (and far away from the solution of the mystery).

"Third Person, Limited Omniscient View" and "Narrative Misdirection"

If your experience was like mine in High School English classes, you probably dread any discussion of "author's perspective," "symbols," or "literary devices." They rarely made the poem, play, or novel any more meaningful in High School and what a bore. I hope this didn't happen to you, but if it did, I promise, if you'll stay awake and catch even half of what I share here about how Ms. Rowling writes, you'll have a much better grasp on how she works her magic, *"Confundus"* charming us all.

The obvious thing we have to remember is that writers have choices. One of the first choices they have to make when beginning a story is the "voice" they will use when writing. No, I don't mean alto, soprano, or tenor. I mean *who* will be telling the story.

Certainly the author is telling the story, I know, but through whom the author tells the story is critical. MOBY DICK, for example, is told from the perspective of Ishmael the survivor, not from the perspective of Herman Melville the author *per se*. Ishmael speaks for himself as "I" or "me" so this perspective is called "First person narration" (because in grammar "I" and "We" are first person, "you" singular and plural are second person, and "he/she/it" and "they" are third person).

The Chase-the-White-Whale story would be completely different if another person told the story (Ahab? Queequeg?) from their equally limited first person perspective or if the story were told from high above the top sail from which God-like height everything can be seen. This God-perspective is called "Third Person, omniscient" because it is a "see all" perspective not restricted to any person's isolated view.

These are the two big options an author has when writing a novel. "Do I tell it from a narrator's experience of the tale à la Dr. Watson in the Sherlock Holmes cases? Or do I tell it as God sees it unfolding in time?" Open up any anthology of Detective fiction (I love the OXFORD BOOK OF BRITISH DETECTIVE STORIES and their AMERICAN DETECTIVE STORIES volume, too) and quickly check to see whether a story is told by a fictional narrator in the "I saw this" and "then we did that" perspective or if the story comes from the author in the role of an all-seeing God.

There are a few variants on these two options, of course, and the one relevant to our getting beneath the narrative surface of Harry Potter is the perspective in which Jane Austen wrote EMMA. This "narratological voice" (sorry!) is called "Third person, limited omniscient view" and telling the story this way is the way that Ms. Rowling pulls off her stunning end of story surprises.

Think for a minute about how the Potter novels are told or flip open any one of the six books in print. With very few exceptions (most notably, the first chapter of the first book and the opening chapters of GOBLET and HALF-BLOOD PRINCE), the stories are told not from Harry's perspective talking like Dr. Watson or Ishmael: "Ron and Hermione and I then pushed our way through the door and saw a wild three-headed dog!" The stories aren't told by God floating above the Astronomy Tower, seeing and telling all: "Then Draco went back into the Room of Requirement to pick up where he left off on Vanishing Cabinet repair."

The perspective of these books splits the difference between the "first person" and "third person, omniscient" perspectives. What this split means in practical terms is that we see all the action in the books as if there were a house-elf sitting on Harry's shoulder with a mini-cam who can also tell us everything Harry is thinking and feeling in addition to what he sees around him. We don't see any more than Harry sees (hence the "limited" in "limited omniscient") but because we're not restricted to Harry's narration it *seems* as if we're seeing a larger bit of the story than if Harry just told it himself.

This last bit of *seeming* is critical because it is our confusion on this point that allows for what literary geeks (and Harry Potter fans) call "narrative misdirection." If you have to remember one thing about how Ms. Rowling writes, make it "narrative misdirection." It's how she wrote HALF-BLOOD PRINCE so that it was a satisfying story and with all the clues we need without "giving away" how the last installment will end.

All "narrative misdirection" amounts to really is our being suckered into believing, because the story is not being told by Harry himself, that we are seeing the story as God sees it. Of course this isn't the case but over the course of the tale our looking down on Harry and friends (and enemies) from "on high", even if "on high" means only from a few feet over Harry's head, we begin to think we have a larger perspective than we do.

This trick works because we like Harry and sympathize with him and his struggles. In short, we begin to identify with how Harry thinks and feels, and, because Harry is not telling the story, we think we have to this position of sympathy and identification with the hero because of our unprejudiced view.

When you've arrived at this position — and, confess, we've all been there, this woman is really good at what she's doing — Ms. Rowling has you wrapped up. She can take you anywhere she wants to take you and make you think almost anything she wants about any character because, by and large, what Harry thinks is what we believe.

Remember our confusion of Professor Snape and Quirrelll as the servants of the Dark Lord in PHILOSOPHER'S STONE? I do. I swallowed Harry's conviction that Snape was evil and made it my own belief. I had all the information that pointed to Professor Quirrelll as the black hat — Ms. Rowling plays by the rules, y'know — but I back-shelved that information as I rushed through the underground obstacles with Ron and Hermione in support of Harry to get to the Mirror of Erised and Snape. Severus, of course, wasn't there and turned out, in the world-turned-upside-down denouement (when Dumbledore tells us how God sees it...), to have been a white hat, despite appearances.

This was possible because of our identification with the orphan boy living under the stairs who was horribly treated by his Aunt and Uncle. We sympathized with him and took his view as our own, though it wasn't his view or an all-knowing one. Pretty embarrassing, but Ms. Rowling uses this same trick in every book — and nowhere more brilliantly than in HALF-BLOOD PRINCE.

I say that because by the time HALF-BLOOD PRINCE opens we've been fooled five times, that is, by each of the first five novels. Many of us have read these books quite a few times (I met a woman and daughter at a book signing that claimed without blushing or laughing at themselves that they had read the five books then in print *seventeen* times). No way were we going to be suckered into the same trap again. But we were.

How she did it is fascinating. First, she turns off the voice we're used to hearing. Instead of a house-elf with minicam on Harry's shoulder we have an elf on the Muggle Prime Minister's shoulder reading his mind in chapter one and another on Bellatrix's shoulder in "Spinner's End." By the time we get to Harry in chapter three, we're ready to resume our comfortable position on our friend's shoulder

— someone we like. If you liked the Muggle Prime Minister and Bellatrix more than Harry and identified more with them than with him, I'm sorry. The ten million of us who gladly leapt onto Harry's shoulder were already deeply hooked into buying his view as God's view or "the truth."

But for you hard-core readers determined not to identify with Harry, Ms. Rowling had another hook or undercurrent to suck you into delusion with the rest of us. For 28 of the 30 chapters, everyone thinks Harry is a nutcase for believing Draco is a Death Eater and that Snape is helping him with his mission from the Dark Lord. If we are resistant in believing Harry to be right in these beliefs, we are in good company; Ron, Hermione, Remus Lupin, Nymphadora Tonks, Mr. and Mrs. Weasley, even Albus Dumbledore also think Harry is just determined to believe the worst of Malfoy and Snape.

But, then, of course, events confirm everything Harry has thought since the book's beginning! Malfoy *was* on a suicide mission from the Dark Lord! Snape *is* his willing comrade and a man capable of killing the beloved Headmaster who is more than a little Christ-like! And everyone in a wave in the Infirmary conclave around Bill apologizes to Harry for doubting him and for believing the best of others like Dumbledore when they should have been hating Snape and Malfoy. Harry is a Prophet!

You're a better reader than I am if the traction of this current didn't pull you off your feet and send you down stream. This isn't just "narrative misdirection." This is judo and Ms. Rowling has a black belt, third dan, in this literary martial art.

The Judo Throw at the Finish of HALF-BLOOD PRINCE

If you don't know anything about judo or its cousin, aikido, let me explain what I mean. The point of these martial arts is to use the force or direction of the opponent to subdue him or her. If someone tries to punch or kick you, the judo response is to "encourage" them to continue in their unbalanced direction and lock them up. Ms. Rowling's judo move is to get us leaning exactly the way we want and then push us over in that direction.

We come into the story as careful readers who have been duped by and large five times. We've all taken oaths, publicly and privately, not to be fooled a sixth time. Everyone else in the book is on our side. "Sure, Harry," pat on head, shared glance with Dumbledore and Hermione, "We know. Draco's the youngest Death Eater ever and you know best about Snape — like all the other times you've been right about Snape. Which would be 'never, ever right about Snape.'" As much as we love Harry, we're not going to be kicking ourselves again at book's end for buying into Harry's jaundiced view. We lean way back from Harry.

But he's right! And everybody that was with us in leaning away from Harry is on the floor apologizing for not trusting in his discernment. This is the crucial difference between the ending of HALF-BLOOD PRINCE and every other Harry Potter book. In every other book's finale we're swearing we won't identify with Harry's view again. We take solemn oaths that *next time* we'll be more like Hermione and we'll see this is one of Harry's mistakes, his "saving-people-thing."

At the end of HALF-BLOOD PRINCE, though, we weren't saying, "I was suckered again! Doggone it!" We were saying, "Wow. Harry was right. Snape killed Dumbledore as part of the plan that the Dark Lord had for Malfoy to do in the Headmaster. Time to line up behind Harry and go Horcrux and Snape hunting on our white hippogriff and in our white cowboy hats."

Ms. Rowling has spun us around from the position toward which we were leaning contra-Harry and forced us into the identification and sympathy mode for Harry's perspective that we swore we'd never accept again.

If you doubt me, turn the pages back to those twenty questions.

Every one of these questions is one we might have asked if we were Hermione. Harry's perspective, alas, is largely an unquestioning perspective. When Dumbledore explains how Severus saved his life when he tried to destroy the ring Horcrux, Hermione would have asked, "How did he do that?" or "Why isn't it treatable more than it is? How serious is this injury?" Harry doesn't blink at the Headmaster's explanation or ask the obvious questions you or I might of a man with this bizarre a wound who was saved by a wizard we believe to be a black hat.

When we accept Harry's non-questioning posture, we're already being swept into narrative misdirection. We think we're learning important information. All we're really getting is a surface explanation. As we can see from the 20 questions, the narrative line actually *raises* more questions in HALF-BLOOD PRINCE than it answers. As good as we tried to be not to be suckered, Ms. Rowling has "rowled" us over again.

And not just in the ending! Think of Harry and what he sees and what we believe in the chapter called "After the Burial." Harry, more than half desperate to get the Slughorn memory, finally takes a swig of Felix Felicis potion. With the liquid luck in his veins, everything goes his way. Ron and Lavender have a row and Dean and Ginny begin the fight that ends their relationship before Harry is out of Gryffindor Tower. Everything is going his way and we are beginning to believe as much as Harry does that nothing can go wrong tonight.

Whenever you think this in a Harry Potter novel, red flags should go up in your brain-housing unit to signal you that you are in serious trouble. Harry runs into Horace Slughorn — just the man we are looking for — and in our excitement and surety that this is all good luck, especially getting the necessary Horcrux memory, we skip over all the information we pick up along the way or have learned before.

We forget that Horace is a more than competent wizard and no slouch at drinking. Are we to believe he doesn't notice that Harry isn't drinking and re-filling their glasses? Sure, Horace is excited about the Acromantula venom and unicorn hair sales he's about to make....

And those greens he's getting from Professor Sprout? Every class we've seen Slughorn teach has been a minimum of real work and the maximum load of "Let's see what you've been able to figure out on your own." Is this a professor that goes to gather greens for his Third Year students at dusk because that will give the potions they're making especially "efficacious"?

And he needs to "change his tie" for Aragog's funeral? He's already said he needs to get some wine, why the second excuse? He needs to check a tie, I think, and maybe ask instructions from someone now that he is close to having the ingredients he needs for his own Potions work. Can he feign drunkenness now and give up the memory to Harry?

We never think to ask. Why not suspect Slughorn? Outside of Lupin, every new teacher at Hogwarts has been either dangerously self-involved or downright dangerous (EVIL) or both. Why don't we assume Slughorn is more than a social parasite? Because that's all Harry thinks he is — and when we see him doing even remarkably suspicious things, we're under the spell of Rowling's Felix Felicis, the magic potion of narrative misdirection.

What Really Happened in HALF-BLOOD PRINCE?

Let's try to answer as many of the questions as we can through several theories of what really happened in HALF-BLOOD PRINCE, always remembering to fight against the current of trusting Harry because of Ms. Rowling's narrative misdirection judo move at the end of the book. The first theory I think answers six of my twenty questions above (numbers 4, 5, 9, 10, 15, and 17 if you want to keep track).

My co-moderator in the August 2005 Discussion Room at http://www.BarnesandNobleUniversity.com (BNU) was Cathy Liesner from "The Leaky Cauldron," a notable Harry Potter fan site. Cathy was struck by the number of references in HALF-BLOOD PRINCE to Harry's very first Potions class way back in HARRY POTTER AND THE PHILOSOPHER'S STONE, chapter 8, "The Potions Master." Cathy figured out that something Snape said in that first class could be an explanation of how Severus helped Dumbledore with his arm. She called this theory "Stoppered Death." I expanded Cathy's theory in the BNU classroom to its present form.

In case you missed the references to this first Potions class, here's a quick review. In chapter 18, "Birthday Surprises," Harry is half-desperate to think of a way to impress Slughorn and clear the way for his handing over the unedited Riddle-asking-about-Horcrux memory that Dumbledore wants. The Potions master gives an impossible *"Find the alchemical antidote"* (yes, he uses the word "alchemical;" see pg. 375) class assignment and Harry is clueless about how to go about applying Golpalott's Third Law. His annotated Potions textbook says only:

> And there it was, scrawled right across a long list of antidotes:
> Just shove a bezoar down their throats.
> Harry stared at those words for a moment. Hadn't he once, long ago, heard of bezoars? Hadn't Snape mentioned them in their first ever Potions lesson? A stone taken from the stomach of a goat, which will protect from most poisons."
> (HALF-BLOOD PRINCE, chapter 18, pg. 377)

The short-cut impresses Slughorn who awards Gryffindor ten points for "sheer cheek" and says for the umpteenth time "Oh, you're like your mother" in admiration. It does not smooth the way for a Horcrux memory revelation, however, far from it, and we're left to wonder at this whole protracted Potions class scene and what it meant. We learn why before chapter's end (we think) when Harry saves Ron's life with a bezoar in Slughorn's apartment.

Ms. Rowling, though, doesn't leave it at that. In the first paragraphs of chapter 21, "The Unknowable Room," Harry and Hermione are having another go at it about the Half-Blood Prince textbook that Hermione thinks is dicey, at best.

> *"Don't start, Hermione,"* said Harry. *"If it hadn't been for the Prince, Ron wouldn't be sitting here now."*
> *"He would be if you'd just listened to Snape in our first year,"* said Hermione dismissively. (HALF-BLOOD PRINCE, chapter 21, pg. 447)

This is a curious throw-away comment. Yes, Hermione had done the assigned work in Potions class and had every reason to be miffed at Harry for taking the short-cut, contrary to directions, and earned Slughorn's approval (again). But, knowing that Harry and Ron can't remember anything scholastic without endless repetition or her explanations, it's curious that even in her pique about the Potions class she thinks Harry could have remembered that first class without some prompting like the note from the Prince. Why does she bring up the first Potions lesson here?

Perhaps to get us to go back and look at that first lesson? Severus makes an aside about his first meeting Harry to Bellatrix and Narcissa in chapter 2, "Spinner's End," that provides some context for what we should look for in that lesson. In answer to Bellatrix's question about why Severus has not killed Harry Potter, he says:

> *"Have you not understood me? It was only Dumbledore's protection that was keeping me out of Azkaban! Do you disagree that murdering his favorite*

student might have turned him against me? But there was more to it than that. I should remind you that when Potter first arrived at Hogwarts there were still many stories circulating about him, rumors that he himself was a great Dark wizard, which was how he survived the Dark Lord's attack....

"Of course, it became apparent to me very quickly that he had no extraordinary talent at all.... He is mediocre to the last degree, though as obnoxious and self-satisfied as was his father before him." (HALF-BLOOD PRINCE, chapter 2, pg. 30-31)

"It became apparent to me very quickly." Say, in the first Potions lesson? What happened in that class in the dungeons?

In a nutshell, Severus insults Harry during roll call, gives a short speech on the wonders of Potions (that he believes will be lost on these dunderheads), and then quizzes Harry on the ingredients for the Draught of Living Death (which Harry produces for Slughorn in *his* first class using the Half-Blood Prince's directions...), on bezoars, and Monk's Hood. He takes two points from Gryffindor for Harry's attempt at humor during this harassment and, later, because Harry didn't prevent Neville from melting his cauldron. Harry is astonished by the evident hatred the Potions Master feels for him and discusses the problem with Hagrid later that afternoon.

So what?

Well, we see in the harassment Severus gives the child Harry that he is looking to see, not so much if Harry is a great Dark wizard in embryo as he claimed in HALF-BLOOD PRINCE's second chapter, but to see if Harry was a Potions genius like his mother. Lily Evans had been able to absorb all of the first year's text as perhaps had his own mother (whose images we have in Hermione who frantically tries to answer Snape's questions). He also begins the attacks and border-line sadism that define his exchanges with Harry until his departure from Hogwarts at the end of HALF-BLOOD PRINCE. Which, of course, could all be an act performed on Dumbledore's orders to maintain his cover.

This extraordinary beginnings having revealed the character of their relationship, though, isn't my point. There are references in this chapter to bezoars and the Draught of Living Death in HALF-BLOOD PRINCE, the latter of which some Dumbledore fans think he was given to seem dead (see Sally Gallo's essay on Horace Slughorn in this collection or Joyce Odell's insights about the Astronomy Tower for more along these lines). But it is the speech that Severus gives that unlocks much of the background in HALF-BLOOD PRINCE.

The class most like an Alchemist's laboratory begins with Professor Snape telling these frightened first years:

"As there is little foolish wand-waving here, many of you will hardly believe

this is magic. I don't expect you will really understand the beauty of the softly simmering cauldron with its shimmering fumes, the delicate power of liquids that creep through human veins, bewitching the mind, ensnaring the senses… I can teach you how to bottle fame, brew glory, even stopper death — if you aren't as big a bunch of dunderheads as I usually have to teach." (PHILOSO-PHER'S STONE, chapter 8, pg.. 137)

"Bottle fame, brew glory, even stopper death." It is this last comment about "stop-pering death" that answers several of the questions that are never explained in HALF-BLOOD PRINCE. In a nutshell, Professor Severus Snape "stoppered" Albus Dumbledore's death when the Headmaster tried to destroy the Slytherin ring Horcrux.

The Meaning of "Stoppered Death"

What does it mean to "stopper death"? It isn't saving a life, obviously or affecting a cure; it is suspending a death that has already happened. When Professor Snape asks his Defense Against the Dark Arts class in HALF-BLOOD PRINCE what the difference is between a ghost and an Inferius (chapter 21, pg. 460), the answer is "Headmaster Dumbledore." In his stoppered death, Albus is quite literally a "dead man walking," something between "a corpse that has been re-animated by a Dark Wizard's spells" and "the imprint of a departed soul left upon the earth." We miss this clue from the Potions class, of course, despite it being an off-the wall question, because we are caught up in cheering for Harry against the sadistic D.A.D.A. master.

Notice that this is not an indefinite process. Severus Snape does not have the *cure* for death. By stoppering the Headmaster's death for, let's say, one year, however, Dumbledore and Snape are forced to be much more aggressive then they might otherwise be in Harry's sixth year. "Suspended de-animation" doesn't last very long. Dumbledore may not have even been on the Astronomy Tower.

Let's look at the 20 questions in light of the possibility that Severus is the reason Dumbledore is in Half-Blood Prince. The "Stoppered Death" theory explains, of course, what happened to Dumbledore's hand [#9] and at least partially illuminates why Dumbledore trusts Snape without reservation [#10]. He cannot share this secret with anyone who is not an accomplished Occlumens because its discovery will mean instant death for the Potions genius. Nonetheless, what reason could he have for *doubting* Severus' loyalty when, except for his potions genius, he would not be present to doubt him? Dumbledore says as much to Harry when he finally explains what happened to his hand:

"Had it not been — forgive me the lack of seemly modesty — for my own prodigious skill, and for Professor Snape's timely action when I returned to

Hogwarts, desperately injured, I might not have lived to tell the tale." (HALF-BLOOD PRINCE, chapter 23, pg. 503)

It answers, too, why Severus would take the Unbreakable Vow with Narcissa even if he knew that Draco's mission was to kill Dumbledore (question #15). For the same reason that he had no qualms about blasting the Headmaster with the *Avada Kedavra* curse on the Astronomy Tower [#5]. As Albus said to Draco on the Tower, *"He cannot kill you if you are already dead"* (chapter 27, pg. 391). Or, if Albus has already succumbed, to blasting his stand-in in an elaborate and very necessary ruse.

Why would Dumbledore give Snape the cursed Defense Against the Dark Arts post, knowing that no one had lasted more than a year in this teaching position [#4]? Because they both knew that the death Severus had stoppered would be evident to everyone before the year was out. If Snape is to survive Dumbledore's death, however, and continue to help the Order defeat Voldemort, the Potions/Defense professor has to leave Hogwarts, and, worse for Severus, cannot be known as the man who "saved Dumbledore's death" for a year. He has to be known as the man who killed Dumbledore. A one-year appointment with an orchestrated, murderous finish is perfect.

And Severus Snape's rage about being called a coward by Harry Potter [#17]? I think I'd lose it, too, if I had to pretend I was a bad guy — by murdering the only man who ever cared for and trusted me — when I was really the Great Physician and beloved disciple — and a young, clueless punk who never bothered to learn the skill that would allow him to be in on the secret (Occlumency) for whom I had made this heroic sacrifice decided to call me the one thing I was not. Severus deserves a badge for self-control rather than a face full of Hippogriff and razor-like claws. I think Snape has to be the "black-hat-who-turns-out-to-be-a-white-hat" in the stunning finish of the last book.

"Stoppered Death" also explains why Dumbledore did a 360 degree turn from his hands-off approach to Harry in PHOENIX and begins tutorial lessons with him. He didn't have the leisure to let Harry mature and live a relaxed life; Dumbledore was already dead and the clock was ticking on the pretense of his life. This tells us in part, too, why Horace Slughorn had to be brought on to the Hogwarts faculty and why Dumbledore was absent from Hogwarts for such long stretches. He had to get as much information about the Dark Lord's Horcruxes — and get them to Harry — as soon as possible. "Stoppered Death" accelerates if it doesn't outright cause most of the action behind the scenes in HALF-BLOOD PRINCE.

Voldemort's Invisible Year

"Stoppered Death" I think gives us the peek behind the narrative that explains much of the mysterious goings on at Hogwarts during HALF-BLOOD PRINCE. We need another theory to give us a cohesive idea of what Voldemort has been up to this year and what his part in the Astronomy Tower murder was.

Before jumping into this theory, though, let's be sure to note that Voldemort is all but invisible this year. We know that he gives Draco Malfoy a suicide mission to kill Dumbledore, a mission in which he is to die either in the attempt on Dumbledore's life or at the hands of the Death Eaters for failing. His mother understands this to be an assignment to punish the Malfoy's for Lucius's mistakes with the diary Horcrux and in failing to recover the Prophecy. Dumbledore echoes her understanding in a later passage.

> *"Ah, poor Lucius… what with Voldemort's fury about the fact that he threw away the Horcrux for his own gain, and the fiasco at the Ministry last year, I would not be surprised if he was not secretly glad to be safe in Azkaban at the moment."* (HALF-BLOOD PRINCE, chapter 23, pg. 508)

Beyond this "fury" and his attacking Lucius by throwing away the life of his son (and torturing both in the process), we see nothing of the Dark Lord. The natural assumption, however illogical or incredible, is that he isn't doing anything this year because we don't read about it.

All together now! Say, "Narrative Misdirection"! It's hard to remember that we're never seeing more than a small fraction of what is going on in this story, locked as we are in Harry's view… We never see what Dumbledore, Snape, or Voldemort are doing or planning except for the few times they cross Harry's line of sight.

Even though we *know* that we're not seeing everything that's going on, part of us believes we have an omniscient view because Harry isn't telling us the story, we're reading about him. Alas and alack, we are caught again in the undertow of the third person, limited omniscient view.

It's happened before. We didn't see Lord Thingy in PHOENIX either and assumed he was sitting on his hands. Out of sight, out of mind — out of luck in figuring out that the Dark Lord had been setting up the trap in the Department of Mysteries' Prophecy vault.

If we assume that Lord Voldemort was at least as active in HALF-BLOOD PRINCE as he was in PHOENIX, we have to be thinking he had more on the stove than punishing the Malfoys with Draco's suicide mission. We can answer questions # 3, 5, 6, 7, 14, and 16 above with a theory of Death Eater intrigue I call "EVIL Slughorn." We know that the new guy every year isn't what he or she seems to be or has a big secret; Sluggo then is either a big hero or a horrid villain. Sally Gallo in chapter three argues that he's the greatest, so let's look at his potential as a bad guy.

Slughorn is EVIL?

The heart of "EVIL Slughorn" is the not-unbelievable hypothesis that Lord Voldemort is not putting all his "kill Dumbledore" eggs in Draco's basket. There is a larger "Decapitate resistance to the Death Eaters by cutting off the Head-Master" plan of which the Draco "torture the Malfoy's" mission is only a side-show. To pull this off — and to keep an eye on Severus Snape — Voldemort needs a man "on the ground" inside Hogwarts. Horace Slughorn is the logical choice for this plant. There are more compelling reasons to believe this than just because "he's the new guy" (as much as prior experience should make us suspect the new guys!).

[Before explaining "EVIL Slughorn," though, a quick aside about why Voldemort needs someone checking up on Snape.

Because he doesn't trust him!

Would you trust an accomplished Occlumens who can just as likely be in Dumbledore's service as your own? I wouldn't and only my children think of me as the Dark Lord (Joke! No letters, please!).]

If Horace is Voldemort's willing or unwilling agent at the School, he is the wizard who bullies and guides Draco simultaneously, he can watch to see if Snape is sharing all he knows with the Dark Lord, and he can monitor Dumbledore's Horcrux search and physical condition (Snape has told the Death Eaters that Dumbledore is wounded and vulnerable; see chapter 2, pg. 31). What evidence, though, do we have that Slughorn is EVIL?

Draco Malfoy tells Professor Snape that *"I've got all the assistance I need, thanks, I'm not alone!"* and, when Snape asks him, *"if you are placing your reliance in assistants like Crabbe and Goyle —"*, Malfoy responds, *"They're not the only ones, I've got other people on my side, better people!"* (Chapter 15, pgs. 323-324)

Besides Fenrir Greyback, who could Malfoy mean? [See "MOURNING FOR HER OWN TRUE LOVE," Chapter 5 in this collection for a LiveJournal discussion of the several Death Eaters who may be on board at Hogwarts in Harry's sixth year.]

I think he means Professor Horace Slughorn. I submit the following points for your consideration. Though none of this necessarily circumstantial evidence is conclusive, taken altogether it is suggestive that the new Potions teacher is a bad egg gone rotten. We should know by now that the narratalogical voice chosen by Ms. Rowling does not give us any straightforward clues. That voice only tells us what Harry sees and thinks and has proven itself to be "dependably unreliable" every year. We are left to pile up the circumstantial evidence and see if it merits a second look to counter Ms. Rowling's narrative misdirection (which tells us the new Potions master is only a comfort-driven, self-important ninny).

1. Horace Slughorn was the head of Slytherin house for many years — and an admirer and mentor of Tom Riddle's;

2. When Dumbledore asks him if his sofa disguise ruse before he and Harry arrives was for him or the Death Eaters, Slughorn "demands" that he explain what that crowd would want with him. Dumbledore explains, *"I imagine they would want you to turn your considerable talents to coercion, torture, and murder"* and asks him if he is not being recruited. Slughorn says he has been in hiding to avoid them. (Chapter 4, pg. 68);

   a. Slughorn is not insulted when the Headmaster in jest or seriously suggests that the Death Eaters would think of him as a natural ally (op. cit.);

   b. Slughorn does not answer the question about whether he was hiding from Dumbledore as well (as he first seemed to be). He is, at best, no ally of the Order of the Phoenix (op. cit.);

   c. At worst, the whole "blasted apartment" Death Eater visit ruse, was a sham to win Dumbledore's confidence that he had not yet been recruited by the bad guys.

3. Slughorn recognizes the ring on Dumbledore's hand on this visit because Dumbledore makes a point of waving it in his face:

   "He shrugged and spread his hands wide, as though to say that age had its compensations, and Harry noticed a ring on his uninjured hand that he had never seen Dumbledore wear before... Slughorn's eyes lingered for a moment on the ring too, and Harry saw a tiny frown momentarily crease his wide forehead" (pg 67-68).

   The student Tom Riddle was wearing this ring when he asked Professor Slughorn about the Horcruxes. Dumbledore does not wear the ring again in the book so it might be assumed he did so here to impress Slughorn with his "collection" or knowledge of Horcruxes;

4. Slughorn, like Riddle/Voldemort, is a collector, albeit of living people and important, influential contacts. He is a "user" of others who only values his students or friends insomuch as their skills (promise) or connections will advance his influence and power;

5. Slughorn gives Harry the Half Blood Prince annotated edition of the N.E.W.T. Potions text. Harry is the big prize Slughorn wants for his collection, the bait Dumbledore uses to bring Slughorn out of retirement.

Horace sets Harry up for great success in Slughorn's class by giving Harry a book that has all the answers to every question and potion in advance. The text is just like his Slug Club invitations; Slughorn is recruiting Harry either because he thinks the "Chosen One" will be able to help him one day when he becomes powerful — or because Slughorn serves or fears the Dark Lord (and knows capturing Harry or even just having access may be useful in the dark future every one fears).

6. When Harry asks him about the Horcruxes, Slughorn shifts from jovial glad hander and Harry's friend to "shocked, terrified" and in a cold sweat bellowing at Harry about Dumbledore and the Horcrux memory (Chapter 17, Scholastic hc pgs. 379-380). "Slug Club" parties cease, if Slughorn later regains his composure and friendliness with Harry. Does Slughorn realize his vulnerability at this time and wonder at how he can get on Voldemort's good side? Or is he terrified that the Headmaster is sending him a signal that he knows what Horace is up to?

7. He is helping Draco, I think, before he accidentally poisons Ron with his never delivered (and why not?) Christmas gift for Dumbledore, if he must be astonished that Malfoy would use him as a conduit. Bellatrix's husband was a Slug Club member or Slytherin intimate we learn from Slughorn's memory; no doubt, they have kept in contact with this collector. Harry's pursuit of the Horcruxes may be what pushed him into active alliance in the "kill Dumbledore" project. If not Slughorn, who is brewing all the Polyjuice potion Malfoy needs for his "crabby goyle friends" (as Helen Ketcham at BNU put it) or the Wolfbane potion he needs for himself?

8. Slughorn's refusal to give the memory to Dumbledore or Harry before seemingly drinking himself into a stupor after Aragog's burial has to count against him. As discussed above, his behavior in gathering greens at dusk so they are especially efficacious and milking Aragog of Acromantula venom makes him a candidate for the brewmeister of the phosphorescent green Cave basin potion. That he had to "change ties" when getting wine and venom bottles suggests he was checking "the ties that bind him" to get approval to feign drunkenness and hand over the memory now that he had what he needed to brew the potion and set the trap;

9. Slughorn's reaction to Dumbledore's murder at Snape's hands clues us in to one, perhaps two things. His response in the meeting of House Heads in MacGonagall's office is,

"Snape!" ejaculated Slughorn, who looked the most shaken, pale and sweating. "Snape! I taught him! I thought I knew him!" (Chapter 29, pg. 627).

a. This is not grief. This is, at best, only embarrassment and concern that someone with whom he has been associated might reflect badly on him, and,

b. If not an act, his evident fear, perhaps, is that his colleagues may not believe his dissociation of himself from Snape…

So what?

If he is not a Death Eater from the get go, Horace Slughorn at least spends the better part of the year trying to play both sides of the field, and rather aggressively. He makes contact with the Death Eaters through Malfoy, Bellatrix Lestrange's nephew, and secretly helps him in his efforts to kill the Headmaster (perhaps by placing the Imperius curse on Rosmerta, if he does seem genuinely shocked that Malfoy has doped his gift; I think Draco pays for that). He tries, at the same time, to recruit or otherwise win favor with Harry in case Dumbledore is successful in collecting and destroying Lord Voldemort's Horcruxes, as he must suspect.

Harry's brazen attempt to get information about Horcruxes, though, shows Slughorn what danger he is in. Dumbledore clearly is not as far down the Horcrux destruction trail as he seemed — and the Dark Lord must know that Slughorn has this memory to share if he wishes. Horace consequently, was put in a position where he had to decide between the Order and the Death Eaters at this point if he were not bad from the start.

Being a selfish coward, Slughorn chooses the Death Eaters. He communicates with the Dark Lord or his minions that he will assist them in their plot to kill Dumbledore, not only by assisting Malfoy with his Vanishing Cabinet repair job, but in sending Dumbledore to the Cave and poisoning the basin in the cave. This answers questions #3, 6, and 7.

We know that he is terrified by the idea of Harry or Dumbledore learning about the Horcrux memory. He is also an accomplished and prodigious drinker. Does he give Harry the Horcrux memory, then, because he suddenly has completely lost his bearings under the influence of spirits (wine!) or is it because the Dark Lord has told him he must and this is a golden opportunity? This is a wizard that Dumbledore describes as *"an extremely able wizard," "accomplished in Occlumency,"* and one who carries antidotes to potions lest he be coerced into spilling his memories (Chapter 17, pg. 372). He's hoodwinked by a boy using a potion he gave the child and by some bottles of wine?

Dumbledore seems to learn something about the cave on the day the cabinets are repaired and Draco can call in his Death Eater friends. Coincidence?

We know that an accomplished wizard has switched out the Horcrux in the basin and left a faux Horcrux with a note seemingly from Regulus Black as well as an impenetrable emerald green potion that Dumbledore "assumes" he must drink. [See Wendy B. Harte's contribution to this collection in chapter two to find out who switched out the Horcrux.]

If Regulus Black left the faux Lord Voldemort Horcrux necklace in its original spot (not the cave) and Slughorn or Voldemort found it, Slughorn could have created with Voldemort's help the trap in the Cave, to include the poisoned potion. Slughorn would only then have to fix the Vanishing Cabinet and cue Dumbledore to the Cave adventure (and tell him to be sure to bring a crystal goblet) on the night of the Death Eater invasion of Hogwarts. The trap would then be sprung.

Hence his terror in the Headmistress' Office on the night of Dumbledore's death. Would he be discovered by these great friends of Dumbledore to be the Judas in their midst? Everything must point to Snape...

After posting the "EVIL Slughorn" theory in the Barnes and Noble University. com Discussion Room I moderate, I was met with a wave of dismissive e-mails and rude hand gestures (sort of). Two readers there, though, pointed out two clues that point to Slughorn being a Death Eater and someone Dumbledore does not trust.

Pat Henderson of Vashon Island, WA, noticed that Dumbledore answers Slughorn's question about how he recognized his disheveled house, which had seemingly been attacked by Death Eaters, by saying there was no Dark Mark over the house. Horace responds:

> *"The Dark Mark," he muttered. "Knew there was something... ah well. Wouldn't have had time anyway, I'd only just finished putting the finishing touches on my upholstery when you entered the room"* (HALF-BLOOD PRINCE, Chapter 4, pg. 64).

What is curious is that he does not deny the ability to make a Dark Mark. We learned from Mr. Weasley at the Quidditch World Cup that it isn't every accomplished wizard that can conjure the Dark Mark. He answers a Hermione question about who made the Dark Mark above the campgrounds by telling us:

> *"Your guess is as good as ours, Hermione," said Mr. Weasley. "But I'll tell you this... it was only the Death Eaters who ever knew how to conjure it. I'd be very surprised if the person who did it hadn't been a Death Eater once, even if they're not now..."* (GOBLET OF FIRE, Chapter 9, pg. 143).

So Horace Slughorn was probably a Death Eater, at least familiar with them, perhaps one of the two Lord Thingy describes at his Re-birthing Party as *"One too cowardly to return… he will pay. One, who I believe has left me forever… he will be killed, of course…"* (GOBLET OF FIRE, chapter 33, pg. 651). I assumed he was talking about Severus and Karkaroff. If he knows Snape is still at Hogwarts in his service, though, this means we have an opening for a "retired" Death Eater, "too cowardly to return" that Voldemort vows to make pay.

This would explain why Horace Slughorn is on the run, why he thinks Dumbledore would believe his house was ransacked by Death Eaters (and that they spread blood on the walls), and why Dumbledore uses Harry as bait to bring Horace back to Hogwarts. He thinks Horace wants to believe in a "Chosen One" that will deliver the magical community from Lord Thingy (and the death sentence "former" Death Eaters live under). As Dumbledore says to Harry after their departure, *"You showed Horace exactly how much he stands to gain by returning to Hogwarts"* (HALF-BLOOD PRINCE, Chapter 4, pg. 74).

It would also explain why there was an opening for a Potions Master and head of Slytherin House when Severus applied for the job. Dumbledore had most likely expelled the Death Eater from his staff during Volde War I.

Cindie Reiter in the United Kingdom noticed, too, that Dumbledore was not bashful about talking in the negative about Horace and asking Harry to consider what he thinks of the new Potions teacher. Harry, of course, accepts him at face value and fails to ponder on why Dumbledore, friend of werewolves, giants, and centaurs feels he needs to plant the seeds of misgivings about Slughorn.

He asks Harry as they leave his house, *"Did you like him?"* Harry stumbles on his answer and the Headmaster jumps in with a longish description of Horace's love of comfort *"and the company of the famous, the successful, and the powerful"* (HALF-BLOOD PRINCE, Chapter 4, pg. 74). This unflattering portrait, a real novelty for Albus who told no one at Hogwarts about the Tom Riddle, Jr., he met at the orphanage, ends with Dumbledore's explanation for this description.

> *"I tell you all this,"* Dumbledore continued, *"not to turn you against Horace — or, as we must now call him, Professor Slughorn — but to put you on your guard"* (op. cit., pg. 75)

Does Harry put himself on guard? Only against over involvement with the Potions Master. He doesn't suspect that Professor Slughorn was a Death Eater — and might be one now…

Voldemort's Plans

The "EVIL Slughorn" theory posits that the Dark Lord had an intricate set of plans to murder Albus Dumbledore in HALF-BLOOD PRINCE. With Horace Slughorn as his willing or coerced agent inside Hogwarts, Voldemort has his heavy hand on Draco Malfoy, an eye on Severus Snape, and a Dumbledore monitor. He sets a faux Horcrux baited trap in the Cave for the weakened Dumbledore and a test for Severus Snape.

Horace brews a potion for the basin with his greens and Acromantula venom, a potion that is essentially a liquid boggart. Anyone who drinks it will live their worst nightmare and beg for death (for a discussion of what Dumbledore sees, see "But Obviously Dumbledore is Not Jesus" in my uppcomming new book later this year, Zossima Press, 2006). Either Horace tips Dumbledore about the Cave and tells him something about a potion (information he might have through "Slug Club" and Slytherin alumni?), or, more likely, Severus Snape is given information by Voldemort that he knows — perhaps even pointedly "allows" — Snape will pass on to Dumbledore.

Dumbledore, nearing the end of his protracted "stoppered death," has little choice except to follow the leads and take Harry to the Cave with him (to pass the Horcrux-destroying torch if he dies in the attempt). He is nearly destroyed by the Slughorn potion but with Harry's help (after rescuing him from the Inferi) he is able to escape. Only to fall into the second part of the trap on the Astronomy Tower, which is also a test of Severus Snape's loyalties and a sacrifice of Draco Malfoy, at least as originally planned.

Voldemort's trap on the Astronomy Tower is not the first trap in which he uses the hero's virtue to draw him in. As we know from the Headmaster's anger with Harry when his young friend seems to imply he is rushing away from Hogwarts and leaving the school unprotected (PRINCE, Chapter 25, pg. 550), Dumbledore has a "Student Protection thing" akin to Harry's "Saving People thing" that Voldemort used to get Harry into the Hall of Prophecy (PHOENIX, Chapter 34).

Having suckered Dumbledore into a life-sapping and vain search for a Horcrux, Voldemort has ordered his cronies to send up the Dark Mark over Hogwarts. The Dark Lord knows the Headmaster will fly to it no matter his condition if he is still alive because he must save his students. Malfoy admits this was the plan in his talk with Dumbledore (PRINCE, Chapter 27, pg. 590).

I think the Dark Lord had two hopes for the Astronomy Tower confrontation above and beyond the killing of Dumbledore. The first is that Draco Malfoy will be killed. Dumbledore says as much to the boy when offering him sanctuary. *"Nobody would be surprised that you had died in your attempt to kill me — forgive me, but Lord Voldemort probably expects it"* (PRINCE, Chapter 27, pg. 592). As his mother said to Severus in Spinner's End, *"Then I am right, [the Dark Lord] has chosen Draco in revenge!"* choked Narcissa. *"He does not mean him to succeed, he wants him to be killed trying!"* (PRINCE, Chapter 2, pg. 34)

Lord Thingy may also have intended the Astronomy Tower confrontation to be a loyalty test for Severus Snape. He assumed Draco would be killed trying to kill the greatest wizard who ever lived — and he undoubtedly knows about the Unbreakable Vow with Narcissa through Bellatrix.

As he doesn't know that Dumbledore is already dead but in "suspended de-animation," the Astronomy Tower confrontation in which the Death Eaters wait for Draco to do the killing looks to be Voldemort's final exam for his most faithful or least trustworthy servant, Severus Snape. If he kills Dumbledore, what doubt can there be of his loyalties even among the jealous Death Eaters? If he fails to kill Dumbledore, he dies for breaking the Unbreakable Vow.

Sounds like just the sort of soul-wrenching position Voldemort would love to set up! All or nothing! The test is set with the cast of players Voldemort sends to Hogwarts via the Vanishing Cabinets. This is not an All-Star team, to say the least. Where is Bellatrix? No, the Dark Lord sends the second team to be sure that Severus will be the man in charge and to pull the trigger on Dumbledore, if anyone gets that close.

What Really Happened on the Tower

Pretty neat plan, eh? Voldemort wasn't just sitting on his hands all year. But how did this plan work out?

I think after Voldemort hears the various reports from the Death Eaters who were there that he will be delighted. Dumbledore is dead, Severus Snape is now a full-time Death Eater who can be given the most horrible of assignments, and the Malfoys have been sufficiently punished by the experience. Unlike his plan for the recovery of the Prophecy, Voldemort's plans to kill Dumbledore, torture the Malfoys, and reveal Snape's true loyalties all seem to have worked out perfectly. If only Draco had died… Oh, well. You can't have everything.

But what really happened?

It could have happened this way:

Albus the Late was un-stoppered by the Cave potion and death quickly spread from his arm through his body. He insisted on his return to Hogsmeade and then again on the Astronomy Tower that Harry get Severus and that he "Do nothing else, speak to nobody else, and do not remove your cloak" (PRINCE, Chapter 27, pg. 582).

The obvious reason that he is calling Severus — the reason that Harry and we assume is his reason — is for medical help. He saved Draco from the Sectumsempra wound Harry gave him and saved Dumbledore from the ring Horcrux disaster. Dumbledore seems to be calling for a medic or Corpsman.

Re-reading the passage in light of "Stoppered Death" and "EVIL Slughorn" I have to think Dumbledore knows he is way beyond re-stoppering before he gets to the Astronomy Tower. If he isn't looking for medical help, though, his call for Severus is either to get him to do the push to death (to maintain Severus' cover as a Death Eater and to save his life from Death Eater attack — a sure consequence of his failing Voldemort's test — and vis-a-vis the Unbreakable Vow) or to say goodbye to his beloved apprentice and try to reconcile him with Harry.

Unfortunately, all Dumbledore's hopes for a death-watch reconciliation between Harry and Severus are blown away by the appearance of Draco first and then the other Death Eaters. He manages, of course, to save Severus' life and value to the Order of the Phoenix as a "deep plant" in Voldemort's camp by sacrificing himself and seeming to be killed by the man who had "saved his death." Dumbledore also works a little final alchemical magic in showing mercy to Draco and preventing his destroying his soul by an act of murder. If his "execution" wasn't pre-arranged with Severus, one assumes his final act was to open his mind to the only Legilimens on the Tower turret and urge him to do the right and necessary thing.

Where does this leave Snape? If "Stoppered Death" and "EVIL Slughorn" are true, then Severus has inherited Dumbledore's mantle as the Chief Wizard in the resistance movement to a Dark Lord take-over, albeit as a double-agent with no contact in the Order. He is responsible, too, for Draco's preservation from further Lord Voldemort punishment and his reconciliation with the good.

Severus is also, it seems, the man to pick up as much as possible where Dumbledore left off in tutoring and supporting Harry, the Prophesied vanquisher of Voldemort. How he is to do this without being able to reveal to Harry the non-Occlumens the real story presents perhaps his greatest challenge. He certainly did a bang-up job of teaching Harry what he must do to prepare for combat with the Dark Lord in the final confrontation at the School gates. *"Keep your mouth shut and your mind closed, Potter!"* and *"No Unforgivable Curses from you, Potter!"* are just the advice Harry needs — if in battle with his raging mentor he may not have been especially receptive to these instructions. Too bad! Dumbledore himself couldn't have said it more succinctly.

Objections

The principal objections to this view of what really happened in HALF-BLOOD PRINCE are that [1] Snape is a sadist and obviously unbalanced in his hatred for Harry (therefore he cannot be a good guy), [2] all the evidence against Slughorn is circumstantial and, though he is a despicable parasite and unprincipled comfort seeker, he certainly isn't EVIL or a Death Eater, and [3] "Stoppered Death" is just too wacky to be true (Ms. Rowling would have had to give us more pointers to this possibility for it to be fair).

Let's roll through these objections one at a time.

About Snape being a vicious Harry Hater and therefore no good, I offer this pointed response of Albus Dumbledore to Minerva McGonagall's objection to Harry's being left with the Dursleys:

> "It's the best place for him, said Dumbledore firmly. "His aunt and uncle will be able to explain everything to him when he's older. I've written them a letter."
>
> "A letter?" repeated Professor McGonagall faintly, sitting back down on the wall. "Really, Dumbledore, you think you can explain all this in a letter? These people will never understand him! He'll be famous — a legend — I wouldn't be surprised if today was known as Harry Potter day in the future — there will be books written about Harry — every child in our world will know his name!"
>
> "Exactly," said Dumbledore, looking very seriously over the top of his half-moon glasses. "It would be enough to turn any boy's head. Famous before he can walk and talk! Famous for something he won't even remember! Can't you see how much better off he'll be, growing up away from all that until he's ready to take it?" (PHILOSOPHER'S STONE, chapter 1, pg. 13).

Dumbledore the alchemist understands the "play of contraries." A force without resistance dissipates while a force meeting resistance concentrates and grows stronger. Dudley is the living example of a child who receives no correction or restraint or punishment. Dumbledore notes in his farewell to the Dursleys in HALF-BLOOD PRINCE that, though they have treated Harry with cruelty and neglect, "he has at least escaped the appalling damage you have inflicted upon the unfortunate boy sitting between you," meaning "Dudders" (chapter 3, pg. 55).

My question about Severus' supposed sadism and cruelty to Harry is, if we subtract the "cruel Potions master" from Harry's Hogwarts experience, haven't we created a Harry Potter that really is the spitting image of James Potter? Without reproof and criticism from Severus, who would take the Boy Who Lived to task? I am left to wonder if there were no "severity" in Harry's life if we would like him very much. Knowing that Dumbledore put Harry in the cruel, negligent home he did — and left him there when he learned McGonagall was right in her assessment of the Dursleys, makes me think that he might have either assigned Severus this job or at least not felt obliged to restrain him.

I am not a Snape apologist. I find his battering of Harry to be bewildering. I also know, though, that a large part of my ill feelings about the Half-Blood Prince is Harry's age-old prejudice that he has from his father and godfather and any adolescent's self-formation around that which they despise. This is the influence of the voice in which Ms. Rowling tells the stories; my view is Harry's view.

It's just as likely that Severus treats Harry as he does to insure that every Death Eater family knows through their children that the Potter-Snape relationship is only unremitting enmity. And the Dark Lord or his Legilimens savvy successor would never find a happy Snape memory between Harry's ears.

I also think, once we step out from Harry's view, we can see why Dumbledore trusts Severus without reservation, even admires him. The Potions master is easily the greatest wizard on staff at Hogwarts and perhaps the greatest Potions maker of the age. His disagreeable personality, what might be called his "aggressive honesty" or "inability to suffer fools gladly," makes his being honored as he should be — for his genius or for his bravery in serving as a double-agent in the first and second Voldemort wars — extremely unlikely. Snape is what Aristotle called a "megalo-psychos" or "Great-Souled Man," proud but with reason, haughty but self-aware.

I think it requires little stretch of the imagination to see Severus as the great hero of the Harry Potter books (which I explain in the last chapter of UNLOCKING HARRY POTTER: FIVE KEYS FOR THE SERIOUS READER, Zossima Press, 2006, which includes my predictions for the Grand Finale). About Horace Slughorn being harmless, even just an amusing "slug on the wall," I submit that this belief and the vehement resistance to "EVIL Slughorn" is evidence of Ms. Rowling's genius with narrative misdirection.

Voldemort has to be up to something beyond punishing the Malfoys this year, and, if he is, he'll need a willing hand inside Hogwarts. If it isn't Severus Snape, who else can this Voldemort agent be *but* Horace Slughorn? Are we to believe it is the Grey Lady or Professor Vector? We believe Horace is affable and harmless because Harry accepts appearances as reality (and isn't very discerning even about appearances).

My favorite objection to "EVIL Slughorn" is that Horace Slughorn is a comic or satiri-cal invention of Ms. Rowling to poke fun (albeit with a sharp stick) at those teachers in secondary schools and universities who create fan clubs and cliques about themselves. These people are unprincipled by definition and self-important, of course, but in always pursuing their creature comforts and the high opinion of others they are incapable of heroic virtue or astonishing vice. Therefore, Slughorn cannot be evil.

I like this objection because it points to Ms. Rowling's satirical purpose in much of what she writes (about the school, the media, and the Ministry...). I really like it, though, because it is almost exactly upside-down.

The reason Horace Slughorn is an excellent candidate for the Dark Lord's servant within Hogwarts is just *because* he is a self-consumed, unprincipled, "beyond good and evil" lover of crystallized pineapple. The greatest supporters of evil-doers are those who do nothing because they are only concerned about their private interests. That Ms. Rowling makes this character seem harmless is to make her point in dramatic fashion (when "EVIL Slughorn" is revealed) that this sort of person is the most destructive and dangerous person when the good are heroically attempting resistance to evil and tyranny.

And to the last objection, that "Stoppered Death" is too wacky and from too obscure a place in the books to be an acceptable clue according to the rules, I can only say "pshaw." Ms. Rowling mentions Dumbledore's horribly disfigured hand and arm in every passage he appears in HALF-BLOOD PRINCE. She points in story and by specific reference to the first Potions class in PHILOSOPHER'S STONE three times in this book and mentions several items from this class that Professor Snape discusses (the bezoar, the Draught of Living Death, etc). Ms. Rowling has more than satisfied the rules by raising an important question — "What's with Dumbledore's hand and arm?" — and pointing to the possible answer, namely, Severus' ability to "Stopper Death." This is only far-fetched if you accept the narrative line as complete, which it clearly is not.

Conclusion: *Half-Blood Prince* is the Best Harry Potter Novel

As I said long ago, when I am asked what I think of HARRY POTTER AND THE HALF-BLOOD PRINCE, my response is that it is easily the best book of the series. I think it is the best book Ms. Rowling has written and is probably better than the series finale can be because it is a masterful showpiece of what she does best as an author.

HALF-BLOOD PRINCE like every other Harry Potter novel is a fascinating hero's journey and alchemical work in which we and Harry are transformed. She advances the four principal themes of the series in this book (choice, change, prejudice, and love's victory over death) and delivers a "wow" transcendent meaning and imaginative experience of death and resurrection. In this achievement alone, HALF-BLOOD PRINCE is as good or better than the other five books in the series.

What makes the sixth book the best book of the series so far, though, is that Ms. Rowling has managed to tell a fascinating and satisfying story, which story also raises more questions than it answers, gives the necessary clues to solving the larger mysteries of the series, and, unbelievably, leaves the reader spinning from the narrative misdirection judo move at the end. In a departure from every previous book, we readers are left thinking at the end of HALF-BLOOD PRINCE that Harry is a Prophet and that we were fools to doubt his intuition about Snape and Malfoy.

The articles which follow in this collection each answers in convincing fashion several of the questions with which we started this chapter. Each also assumes you understand "narrative misdirection" and the deft way Ms. Rowling manipulates our attention away from information she is obliged to show us (the 'shipping passages of PRINCE were ideal for this work, as she all but said in the Mugglenet interview, given the frenzied state of Fandom on this side issue before publication).

The better ones, in fact, show why my "EVIL Slughorn" theory is wrong-headed or worse; Sally Gallo even argues persuasively that, rather than the villain, Professor Slughorn is the great hero of HALF-BLOOD PRINCE who affects the greatest switch-and-disappearance act in the history of Hogwarts or stage magic. If you remember why HALF-BLOOD PRINCE is the best Harry Potter novel and how narrative misdirection works and forget or disagree with "Stoppered Death" and "EVIL Slughorn," I will have done my job and can pass the baton to W. B. Harte happily. For my best guesses about when Dumbledore died, "stoppered death" undone, and how the two great Potions masters created a staged death on the Astronomy Tower, I hope you'll read the last chapter in my UNLOCKING HARRY POTTER. I explain there how Severus plays Dumbledore throughout Half-Blood Prince, from picking up Harry at the Dursleys to the scene in the Cave, and and his being the Gryffindor/Slytherin Hermaphrodite and hero of the books.

As I said in the Introduction, though, our purpose here is not to write spoilers before you even have the last part of the story. We are, rather, determined to challenge you to probe canon and speculate boldly to see how Ms. Rowling will finish the world's best selling book with the "biggest twist" in English Literature. The writers here will speak confidently about what must have happened in HALF-BLOOD PRINCE. All of us are as certain, however, we will be surprised and delighted by all we missed when the whole story is told. Until then, however, hold on for a long, hard look in the coming chapter at R.A.B. and the probability that he switched the Horcrux in the Cave *before* it was placed in what Joyce Odell calls the "Birdbath of Doom."

Wendy B. Harte

Wendy Bierman Harte has had a 20 year career in the marketing research industry, focused on consumer packaged goods. She has worked for Coca-Cola Bottling, comScore Networks, and Information Resources, Inc. where she is currently a Vice-President. Wendy is a specialist in the area of data interpretation.

Wendy has a Bachelor of Arts degree in Economics, and a Masters in Business Administration. She resides in the Bay Area of Northern California with her husband and two young children who never seem to tire of playing "Prisoner of Azkaban" on their home pc. You can find her Harry Potter related musings in "The Chamber of Mom" at:

http://professor_mum.livejournal.com

Wendy first purchased the Harry Potter books in 2003, assuming that she would read them aloud to her oldest child. The kids have yet to pry the books out of their mother's hands. Wendy is an avid reader of mysteries, historical fiction, biographies of Elizabethan era men and women, children's books, and of course, anything related to Harry Potter.

ACKNOWLEDGEMENTS:

I would like to most gratefully acknowledge Joyce Odell, John Granger, and Daniela Teo. Their highly perceptive influences inhabit my work. I would also like to give special thanks to Wendy Swiggett, the Bierman Family, and Paul, Lila and Spencer Harte for their support. I'd also like to acknowledge these excellent resource sites: hp_essays on Live Journal, Mugglenet, The Leaky Cauldron, The HP Lexicon, Madam Scoop, The Quick Quotes Quill, Wikipedia, Red Hen Publications, and The Hogwarts Professor.

The Curse of the Black Family Tree

Do not seek evil gains; evil gains are the equivalent of a disaster
– Hesiod Works and Days; Greek Philosopher, 800 BC

B LACK FAMILY EMPHASIS:

I think most of us who invest time in unraveling clues in the Harry Potter series well know that J.K.Rowling is not one for emphasizing idle coincidences (except, perhaps the Mark Evans brouhaha, which she quickly and deftly swatted aside). Given the long gap between HALF-BLOOD PRINCE and Book 7, Jo apparently felt the need to dangle a snack to her hungry readers with a hand-drawn Black Family Tree created for a charity auction in February 2006.

We first learn of the Tree in ORDER OF THE PHOENIX Chapter 6:

> *"The tapestry looked immensely old; it was faded and looked as though doxies had gnawed it in places; nevertheless, the golden thread with which it was embroidered still glittered brightly enough to show them a sprawling family tree dating back (as far as Harry could tell) to the Middle Ages. Large words at the very top of the tapestry read:*

> ### *The Noble and Most Ancient House of Black*
> ### *"Toujours Pur"*

While Sirius spends time in this chapter pointing out various family players and those whose existence has been conspicuously erased, we don't get a very complete view of all the characters present. The recently published, and very detailed Black Tree makes clear how, through blood and marriage, Nymphadora, Draco, Neville, Crabbe, Burke, Barty Crouch, Bellatrix, the Weasleys, and perhaps even Harry are all related through the Blacks.

Why did Ms. Rowling publish this specific multi-generational family tree when she has, besides the honorable BOOK AID fund-raising angle? While she did address Black Family history in ORDER OF THE PHOENIX, in HALF-BLOOD PRINCE she really focused her emphasis on Tom Riddle's back story, excluding other wizarding families except as they intersected with the Dark Lord's development. Maybe Jo realized that the clues for the R.A.B. Locket switch caper, which came to light in HALF-BLOOD PRINCE, were a bit too scant, even for her careful readers. It's with this in mind that I started to obsess on Jo's latest hint, and came to this conclusion: it just cannot be without significance that both Regulus Black and his father Orion Black died in the same year, 1979, a fact we learn from the just published Black Family Tree.

Before we begin speculating about Black Family events from 1979, let's give up the pretense that R.A.B. is anyone else *except* Regulus Black. Jo told us directly that Regulus would be a "fine guess" during her lengthy July 16th 2005 interview with Mugglenet and the Leaky Cauldron. In the Dutch edition of the Harry Potter novels Regulus and all Black surnamed family members have their last name translated as "Zwarts". Correspondingly, the locket note in HALF-BLOOD PRINCE is initialed "R.A.Z.", so that seems proof enough. There is no telling if Jo allowed this to happen on purpose or not. My guess is no — it just slipped by during the Dutch translation of Chapter 1 of SORCERER'S STONE and the die was cast for all remaining books (the single reference is from Hagrid: "Young Sirius Black lent it to me"). The international translations are released time lagged from the British and American editions.

Returning to the July 2005 Mugglenet/Leaky Cauldron interview, here's what Jo had to say after she referred to Regulus as "a fine guess" for the identity of R.A.B.:

ES: *What's one question you wished to be asked and what would be the answer to that question?*

JKR: Um - [long pause] — such a good question. What do I wish I could be asked? [Pause] Today, just today, July the 16th, I was really hoping someone would ask me about R.A.B., and you did it. Just today, because I think that is — well, I hoped that people would.

MA: *Is there more we should ask about him?*

JKR: There are things you will deduce on further readings, I think — well you two definitely will, for sure - that, yeah, I was really hoping that R.A.B. would come out.

MA: *Forgive me if I'm remembering incorrectly, but was Regulus the one who was murdered by Voldemort —*

JKR: Well Sirius said he wouldn't have been because he wasn't important enough, remember?

MA: *But that doesn't have to be true, if [R.A.B.] is writing Voldemort a personal note.*

JKR: That doesn't necessarily show that Voldemort killed him personally, but

Sirius himself suspected that Regulus got in a little too deep. Like Draco. He was attracted to it, but the reality of what it meant was way too much to handle.

So, Jo's greatest wish in July 2005 was for readers to reflect on R.A.B., and in February 2006 she publishes the Black Family tree. That's a lot of purposeful emphasis, if you ask me. Putting the Black Family Tree under a microscope, is not running down a rabbit trail, but pursuing an important piece of the story line puzzle. The Tree is an important secondary septology resource, much like Jo's FANTASTIC BEASTS AND WHERE TO FIND THEM, and QUIDDICH THROUGH THE AGES. Both books contain many series clues, and both were written for charity.

The sub-title below Jo's hand drawn tree reads: "there are many stories between the lines". We'll take Jo at her word, and assume that there is something important that needs to be inferred from the phrase. What we'll discover is rather surprising: that the fruits of the Black tree, including Sirius, Bellatrix, Regulus and the Malfoys, Slytherins all, have proven to be downright poisonous to the Dark Lord. Their handling of his Horcruxes make them, almost as much as Harry, Voldemort's bane.

Narrative Misdirection:

Back to ORDER OF THE PHOENIX Chapter 6, Harry and Sirius are examining the Black family tapestry, and Sirius relates these four key plot points:

1. Sirius hates his family due to their pure-blood mania;
2. Sirius states his younger brother Regulus joined the Death Eaters. His parents did not, but they supported Death Eater goals;
3. Sirius thinks that Regulus was likely killed on Voldemort's orders, but the deed was done by other Death Eaters. Regulus himself wasn't important enough to be personally killed by the Dark Lord himself; and
4. Regulus had a change of heart and tried to back out of the organization, and that is the reason why he was killed.

If there's one thing we know about Jo, it's that her characters are often incorrect with their interpretation of events. There is no better example of this than Harry — think about how wrong he was regarding Sirius Black for over 300 pages of PRISONER OF AZKABAN. In fact, everyone (except Peter Pettigrew) had their facts incorrect regarding Sirius and the crime he was accused of. This technique has been nicely dubbed "narrative misdirection", and in simple terms it means that as we view the story filtered through a character's eyes, opinions, and life experiences, we can purposely be drawn to a premature and incorrect conclusion. The reader becomes mislead as the characters bring their prejudices and judgments to bear upon the situation. Jo herself says: "…mine are very character-driven books" (Mugglenet/Leaky Cauldron interview July 2006). [See Chapter One of this book for a longer discussion of narrative misdirection.]

Sirius' first two statements above are facts. But, he doesn't know the specific details regarding points 3 and 4. Both of these ideas about Regulus' death are just his conjecture at this point in the septology. How and why Regulus died, consequently, is anything but established and that he died in the same year as his father seems doubly curious.

Our primary interest in Regulus remains on his ability to pull a double cross or switch with Voldemort's Locket Horcrux. Let's look at this deed, like we would a crime, with an eye on why he might have died so near in time to his father's demise.

The Crime:

In a criminal investigation, a detective's job is to interview suspects and review evidence to solve the crime. They have to trace motives (why something occurred), means (how it was executed), and opportunity (the specific timing of said crime) to solve the 'whodunit', with the assumption that there are few perfect crimes. We'll treat the R.A.B. Locket switch caper as a crime and try to figure out what happened given logic, slim canon references, and the Black Family Tree:

Motive (Why Something Occurred):

- Regulus discovered a secret during his short Death Eater tenure (sometime between June and December 1979) that was so sensational that it caused him to want to leave Voldemort's service. He spent his entire childhood being raised in a household which supported pure blood superiority, and after just a few short months of adult service, he wants out. Therefore, this 'secret' would have to be inflammatory, and something that crossed his relative boundaries of decency to cause such a reversal

- We can assume that Voldemort has taken care that a very specific secret remain unknown

- Did Orion pre-decease his son in 1979? A son avenging his father's murder is indeed a powerful archetype. In classic literature we might think immediately of Shakespeare's HAMLET, or the ORESTIA, or, yes, our own HARRY POTTER. If Orion did meet an untimely demise, that event could provide Regulus with motivation to turn against the Dark Lord. Given Orion's security concerns (Grimmauld Place was Unplottable) you must wonder how someone managed to murder him at all. The death/murder of Regulus' father does not pass the definition of being a "secret" given that the Death Eater manifesto is about ethnic cleansing. Orion would have been a general supporter of this point of view

Means (How it was Executed):

☞ Despite excellent Fandom theories involving house elf assistance, it just stretches the imagination that 18 year-old Regulus could have successfully executed the Locket switch right under Voldemort's nose without a more accomplished wizard accomplice. What wizard or witch, though, especially among the Death Eaters would knowingly assist this young man on a virtual suicide mission contra Voldemort? The Locket Horcrux switch is a complex crime with so many unknowns regarding means and opportunity: discovery of the Cave location, learning the trick necessary to enter the Cave (even "Dumbledore" sweated a bit over that), knowing the magic to navigate safely to the center of Lake Inferi, the potion barrier, the switch, retreat, not to mention animated dead bodies. These books are about the skill and luck of Harry Potter, not Regulus Black. We need something less complicated or less implausible than Regulus solo or leading a team of commandos on a mission to steal, switch, and replace the Locket Horcrux

☞ The fact that the note inside the fake locket referenced the word "Horcrux" meant that Regulus clearly understood what that particular magical term meant: murder and the splitting of one's soul to achieve immortality, or, at least the condition of not being able to be killed. There would have been no plot to switch the lockets unless its purpose as Voldemort's death defier was understood by R.A.B.

☞ Whereas Dumbledore states in HALF-BLOOD PRINCE that Voldemort believes that no one else is aware of his Horcruxes, he must be mistaken. We know Horcruxes were supposed to be a forbidden subject at Hogwarts, but the Black family clearly has a fascination with the Dark Arts, and likely has a Dark subject matter library (recall "NATURE'S NOBILITY: A WIZARDING GENEALOGY" in the Drawing Room?). Recall that young wizards tend to be home schooled before they enter Hogwarts, and you can easily assume the topics and reading matter the Blacks might have offered their children

☞ Why place the Horcrux Locket in the Cave of all places at all? It's because it is Lord Voldemort's specific wish that the Locket be hidden there for the Cave's booby-trapped protection and its symbolic power. Regulus, therefore, must have been part of the plan to hide the Horcrux in the Cave or learned of the plan if he placed the faux Horcrux Locket in the basin

☞ Voldemort completely trusted the person in charge of placing the Horcrux on the island as he apparently was unaware of the switch. Someone has reported "mission accomplished" to him, and Voldemort believed it to be true

Opportunity (Timing for the Plan): ·

☞ If he did not know about the plot in advance and prepare accordingly, in order for Regulus to switch the Slytherin Locket and pen a revenge note, he would need both access to the locket and privacy to pen his 'gotcha' note

☞ Only Regulus himself, shielded from close view, could have placed the fake locket into the Stone Basin potion. Anyone else participating in its placement would see that it didn't look like Slytherin's locket. Even Harry noticed this nearly immediately after he found the Fake Locket next to Dumbledore's body

☞ It has been theorized that only a wizard with a Dark Mark could place the Locket into the basin potion. Regulus would qualify in this regard, as would Bellatrix. This might be true, but isn't necessary. Either via the Dark Mark or some other means, Voldemort has set up some mechanism for someone other than himself to place the item there. Think of an open safe — anyone who has access to the bank can put gold inside of it, but once you close it and spin the lock, the gold is safe from all who don't know the combination

R.A.B.'s Opportunity:

These crime scene elements led me to the conclusion that Voldemort must have entrusted the Horcrux Slytherin Locket and the concealment assignment to Regulus' older cousin *Bellatrix Lestrange*. Voldemort did not place the Locket in the Cave himself otherwise he would have placed the real one there. I am just going to assume for the rest of my argument that Lord Voldemort didn't place the Locket and *then* R.A.B. switched it out because of the sheer complexity of such an enterprise. The details which follow still jive well with canon to make such an assumption.

Recall this mysterious quote from Bellatrix in Half-Blood Prince Chapter 2: *"The Dark Lord has, in the past, entrusted me with his most precious… "* Bellatrix's remark " … in the past" could easily refer to 1979, before she entered Azkaban.

We do have a precedent for Voldemort entrusting one of his Death Eaters with a Horcrux assignment in the past: he gave the Tom Riddle Diary to Lucius Malfoy before his fall at Godric's Hollow.

If Bellatrix was in charge of the Slytherin Locket, Regulus' switch opportunity almost certainly occurred at the Black Family home: Grimmauld Place. Sirius states that his father placed many charms on their home and it was Unplottable (i.e. it can't be located on a map). I'd suspect that only immediate Black Family members might be allowed to know of its exact location and as such, cousin Bellatrix might be able to access Grimmauld Place, but other non-related Death Eaters would not. It is also possible that the Black family home was a Death Eater meeting place (at least for the Black family participants), making it ironic that years later it would become the headquarters for the Order of the Phoenix. There is no evidence in canon for this, except, of course, the descriptions of the Slytherin styled hardware there. The most compelling clue that a switch might have taken place at Grimmauld Place is the existence there of a heavy locket that no one can open — a locket that careful readers with good memories assumed was the Horcrux locket as soon as they learned the one from the Cave was a fake. In HALF-BLOOD PRINCE Chapter 10, Marvolo Gaunt grabs his poor daughter by the necklace chain she is wearing to show Bob Ogden that they are indeed Slytherin's heirs. Jo describes it as "a gold chain" and "a heavy gold locket."

R.A.B.'s Motivation:

In discussing *why* Regulus would do the switching deed above, I noted it was probably consequent to a discovery about Lord Voldemort, something the Dark Lord didn't want known. Well, how many secrets does Lord Voldemort have to be discovered? He secretly adores taffy? No, he's been set up to be an unkillable psychopath — what could possibly embarrass the Dark Lord? Is it an unknown secret the Jo has withheld from us and will spring at the 11th hour in Book 7? No, that just isn't her style: Jo must have already provided us a clue to reason it out. Whatever the secret is, we should assume that R.A.B. has 'discovered' it despite or even because of Voldemort's taking some care for it to be kept secret.

It seems safe to assume from evidence in canon that the secret that the R.A.B. note refers to is this: that Lord Voldemort, the Heir of Slytherin, is really a half-blood wizard — and this makes Voldemort not only a hypocrite but an unworthy leader, at least to the Blacks whose family motto is "Toujours Pur" or "Always Pure"

Some sleuths have suggested that Regulus turned against his master because he objected to the creation of Horcruxes in principle. This theory just doesn't wash. Why would Dark Wizards involved in the quest for racial purity object to murder? Purifying the wizarding race doesn't involved sending Mudbloods, Half-Bloods, and other objectionable creatures to a humane detention camp. Ethnic cleansing is a call for murder.

Dirty laundry that the supreme leader of Salazar Slytherin's noble cause is not who he claims to be isn't truly inflammatory in and of itself — it's just troubling for its hypocrisy. But this secret, if it was combined with the unjust murder of a teenager's family member, might spark a bonfire of emotions. Even little racists love their mum and dad in Jo's world. Young pure-blood Draco Malfoy, for example, isn't the most sympathetic character, but he does spend the entire sixth book frantically trying to protect his parents from Voldemort's wrath.

Principles of Wild Guesswork:

"From this point forth, we shall be leaving the firm foundations of fact and journeying together through the murky marshes of memory into the thickets of wildest guesswork." Dumbledore, HALF-BLOOD PRINCE Chapter 10

We don't have much literary canon to reconstruct the elaborate back story that links the Harry Potter series together. That's why the Black Family tree proves so useful. But there are certain ground rules for good theories that most of Jo's careful readers agree upon:

1. You can't invent magic. If Jo hasn't demonstrated a spell (ex: the Avada Kedavra protection spell), it can't be created to explain anything. The exception is magic that she says exists, such as the Horcrux Creation spell. We don't know its name, and it certainly hasn't been demonstrated, but we know that it is a process that few wizards have accomplished: *"There is a spell, do not ask me... "* says Slughorn (HALF-BLOOD PRINCE, Chapter 23)

2. All of her character's points of view are filtered through their prejudices and desires, and can be wrong as well as right. Their interpretation of events should not be automatically trusted, and this includes the seemingly omniscient narrator who tells the story as if looking over Harry's shoulder. The characters in Jo's world are flawed human beings and creatures so their testimony isn't always what it seems

3. You can, however, firmly trust the roles and functions of magical elements that she has demonstrated for us: a spell (*Accio*), a creature (House Elves), transportation (the Floo Network), magical principles (time travel), or a place (the Department of Mysteries). She is usually quite clear when it comes to establishing magical boundaries (ex: you can repair a broken bowl but not return the potion contents)

4. Jo applies "echoes" to characters and events to emphasize that the past and present are linked in the Potterverse. If something is familiar to you (ex: both Harry and Voldemort are orphans), it has been purposefully written that way for you to pay attention

5. Jo often writes situations with more than one clear interpretation. It is the readers' job to look carefully at the slim nuggets of canon support and develop a unifying theory, minimizing disconnects

6. While Jo has dozens of notebooks in her private office with the backstory, she isn't 100% perfect with details. Jo has a little trouble with math (ex: the birth/death dates of characters), but her Potterverse, for the most part, hangs together well and elegantly

7. The series runs on two parallel tracks: what Harry observes and what else goes on behind the scenes. 'Behind the scenes' might refer to the past (i.e. the Four Founders) or it might refer to the goings on in the present outside of Harry's point of view (i.e., activities at the Ministry of Magic). Don't forget that you're never getting even half the story

8. Lastly, Jo has quite a few storylines to unify in Book 7. The US Hardback edition ORDER OF THE PHOENIX is over 870 pages in length, and she has stated she doesn't want the final book to be quite that long. The puzzle pieces, though, will all have to fit together in the end. Because of the need for a satisfying conclusion in a certain number of pages, all mystery-solving theories must pass what some have termed "a simplicity test." I basically agree, but PRISONER OF AZKABAN is anything but a simple story, so I will re-label this requirement as 'a non-contortion test.' All solutions must be linear, not conflict with any clear facts, and fit together in the spirit and space of a tale well told

As such, here is my re-enactment of what might have happened in 1979, the 'means' for the Locket switch. I have combined canon sources, conjecture, and the principles detailed above.

The R.A.B. Caper Imagined:

In HALF-BLOOD PRINCE, Albus Dumbledore escorts Harry into a memory he received after visiting an Azkaban prisoner named Morfin Gaunt. It's difficult to pinpoint when Dumbledore made this prison visit. All the Headmaster tells us is that he extracted Morfin Gaunt's memory, with difficulty, shortly before Morfin's prison death. Dumbledore states that he tried to use the extracted memory to secure Morfin's release, but Morfin passes away before the Ministry reached a decision.

We don't know the date of Morfin's death (we sure could use a family tree), whether it was closer to 1942 (when Tom Riddle might have visited his Uncle) or more recently (closer to the peak of Voldemort's power in the late '70's). It's a huge range, but, heading into the speculative thicket, let's suppose the not unlikely possibility that a Ministry Official, who is a Death Eater sympathizer, has taken note of Dumbledore's visit, either at Azkaban or, more likely, consequent to Dumbledore's appeal for Gaunt's release.

Perhaps this Ministry insider is one of Sirius and Regulus' grandfathers, Arcturus (paternal: 1901-1991) or Pollux (maternal: 1912-1990) In ORDER OF THE PHOENIX, Chapter 6, recall that the kids during the clean-up of Grimmauld Place, found an Order of Merlin, First Class that had been awarded to one of Sirius's grandfathers (not named) for "Services to the Ministry." Sirius discounts its value, tossing it in a trash bag and says "It means he gave them a load of gold". I suggest that this Ministry insider is Arcturus rather than Pollux Black, because it is Arcturus' son Orion Black who ends up dead in 1979, not Orion's lovely wife and second cousin Walburga, who is Pollux Black's daughter.

As per someone's request or perhaps on his own initiative, Arcturus, who in the past has provided some great 'Service to the Ministry,' goes to Azkaban and speaks with Morfin Gaunt in his cell. He wants to check Dumbledore's information, as we know from HALF-BLOOD PRINCE that memories can be tampered with. While Morfin was a hostile customer, Dumbledore did successfully use Legilimency on him, and was able to secure the Tom Riddle memory that he later showed to Harry. If you recall from ORDER OF THE PHOENIX, when Snape gave Occlumency lessons, Harry was able to perfectly recall what memories Snape had accessed.

Arcturus tells Morfin that he is representing both the Ministry and other sympathizers. He explains that the Black family is secretly in support of the Slytherin family, and he needs to hear again what the blood traitor Albus Dumbledore discovered on a recent visit. And what he learns from Gaunt is this: that some Parselmouth boy, looking for Morfin's father Marvolo, visited Morfin in the Gaunt home. This young man, Morfin's memory reveals, looks exactly like that Muggle Riddle who married and ran off with his sister years ago. That Muggle returned without his sister in tow and now lives in the big Riddle mansion nearby. Oh, and by the way, the Muggle left her and must have stolen Slytherin's Locket. Dumbledore may or may not have shared this last part of the story with the Ministry as the subject dealt with his secret Tom Riddle inquiries.

Later, Arcturus discusses this story with his son as the Slytherin Locket has been mentioned before as part of Black Family lore. His son Orion Black is also quite intrigued as he knew a Tom Riddle at Hogwarts, a wizard assumed to be a Pure Blood. As a matter of fact, this Morfin memory has several Black family intersections:

☞ The Blacks attended Hogwarts with a Tom Riddle:
  - 1925–1985: Walburga Black (Hogwarts 1936-1943)
  - 1926 (December)–NA: Tom Riddle/Lord Voldemort (Hogwarts 1938-1945)

- 1929–1979: Orion Black (Hogwarts 1940-1947)
- They recall that Tom Riddle lived in a Muggle orphanage during the summer months.

👉 Tom Riddle had a group of Slytherin friends around him at Hogwarts: Nott, Rosier, Mulciber, Dolohov, and Avery, all of whom became Death Eaters. Tom Riddle's name is not mentioned among these friends group any longer

👉 Tom Riddle used to work for Arcturus' distant cousin Herbert Burke and vanished, without a trace, along with some valuable artifacts. One of these artifacts was said to be the Slytherin Locket

Perhaps Arcturus and Orion decide to mind their own business given the troubling family connections. They file Morfin's memory of Tom Riddle away. But fast forward to 1979, and the Black's youngest son Regulus has signed up for Lord Voldemort's Death Eaters. Walburga thinks he is a "right hero", but Orion is secretly alarmed. He relates Grandpa Arcturus' story about the mysterious Tom Riddle and the missing Slytherin Locket to his younger son. Regulus tells his father that the information is a big "so what", and not to worry

But security conscious Orion can't let it drop, concerned as he is about Regulus since he is already estranged from his oldest son Sirius. So he asks a few innocent questions of his old Hogwarts' Slytherin pals, or his cousins the Lestranges, or, more likely, someone at Borgin and Burkes shop. Big mistake. Whoever he asked, if they knew what was good for them, let Lord Voldemort know that someone was asking questions about Tom Riddle and a Locket. This news, in 1979, coming on the heels of a mysterious prophesy predicting his downfall, must have sent off loud alarm bells in Lord Voldemort's inner sanctum.

No one knows the exact details of what happened next (except Jo), but, we do know from the Black Family Tree that Orion Black dies in 1979 at the age of 51, still young-ish by wizard standards. The average age of all blood related Black Family Tree males who pre-deceased him (excepting his great-uncle, the first Sirius Black who died as a boy) is 68 years old. Something suspiciously tragic has occurred to the Black Family.

We can guess that Orion is just found dead and assumed to have died of natural causes (*Avada Kedavra* leaves no physical injuries). If nothing else, the reported cause of Orion's death is ambiguous or, if murder is assumed, there are no obvious suspects. Maybe Orion's body was never found, and that is why there is no portrait of him at Grimmauld Place.

Regulus may have been a foolish young man for getting involved with the Death Eaters, but we can assume from Slughorn's admiration that he was capable of reading between the lines of his father's sudden death or disappearance. His worry-wart father had probably spoken to the wrong Slytherin about Grandpa Arcturus' crazy Tom Riddle story, and he ended up dead shortly thereafter. Regulus perhaps had naively assumed that his family was untouchable as several Black Family relatives were in the Death Eaters (himself, Bellatrix, and her husband Rodolphus among others). Morfin's Tom Riddle tale, therefore, must be a story that Lord Voldemort meant to keep secret.

Imagine Regulus asking himself, "Does this mean that Tom Riddle is really Lord Voldemort? If true, then Salazar Slytherin's noble cause is being led by a half-blood or a mudblood who killed my father." Now we have finally entered "inflammatory" territory, as an idealistic young man's personal, family, and ideological boundaries have all been crossed.

Around Halloween 1979 approximately, the Dark Lord was made aware of Sybil Trelawney's prophesy which foretold his downfall via a child who would become Voldemort's vanquisher. Note that 10/31/79 plus 40 weeks puts us precisely at 7/31/80, Harry's birth date. The fact that the subject of the Slytherin Locket surfaced around this time as well, would have been a very troubling turn of events especially in combination to Lord Voldemort. So the Dark Lord asks one of his inner-most circle, one who has access to Grimmauld Place, to do a most urgent and secret errand for him. He normally trusts no one, but there is a certain Death Eater who would be quite useful for this particular assignment.

Voldemort enlists Orion Black's niece, Bellatrix Lestrange, to carry out a two-pronged mission with these instructions:

"First, interrogate Orion's wife Walburga and make sure she is not that aware that I posses Salazar Slytherin's Locket. I believe that Orion might have been poised to betray me with some information he obtained.

"Next, you are to hide the Locket in a safe but secret place that I have prepared. This place is protected by Inferi so you might want to bring your cousin Regulus along to help you with them should they become excited. I am quite close to ensuring immortality for myself and I will do the same for all my loyal Death Eaters as we purify the wizard race. You are my chosen one and no one else knows this information."

Bellatrix is surprised regarding her Aunt and Uncle, the Blacks, but she is also flattered and determined not to fail. Bellatrix appears at Grimmauld Place or, more likely, she is escorted there by Regulus under the pretext of consoling Walburga (who we have seen as being an unattractive screeching piece of work). When they arrive at this secure location Bellatrix tells Regulus that they have been honored with a very special mission for the Dark Lord that will take place that very evening.

He questions her and she tells him quite indiscreetly: "Guess what I think the Dark Lord has accomplished? Immortality!" Or perhaps he just overhears a conversation between Bellatrix and Rodolphus. Bellatrix has speculated correctly that Voldemort must have mastered the ancient Horcrux spell. But, before they go on Voldemort's mission, Bellatrix tells her young cousin, she needs to speak with and console Regulus' mother on the death of her husband, "dear Uncle Orion." She leaves Regulus in the drawing room so she can perform Legilimency on the Widow Black, who, it turns out, knows nothing about Morfin's memory, recent Tom Riddle mentions, or the Slytherin Locket.

"Horcrux? Immortality? Mission?" Regulus' young head must be spinning. Perhaps Bellatrix has given Regulus a package for safe-keeping or to impress on him the importance of their mission. Or perhaps Bellatrix in her excitement, is careless with her belongings (Regulus is a fellow Death Eater, after all) while she slyly interrogates Aunt Walburga in private.

Regulus looks inside her cape or bag and discovers a wrapped heavy locket with a gigantic $\mathcal{S}$ on it — most likely Salazar Slytherin's. A quick trip to Grimmauld Place's library clarifies the unknowns. His father had apparently stumbled upon a secret worthy of protection by murder: Voldemort must be the mud-blood Tom Riddle, but, Regulus decides, this half-blood murderer who dared to kill a pure-blooded Black who knew his dirty secret is neither fit to own nor profit by the Slytherin House founder's locket!

Regulus understands that he can't destroy one of the greatest wizards in history, and he won't be alive long enough to spread the truth, particularly with skilled Legilimens Bellatrix inside normally secure Grimmauld Place. Regulus realizes that he has a unique opportunity, that very second, to avenge his father's death. He summons Kreacher and commands the house elf to find a similar locket in his Mistress' jewelry box, but tell no one. When he returns, they exchange lockets and he tells Kreacher to hide the Slytherin Locket and again, tell no one. Kreacher *must* obey. Alone, Regulus composes the R.A.B. note, places it in the fake locket, and replaces the re-wrapped locket.

A spontaneous crime of opportunity!

That night Bellatrix and Regulus head for the Cave, and offer the necessary blood tribute to enter. Bellatrix at last tells Regulus the plan: only a single wizard can go in the boat across the lake. As Bellatrix is more powerful, she will manage the Inferi. "Take this package and place what is inside of it into the Stone Basin," she orders him. He complies, nervously crossing the lake and placing the fake Horcrux in the potion, well out of view from Bellatrix on the distant shore. After the Fake Locket is safely placed, Regulus returns in the small boat. I think we can assume based on Harry's experience with Occlumency lessons with Severus (PHOENIX, Chapter 24) that Regulus' excitement and righteous anger about what he has learned that night makes his mind an open book to Bellatrix the Legilimens.

She reads what he believes and some part of what he has done.

A furious argument and fight ensues, and Bellatrix acts quickly to silence the young traitor Regulus Black (just like his father and brother!) and pushes his body into Lake Inferi. It is the ultimate act of loyalty as a Death Eater — sacrificing your own family blood in protection of the Dark Lord! Recall that she screeches at Snape in HALF-BLOOD PRINCE, Chapter 2: *"He shares everything with me... he calls me his most loyal, his most faithful... "*. Indeed. Perhaps, too, she is terrified that Voldemort will discover that Regulus had overheard her say the locket was a Horcrux.

Or, could Voldemort have been planning Regulus' death in the Cave from the 'get go'? Perhaps he got wind that Regulus was shaken by his father's death. Lupin does state that Regulus was dead only a few days after turning against the Death Eaters. Maybe Voldemort purposely suggested that Bellatrix take her cousin along precisely because he knew that Bellatrix would deal with him there decisively, if need be. The Cave would be an excellent spot for a fanatical Death Eater to discreetly deal with another less committed follower.

What Voldemort couldn't have anticipated would have been Regulus' discovery of the Horcrux secret and making the switch. After Bellatrix serves her cousin up to the Inferi, she is unable and unwilling to do anything else but escape the Cave. If she did learn about the switch, she could do nothing about it, except hope the Dark Lord would not discover what had happened.

The Cave, Chapter 26 in HALF-BLOOD PRINCE, utilizes the words "black", "blackness", "mirror", and "green" so many times, all terms related to the Black Family. Harry even spots a dead wizard in Lake Inferi, his robes floating in the water. The rest of the Inferi are described as wearing just rags. Does Harry see his godfather's younger brother just below the water's surface?

Assuming the essence of this imagined scenario to be more or less on target, Sirius was right regarding the big picture of his younger brother's death. Regulus wanted out of the Death Eaters but wasn't killed by the Dark Lord himself. Sirius, however, had no access to the details of the crime executed by others. If the above scenario is true, Bellatrix has murdered both of her Black family cousins, Regulus and Sirius.

The fact remains that Bellatrix Lestrange, by accident or by negligence, allowed the Slytherin Locket to slip out of the Dark Lord's possession. Does she know about the switch? She plainly asks Snape in HALF-BLOOD PRINCE, Chapter 2, why he cannot reveal the location of the Order of the Phoenix's Headquarters. He tells her that he is not the location's Secret Keeper. Why does she need reminding of magic that she likely understands quite well?

As suggested above, perhaps Regulus told her what he had done before he died or she performed Legilimency on him as he returned to shore. Maybe Bellatrix would like to search Grimmauld Place before her boss gets wind of what she has allowed to happen on her watch. He was quite furious when he discovered what Lucius Malfoy allowed to happen. As we'll see momentarily, Bellatrix isn't the first or the last Black Family Tree member to have inadvertently sabotaged her master's means to immortality.

R.A.B.'s Note:

Keeping the scenario of Regulus' motivation, means, and actions to switch out the locket Horcrux with a look-alike before getting to the Cave as imagined above firmly in mind, let's look at his note to Voldemort in the Fake Locket and see what it tells us.

> To the Dark Lord
> I know I will be dead long before you read this
> but I want you to know that it was I who discovered your secret.
> I have stolen the real Horcrux and intend to destroy it as soon as I can.
> I face death in the hope that when you meet your match,
> you will be mortal once more.
> R.A.B.

...and look at the crest above the Black Family Tree (redrawn here):

Toujours Pur

The Black family crest has an upside-down **V** chevron type shape with a short sword underneath. The shield is flanked by a ribbon with the motto "Toujours Pur" and decorated with stars and dogs. The mirrored triangle or diamond format of the fake locket note seems to rather purposefully mimic the triangular shape of the Black Family crest. A more direct explanation of the note's diamond shape comes from Astronomy. The stars and constellations Arcturus, Regulus, Sirius, and others are all within two celestial triangles that make up a pattern of stars know as "The Great Diamond of Spring".

I assume that Regulus believed that Voldemort would read his 'boo hiss' note sooner versus later. Therefore, Regulus's bold claim that "it was *I* who discovered your secret" might have been made to emphasize that Regulus is the only Black family member who knows anything about Voldemort's secret. His mother does not, Bellatrix confirmed this, and no one is in touch with Sirius.

Lord Voldemort's Plan B:

The last chapter of HALF-BLOOD PRINCE has Harry reviewing the remaining Horcruxes he needs to collect and destroy:

> *the locket... the cup... the snake... something of Gryffindor's or Ravenclaw's...*
> (HALF BLOOD PRINCE, Chapter 30)

Why did Lord Voldemort trust his Death Eater minions with the Locket and Diary without applying Secret Keeper magic or an Unbreakable Vow? Perhaps Voldemort prefers to avoid the sort of magic which relies on the human characteristic of trust or the intimate touching of hands.

But as mentioned previously, there is a precedent for Voldemort using a loyal Death Eater to safeguard a Horcrux — Lucius Malfoy and the Tom Riddle Diary. You have to ask yourself again, "Why did Voldemort utilize his lieutenants when we were told that Voldemort prefers to work alone?"

Someone has made an ominous prophesy concerning The One who will have the power to vanquish the Dark Lord — Death is the Dark Lord's greatest fear — Jo has told us so. Even though he is only aware of the first part of Trelawney's prophesy, Lord Voldemort must react to the vulnerability. He may have decided his priority should be discovering the identity of this future menace and eliminating the supposed Vanquisher. But he also devises a Plan B in case he fails with his first priority: to carefully hide his Horcruxes should the prophesy come to fruition. Of the Horcruxes we know about, [1] the Dark Lord buries the Ring Horcrux under the Gaunt family ruins himself, [2] he sends Bellatrix and Regulus to put the Locket Horcrux in the Cave's Stone Basin, [3] and Lord Voldemort gives the Diary Horcrux to Lucius for safe keeping in Malfoy Manor. This leaves a few additional Horcruxes that need hiding. Let's take a long look at Draco's trip to Borgin and Burkes at the beginning of HALF-BLOOD PRINCE to see if we can spy another one.

Bite or Mark?

Whenever Jo interrupts or hides something, we know it must be rather significant. Harry Potter Fandom has focused its energy on two theories for Borgin's startled reaction to Draco in Chapter 6 of HALF-BLOOD PRINCE. Draco must have either (A) a Dark Mark or (B) a Werewolf bite on his arm. Both of these are indeed incendiary flesh marks that Draco could display to provoke a strong response from Borgin. I have a feeling, however, that Draco displayed neither Dark Mark nor Werewolf bite to Borgin.

If it were a Werewolf bite, it doesn't make sense that Draco would tell Borgin not to tell his mother about their conversation. I don't think Draco would want to make it public, in any forum, that his blood was contaminated. And I don't think it is the Dark Mark either based on a comment Draco makes on the Hogwarts train along the lines that he doesn't need to be fully qualified to be useful to Lord Voldemort. Draco is an underage wizard and could not apparate to the Dark Lord when called (particularly from Hogwarts) so there would be little advantage in branding him with a Dark Mark and no small risk.

I think Draco displayed something else to Borgin that clearly communicated his powerful association with the Dark Lord. The scene at Borgin and Burkes:

> "No?" said Malfoy, and Harry knew, just by his tone, that Malfoy was sneering. "Perhaps this will make you more confident."
>
> He moved toward Borgin and was blocked from view by the cabinet. Harry, Ron, and Hermione shuffled sideways to try and keep him in sight, but all they could see was Borgin, looking very frightened.
>
> "Tell anyone," said Malfoy, "and there will be retribution. You know Fenrir Greyback? He's a family friend. He'll be dropping by from time to time to make sure you're giving the problem full attention"

Then later:

> "Not a word to anyone, Borgin, and that includes my mother, understand?"
> (both quotes from HALF-BLOOD PRINCE, Chapter 6)

If Jo is monitoring fan cyberspace, she must be utterly delighted that we have walked into her trap of working on only Theory A (Dark Mark) or Theory B (Werewolf Bite). Theory B seems emphasized with the Fenrir Greyback threat. But let's review that scene in Borgin's shop again. What the trio observed through the window was:

☞ Draco displaying something out of their field of vision to Borgin;

☞ Borgin reacting with a frightened look on his face;

☞ Draco playing the Fenrir Greyback card to optimize cooperation; and

☞ Then Malfoy dramatically leaves the premises, but not before telling Borgin that he must not tell his mother Narcissa what was seen

It is Harry who concludes that Draco must be branded with the Dark Mark (Theory A) as earlier in the same chapter he saw a reaction when Madam Malkin touched Malfoy on his left arm. He concludes that Draco must be a Death Eater, but Hermione disagrees. Jo has left this scene seemingly open to just two interpretations.

Return to the Chamber of Secrets:

> *"Malfoy, the Heir of Slytherin?" said Hermione skeptically.*
> *"Look at his family," said Harry, closing his books too. "The whole lot of them have been in Slytherin; he's always boasting about it. They could easily be Slytherin's descendants. His father's definitely evil enough."* CHAMBER OF SECRETS, Chapter 8

Readers know where this particular logic path led us: Harry was wrong and Hermione was right to be skeptical. Jo often speaks directly to us via the voice of Hermione with clear wisdom, particularly when the girl isn't emotional. So while HALF-BLOOD PRINCE is all about Harry's growing intuition, I think he is in fact mistaken in regard to his interpretation of the Borgin scene. I suggest that Jo has set the Borgin scene up for exactly a Theory A or Theory B conclusion, but she is misdirecting our attention away from another possibility.

Jo is a literary Magician. One guiding principle of magical performance is to "force" specific playing cards onto an unsuspecting participant so it appears to be chance, but in reality, the magician is in control of the trick's outcome from the very beginning. It is no wonder that Book 6 prominently features Horace Slughorn, no doubt drawn against a famous real life illusionist named Horace Goldin whose autobiography was entitled IT'S FUN TO BE FOOLED (1937).

Let's review the story elements present in HALF-BLOOD PRINCE, Chapter 6, and think about what they echo in CHAMBER OF SECRETS, Chapter 4, "At Flourish and Blotts:"

☞ We are in Diagon Alley before school begins;

☞ A trip to Flourish and Blotts to buy textbooks with the Weasleys;

☞ Nasty words between the trio and Malfoys are exchanged;

☞ An invisibility cloak is utilized;

☞ A visit to Borgin and Burkes made overtly by Malfoy, secretly by Harry;

and

☞ Dark objects are observed: the vanishing cabinet, the opal necklace

Does it seem like Jo is calling our attention to a Dark Mark, (an element introduced in GOBLET OF FIRE)? Does it seem like Jo is calling our attention to a Werewolf Bite (from PRISONER OF AZKABAN)? No, it seems more like she might be calling our attention to an important element from CHAMBER OF SECRETS that is conspicuously missing from the list above. Something that was last seen in the possession of the Malfoy family, maybe? How about the *Tom Riddle Diary?*

If anything, the Werewolf Bite and the Dark Mark are both important as they intersect in the climax chapter of the story: "The Lightning Struck Tower." In HALF-BLOOD PRINCE, Chapter 6, Jo is calling us back to the CHAMBER OF SECRETS so we will recall the Horcrux diary.

What do these five sentences from CHAMBER OF SECRETS tell us about Tom's diary?

Pg. 231 US Paperback, Harry: *"He opened it eagerly. On the first page he could just make out the name 'T.M. Riddle' in smudged ink."*

Pg. 335 Dumbledore: *"He held up the small black book with the large hole through its center, watching Mr. Malfoy carefully."*

Pg. 336 Dumbledore: *"Very fortunate the diary was discovered, and Riddle's memories wiped from it."*

Pg. 337 Dumbledore: *"I would advise you, Lucius, not to go giving out any more of Lord Voldemort's school things."*

Pg. 337 Lucius: *"Mr. Malfoy ripped the sock off the diary, threw it aside, then looked furiously from the ruined book to Harry."*

These passages tell us that the diary is small, has Tom's Riddle's abbreviated name written in it, Dumbledore has linked Riddle and Voldemort directly together, and that the diary was last seen leaving Hogwarts in the hands of Lucius Malfoy.

Books are a significant "echo" to the past linking both CHAMBER OF SECRETS and HALF BLOOD PRINCE together:

☞ Harry is involved with a mysterious book with links to the past in HALF-BLOOD PRINCE (same situation in CHAMBER OF SECRETS);

☞ Ginny and Hermione question the wisdom of a relationship with an unknown author in HALF BLOOD PRINCE, a clear repeat of advice given for the Tom Riddle diary; and

☞ In HALF-BLOOD PRINCE Draco is shown crying in the bathroom to Moaning Myrtle. Myrtle first identified the Diary in her bathroom to Harry in CHAMBER OF SECRETS

Even normally unobservant Hagrid notices the parallels: *"Chamber o' Secrets all over again, isn' it?"* (HALF-BLOOD PRINCE , Chapter 19)

Tom Riddle's Diary:

The Diary was the earliest Horcrux that Jo introduced, but it wasn't given a name or a function in CHAMBER OF SECRETS. Lucius Malfoy received the Diary shortly before Voldemort fell, and he was to hold onto it until given orders. Lucius claimed, however, to have believed that Voldemort was gone, and decided to deploy it for his own personal benefit. He planted the Diary on the daughter of his Ministry nemesis Arthur Weasley both to discredit Arthur's work and to open up the Chamber of Secrets. But instead of ridding the school of mudbloods, Voldemort's Diary Horcrux is disarmed by Harry with a Basilisk fang. As such, Lucius became the second Black Family tree member to negligently betray the Dark Lord's trust.

At the train station before he departs for his 6th year, Harry has a discussion with Arthur Weasley about his "Draco is a Death Eater" suspicions:

"I doubt it, to be honest, Harry," said Mr. Weasley slowly. *"You see, when Lucius Malfoy was arrested, we raided his house. We took away everything that might be dangerous."*

"I think you missed something", said Harry stubbornly (HALF-BLOOD PRINCE, Chapter 9)

Arthur tells Harry that all potentially dangerous objects have been removed from Malfoy Manor in a recent raid, but Harry's statement above feels like a direct hint from Jo — we missed something.

We know that the Riddle Diary is a disarmed Horcrux. It's a ruined blank diary with a hole through it, and it could have easily been missed by Arthur's crew or spirited away earlier by Draco following his father's arrest at the end of ORDER OF THE PHOENIX. Recall that Draco knows where Lucius keeps his most precious relics:

"But luckily, we've got our own secret chamber under the drawing-room floor — " (Draco, CHAMBER OF SECRETS, Chapter 12).

Your next questions are probably, "Would Borgin comprehend what the ruined Diary represented, and would he have reacted to it in a frightened manner?" In CHAMBER OF SECRETS, Dumbledore links the identities of Riddle and Voldemort directly to Lucius Malfoy. Borgin would certainly have known of

Tom Riddle from the shop's former partner, Burke. He could have been thinking about the deceased Orion Black who may have asked for advice regarding Tom Riddle many years ago, given the R.A.B. scenario imagined prior. Dumbledore gives us information though, to put Borgin's reaction in perspective. In Chapter 17 of HALF-BLOOD PRINCE he says *Few who knew him then are prepared to talk about him; they are too terrified."*

In the shop, Draco could have brandished the book and held it open to the title page. The name T.M. Riddle would have certainly meant something to Borgin. Tom Riddle was a former shop assistant who disappeared with some important Dark items right after one of the shop's best clients was found murdered, supposedly by her House elf. Yes, Hokey the Elf took the blame, but the point remains, Riddle was gone along with some important relics that Hepzibah Smith's family would have known to be in her possession. They may have even blamed Borgin and Burkes store directly for the disappearance.

After Draco leaves the store, Mister Borgin's expression changes from fright to concern:

> *"Inside the shop, Borgin remained frozen; his unctuous smile had vanished; he looked worried."* (HALF-BLOOD PRINCE, Chapter 6)

I think it would be enough for Draco to say to Borgin: "This diary used to belong to Lord Voldemort and it was used to open up the Chamber of Secrets". Borgin is most likely a Hogwarts graduate and would be familiar with the dark legend of the Chamber if he didn't know about the events of Harry's second year. Perhaps we are supposed to notice the echo with Dumbledore displaying the disarmed Slytherin ring to Slughorn to gain his cooperation and Draco displaying the disarmed Diary to Borgin to gain his as well. Both Draco and Dumbledore are very busy schemers in Book 6.

Movie Side-Bar:

Now I completely concede this does not count as canon (only Jo's writing or interviews are considered canonical by Fandom) but in the extended film version of CHAMBER OF SECRETS we have this deleted scene, an exchange written by screenwriter Steve Kloves:

Lucius Malfoy: *Anyway, I brought you items from home that might prove embarrassing should the ministry call, poisons and the like...*
Borgin: (Gasps as he examines content of box) *Look at this!* (the audience cannot see what he is reacting to)
Lucius Malfoy: *That particular item is not for sale!*

Borgin: *I don't understand. It has unique qualities. I wouldn't want to see it fall into the wrong hands.*

What Steve Kloves was trying to highlight in this scene was that Malfoy had a magical item on him when he left Borgin's for Flourish and Blotts (i.e. the Horcrux Diary). Borgin is shown in this scene to clearly recognize the diary's power. On this same DVD, there is an interview between Kloves and Rowling and they make it clear that there is quite a bit of trust and collaboration between the two. Take the point below, for what it is worth, from the interview:

Steve: I will sometimes ask Jo. I will say, you know, this detail, you just seem to have cast just a bit more light on this in this scene than the other details. Sometimes I'm wrong, but often she'll say "No, that is going to play." There's one thing in Chamber, actually, that Jo indicated will play later in the series. The hardest thing for me, honestly, is I'm writing a story to which I do not know the end. (Steve Kloves/JKR Interview for COS DVD — February 2003)

It's important to note however, that there is no mention of the Diary during the same scene in Jo's published version of CHAMBER OF SECRETS.

Draco's Dud Diary:

What might the Tom Riddle Diary have represented to Draco? A good luck amulet to assist him with his life or death task, perhaps. There is an emphasis on amulets in HALF-BLOOD PRINCE. Outside of Flourish and Blotts bookstore, for example, our attention is purposely drawn to a sign that reads: *Amulets — Effective against Werewolves, Dementors, and Inferi.*

Draco may have initially spent some time trying to make the Diary work, which it would not (meaning, he could have brought it into Hogwarts and the Dark Magic detectors would not have gone off). But I'm sure he realized that the Diary's value was in its collectable status. From recognizing the value of the Diary, however damaged, as a collectable, it is a short trip to realizing: who in the entire Wizarding world does Draco know that would value and pay for this particular Dark item, working or not? Only Mister Borgin. And, if Draco went to the shop to confirm this thought as well as win Borgin's help, he succeeded. Borgin did react strongly to viewing the Diary.

It is probably with funds gained from the sale of the Diary to Borgin, that Draco gets the money he needs to purchase the cursed Opal Necklace he uses to try to kill Dumbledore. Recall that the necklace we first saw in CHAMBER OF SECRETS gets a special mention again during Hermione's klutzy conversation with the store keeper. Borgin points out that the cursed item is very costly at 1,500 galleons.

While the Malfoys are considered wealthy, I doubt that Draco had 1,500 gold galleons in his piggy bank at Malfoy Manor. He can't ask his mother, and his father is in prison. Draco warns Borgin not to tell his mother about his visit, so I suspect that Draco is operating alone.

Jo thoughtfully drops a handy hint that addresses access to money in HALF-BLOOD PRINCE exactly during the time frame when getting hands on funds would be quite significant for Draco. Before Harry and the Weasley's depart for Diagon Alley, Bill hands Harry a sack of galleons and states that it has been challenging to get gold out of Gringotts Bank nowadays as the goblins have clamped down on security.

A much more elegant alternative is to assume that Draco traded the Diary in *barter* for the Opal necklace. Besides the recent awkward inquiry by Hermione, I'm sure no one else had expressed interest in that particular necklace for ages. You can easily assume that Borgin was secretly glad to be rid of the item.

The Opal Necklace:

When and how did Draco obtain the expensive Opal necklace, and get it into Rosemerta's hands? After the trip to Diagon Alley (approximately August 3rd according to the calendar calculations of the online HP Lexicon), there is only a month until all of the students board the train (September 1st). Draco must have made the necklace purchase or barter during the August interval.

But how did he get it to Hogsmeade? He might have been able to bring the necklace on the Hogwarts Express, but such a Dark object wouldn't have made it into Hogwarts. We know that Draco has an alibi during the necklace incident (he's in detention under McGonnagall's watch). There is no trip to Hogsmeade for students between September 1st and the first weekend trip (either October 12th or October 19th, again according to the Lexicon). All communications in and out of the castle are being monitored. So how exactly did Draco's criminal enterprise go down?

The Necklace Caper Imagined:

Sometime after the meeting in which Voldemort tasks Draco with Dumbledore's murder and the boy's trip to Diagon Alley, Draco hatches a backup assassination plan, perhaps inspired by his recent detour to Knockturn Alley. Borgin didn't seem too confident regarding the Vanishing Cabinets and Draco must succeed at all costs.

In a subsequent visit Borgin may have told Draco that a suspicious young girl nearly his age with bushy hair inquired about the Opal necklace minutes after he left the shop. Draco knows that Hermione was in Diagon Alley that day, and if Miss Smarty Pants thought that the necklace was interesting, it might just prove to be a most promising weapon. I suggest that Draco traded the Riddle Diary for the deadly Opal necklace — it may have felt like an excellent gamble based on the necklace's card description alone: *Cursed — Has Claimed the Lives of Nineteen Muggles to*

Date. Then Draco boarded a train for Hogsmeade, imperiused Rosemerta (with Aunt Bella?), and left the brown-bagged cursed necklace there on the premises of the Three Broomsticks. To hide his connection with the cursed object, he planned to make the compliant Rosemerta dupe a less suspicious looking girl student into carrying the cursed necklace into the school, and into Dumbledore's hands. If the caper fails, it can be blamed on the poor unsuspecting student.

> *Dumbledore closed his eyes again and nodded, as though he was about to fall asleep. "...of course... Rosemerta. How long has she been under the Imperius Curse?"* (HALF-BLOOD PRINCE, Chapter 27)

A timeline answer isn't provided. Draco just sneers back that Dumbledore has finally figured the puzzle out.

While Draco does have a perfect alibi to distance himself from the necklace crime, I think it is important to point out that for some reason known Slytherin poser Blaise Zabini is observed hanging around the Three Broomsticks right as the necklace plan is set into motion. Perhaps he was going to follow the chosen cursed student back to school and create a distraction before Filch could do a thorough search. Several times during HALF-BLOOD PRINCE Filch's security skills are called into question

Alternatively, some in fandom have proposed that we are seeing Polyjuice Draco, and he and Zabini have traded spots temporarily.

Third Horcrux, a Charm?

It is very possible that the laundry list of Horcruxes Harry has to locate and destroy is closer to complete than he knows. Consider the possibility that the cursed Opal Necklace is a Horcrux. Besides being in Hogwarts thanks to Draco's murderous machinations, it has probably been disarmed by Snape. The Opal Necklace could be one of the early Horcruxes created by Tom Riddle, while still employed at Borgin and Burkes. Borgin and Burkes is a store which specializes in Dark magic and Founder's artifacts, and Tom Riddle was a determined collector. Perhaps he discovered on his own that the necklace was connected with a Founder and elected to hide it in plain sight. A card declaring that the necklace was cursed would keep most folks from examining it closely, or even Borgin from moving it out of the display case.

Could the Opal Necklace be the Ravenclaw relic Dumbledore mentioned? Both ravens and opals are considered unlucky elements. The opal was sometimes referred the as 'Eye Stone', as it might strengthen one's eyesight. It's also been called 'Thieves Stone' as it was thought to make one invisible. Ravens are intelligent birds. They are known for their sharp vision, their keen attraction to shiny objects, and for their scavenging ways, so that might be the link between opals and ravens right there. Ravenclaw, after all, is known to be the brainy and pretty house. Finally, a slight touch of the necklace caused Katie Bell to rise into the air. She is described as a graceful bird, about to take flight.

Recall that Dumbledore said that only Professor Snape had the knowledge to help save his life after he disarmed the Slytherin Ring. When last seen, the Opal Necklace was wrapped in a scarf in Filch's hands on its way to Snape's office in Hogwarts. It makes sense that Snape would know how to handle it, and disarm the cursed Opal Necklace. If the curse turns out to have been the Horcrux placed within it, Severus either disarmed it like the Ring Horcrux and notified Dumbledore or put it in a safe place. Even if Severus turns out to be EVIL!Snape, I doubt Dumbledore lost track of the necklace such that Snape could spirit it away after the Tower incident.

And, if this item proves to be the Ravenclaw artifact, that would make it the *third* Horcrux that a Black Family Tree relative has let fall into someone else's hands:

1. Bellatrix with Regulus' sacrificial switch delivered the Locket Horcrux to the future home of Dumbledore's Order;

2. Lucius gave the Diary Horcrux to Ginny Weasley on her way to Hogwarts, Dumbledore's dominion

3. And now Draco, the youngest person on the Black Family Tree, son of Narcissa Black Malfoy, has managed to bring the Ravenclaw Horcrux forcefully to Dumbledore's attention

These three Horcrux blunders combined with Bellatrix and Lucius' failure to retrieve the globed prophesy in ORDER OF THE PHOENIX makes one wonder if the Black Family legacy is really Voldemort's curse. They are the corporal embodiment of a reverse Felix Felicis: all of Voldemort's efforts tend to fail with a Black Family member involved. Perhaps Voldemort was drinking unicorn blood prior to SOR-CERERS' STONE. If he was, it would make this SORCERERS' STONE line from Firenze the Centaur quite prophetic: "...and you will have but a half-life, a cursed life, from the moment the blood touches your lips". But there is yet another Black Family disaster to be uncovered, the law of unintended consequences unleashed.

Why Sirius Died:

Question: *Why did you kill Sirius? It made me very sad*
JK Rowling: I'm really, really sorry. I didn't want to do it, but there was a reason. If you think you can forgive me, keep reading, you'll find out. [I feel really guilty now].
World Book Day Chat, March 2004

If the R.A.B. Locket caper scenario is true, than it becomes clear why Jo killed off Sirius at the end of ORDER OF THE PHOENIX: so Harry would inherit Grimmauld Place and ultimately uncover the Slytherin Locket. It is a situation that was created precisely by Bellatrix who murdered her cousin Sirius, ending the direct Black bloodline.

In Chapter 4 of HALF-BLOOD PRINCE Jo emphasizes this inheritance when Dumbledore comes to collect Harry from the Dursleys' home. In fact, Jo spends quite a few pages in this chapter emphasizing two points:

1. Harry is the new owner of Grimmauld Place despite a Black Family tradition of handing the house down to the next male with the name of "Black", and

2. Harry is the new master of Kreacher

Jo foreshadowed the importance of these two elements at the end of ORDER OF THE PHOENIX Chapter 37:

Dumbledore says to Harry: *"Kreacher lied... you are not his master, he could lie to you..."* (Page 829, US Hardback)

Dumbledore says to Harry regarding Kreacher *"But I am a sufficiently accomplished Legilimens myself to know when I am being lied to and I... persuaded him... to tell me the full story... "* (Page 832)

These two quotes, in concert with the R.A.B. caper scenario above should help her careful readers understand that:

1. Both Regulus and Sirius are dead. By killing them both, Bellatrix has facilitated Harry's inheritance

2. Harry can search for the Slytherin Locket Horcrux at Grimmauld Place in private now that he is the true owner

3. Harry now has mastery of Kreacher who must tell Harry directly what he knows of R.A.B. and the Locket plot, if asked

4. Harry now owns any Dark Arts books from Grimmauld Place. Hermione can get busy researching Horcruxes in much more depth than the books she might be able to access in the Hogwarts' restricted section

5. Dumbledore must have first uncovered the R.A.B. caper when he performed Legilimency on Kreacher. Kreacher may or may not know of the Cave, but a mental x-ray would tell Dumbledore that he was quite close to finding the Slytherin locket

Conclusion:

Ms. Rowling has asked us to give the Black Family Tree that we only saw in outline in ORDER OF THE PHOENIX a much closer inspection. The R.A.B. note in the fake Locket Horcrux, her comments in interviews suggesting the importance of Regulus Black, and the detailed BOOK AID Black Family Tree she made public in February, 2006, are all pointers to the centrality of the Blacks. The remaining Horcrux mysteries and Harry's ability to find and destroy them all largely depend on our ability to understand what we have not yet seen, invisible to us because they are puzzles wrapped in Black.

Voldemort has no greater enemy, it seems, than the Death Eater fruits he has gathered from under the Black Family Tree:

- Regulus and Bellatrix *bring* the Slytherin Locket Horcrux to the Order of the Phoenix Headquarters.

- Lucius *sends* the Diary Horcrux to Hogwarts

- Draco may have used the same Diary to *hand* the Ravenclaw Horcrux to Dumbledore in HALF-BLOOD PRINCE

- Bellatrix and Lucius *fail* to collect the prophesy and allow its full contents to remain unknown

- Bellatrix's *murder* of Sirius causes his family home and house elf to fall directly under Harry's control

The Black Family is the underlying bane of Voldemort's cursed existence. One cannot help but wonder what other unknown consequences of Black Family blunders await Lord Voldemort. As such, it seems like the 7th Book could easily be titled: HARRY POTTER AND THE BLACK FAMILY CURSE.

Advantage: Harry!

Sally March Gallo

Ms. Gallo lives in Virginia with her husband and their four children. She has a BFA in Theatre and an MFA in Creative Writing, both of which came in handy for the writing of this essay. She wishes to thank Jo Rowling for the gift of Harry Potter, which has had such profound personal impact that one wonders how it could have been intended for the whole world.

How Dumbledore and Slughorn Used Magic — and Stage Magic — and Fooled Us All was originally published in The Leaky Cauldron's essay project Scribbulus, premiere edition, under the title Dumbledore is Not Dead. The Leaky Cauldron and the author, Sally M. Gallo, have granted permission to the publishers of Who Killed Albus Dumbledore to reprint this essay.

Editors' Note: as stated above, this essay was originally posted early in 2006, long before Ms Rowling made her public statement at Radio City Music Hall that Albus Dumbledore was "definitely dead."in August of that year.

Ms. Gallo's insights about what happened on the Astronomy Tower tell us, in brief, how the events on the Tower could have unfolded if Albus Dumbledore died before his staged death. With the two Potions Masters left after Dumbledore's demise to teach Harry about Horcruxes, save Draco, and maintain Severus' cover as a Death Eater, Ms. Gallo's theory about Horace Slughorn answers almost all the "how" questions. Read on to learn the value of seeing Horace Slughorn in a heroic light.

It is not necessary that a theory be correct to prove to be of value. Even failed theories can turn up bits of gold. Nor do you have to stop playing with a theory should it turn out to be Leprechaun gold and fades away with the morning.

How Dumbledore and Slughorn Used Magic — and Stage Magic — and Fooled Us All

Originally published in The Leaky Cauldron's Scribbulus essay project

IN THE JULY 2005 MUGGLENET/LEAKY CAULDRON INTERVIEW, during a discussion about the death of the mentor in the fantasy genre, J. K. Rowling added that "the question is when and how." An editorial discrepancy raised the question again; in the Scholastic edition, several lines from Dumbledore to Draco remain that don't appear in the Bloomsbury edition, including, "he cannot kill you if you are already dead." (pg. 591) This discrepancy, along with Rowling's comments from the interview, imply that the question of Dumbledore's death was not answered in HARRY POTTER AND THE HALF-BLOOD PRINCE and opens up myriad possibilities.

One trail of clues in the text leads to one possibility out of the many that seems more plausible than most. It appears that Slughorn had switched places with Dumbledore for the trip to the cave, and that both Slughorn and Dumbledore avoided death that night, as did Snape by default. The indications I've enumerated in the pages that follow are striking in and of themselves, and more so when we realize that "Muggle Magic" makes its first appearance in the series here in this book, seemingly by no coincidence. Slughorn's staged death in chapter four is underscored by the twins' stocking Muggle magic tricks in their shop — and the events in the cave, on the tower, and at the funeral, it can be argued, are similarly well-stocked with misdirection, illusions, and gimmicks, all performed with the benefit of the real magic that exists in the "Potterverse." The tricks and traditions of stage magic go back centuries and across cultures, but a common thread seems to connect them all: technique. In a 1641 booklet by writer John Ady, King's magician, HOCUS POCUS, is described as using "a dark combination of words, to blind the eye of his beholders, to make his trick pass more currently without discovery, because when the eye and the ear of the beholder are both earnestly busied, the trick is not so easily discovered, nor the imposture discerned." (Edmonds, pg. 42) Harry discovered this firsthand, trying to discern how Slughorn was collecting the Acromantula venom, and perhaps experienced more misdirection in the cave and tower scene.

Further research into the art of stage magic reveals a colorful character from the Golden Age of Magic, a magician by the name of Horace Goldin, who bears an uncanny resemblance to Horace Slughorn. Quite similar to Rowling's descriptions of Slughorn, Goldin was pompous and extremely nimble-fingered, "an unlikely figure for a magician... , round and fleshy, with an oversized nose and thinning hair" who nonetheless "had mastered the dashing, graceful gestures of a swashbuckler." (Steinmeyer, pg. 284) Horace Goldin developed a silent and fast-paced routine, reminiscent of Slughorn's two-minute staged death. As a novice, Goldin idolized a more seasoned magician called the Great Albini (how similar to "Albus"). Goldin had a framed portrait of Albini he'd prominently displayed; one evening after a particularly strong performance from Goldin, Albini called on him and taught him the secret of his famous Egg Bag trick, then signed the portrait. (This trick was attributed to a conjurer with another familiar name, Isaac Fawkes, in 1736, according to Edmonds, pg. 43). Albini and Goldin later became peers and rivals, a dichotomy that seems to be characteristic of many of the relationships between the more famous magicians of the Golden Age of Magic. It should also be noted that Goldin had a big act called "The Tiger God" that he toured extensively, the star of which was his pet tiger named Lily.

Milbourne Christopher says of Horace Goldin in THE ILLUSTRATED HISTORY OF MAGIC: "I met Horace Goldin in London in the fall of 1936. At sixty-two he was stout, wore his reading glasses on a black ribbon around his neck, and carried a cane. The tiepin in his cravat sparkled with the jewels he had received from Kings and Queens... 'Confidentially,' he said, 'I have the best act in the world. You must see it as my guest.' I accepted his invitation... I sat in the front row... Albini's 'Egg Bag,' to which Goldin had added various comedy touches, delighted the audience... Before the curtains closed, Goldin caught a bullet fired at him from a rifle, on the china plate he held in front of his chest." (pgs. 315-16) Goldin was noted for this trick, and coincidentally (or not), Dumbledore's hand is over his chest during the entire tower scene.

Slughorn's connection to the theme of stage magic strongly supports the argument that the scene at the cave and atop the Astronomy Tower was riddled with the tricks of the trade; even more so, the textual indications that Slughorn stood in for Dumbledore are powerful images in themselves. Still, without a careful reading of the series, it's more challenging to tease out from the text answers to some of our questions about why this would have occurred. First, what does Dumbledore gain from faking his death? The simplest answer might be that he remains alive — but Dumbledore's been possessed of a mission to destroy Voldemort throughout the entire series, and in light of that, to assume that the events on the tower are as they appear, and that Dumbledore in essence allowed Snape to kill him, seems contradictory. By faking his death, he's afforded himself the freedom to continue his mission undetected and Snape to retain his cover as a double agent. Furthermore, if indeed Slughorn is impersonating Dumbledore on the tower, then Draco isn't failing the task we understand to be to kill Dumbledore, but rather he's failing to kill Slughorn, and thus the terms of the Unbreakable Vow are evaded. A second question might wonder what evidence is there that demonstrates Slughorn would be willing to take such an action; careful attention to the scene in Hagrid's hut reveals that Slughorn was uncertain until that night that Harry was indeed the Chosen One and that there was any purpose to be served with handing over the proper memory. Once he's made the connection that Harry is willing and perhaps able to attempt to defeat Voldemort, Slughorn commits to the mission himself, evident in his parting with the memory of his own free will.

Other questions also arise: Where is Dumbledore during the events of the cave and tower scenes; how do we understand the Avada Kedavra curse we saw on the tower; what can we take at face value and what is misdirection? These are questions I intend to briefly address following the primary focus, a discussion of the details that lead to the conclusion that Slughorn did indeed stand in for Dumbledore that night, in a loose progression of the events as they occurred. Subheadings will be provided to help stay on track, and all quotes of the Potter series are Scholastic first editions.

The "Five Minutes"

It seems highly likely that Slughorn stood in for Dumbledore for the cave visit with Harry and the confrontation on the tower. The switch would have taken place during the five minutes in which Harry goes to give the Felix to Ron and Hermione, and in reverse at the base of the tower after being lowered safely to the ground. Although Slughorn questionably has a store of Polyjuice Potion in his classroom when the school year begins, and it would seem the obvious choice for a means for a switch, I think what's more likely, since Switching Spells have been brought up in the series and not used (as far as we know), that two skilled old Wizards like Dumbledore and Slughorn might have other means for switching places at their disposal.

Before they head off to the cave, Dumbledore directs Harry to go get his Invisibility Cloak (pg. 551), although he should have expected Harry to already have it, as he'd told him to keep it on him at all times, even at Hogwarts. (pg. 79) Then he tells Harry to meet him in the Great Hall in five minutes. It's been suggested that Dumbledore took this opportunity to put up his portrait; perhaps by simply resigning from his post as Headmaster, his portrait would go up automatically. It's also enough time to arrange for Slughorn to meet Harry in the Great Hall. Dumbledore's opening scene with Harry is framed by two impostor checks. First, he admonishes Harry for assuming that he is indeed himself (his favorite jam is raspberry); then we see a person who can appear to be someone other than himself (the Slughorn "chair"). Then directly after Dumbledore leaves the Burrow, Arthur insists on impostor-checking with Molly. Despite this, Harry never does verify Dumbledore's identity.

Slughorn would probably be instructed to Apparate to the correct location; but it may be that Slughorn is uncomfortable with Apparating because of his size: We see him taking the train to Hogwarts, plus we learn from Ron that Charlie Weasley had trouble passing his test, and in the same breath Ron mentions Charlie's size. Although Ron's point was that he wouldn't tease Charlie because he didn't want to risk a fight with him, Rowling's instructed the reader that Apparating is difficult for the heavy-set. Earlier in the book, Dumbledore does not count to three, and he asks Harry to grip his arm. The Apparition to the cave follows a different pattern. Dumbledore counts to three, and does not ask that Harry grip his arm. There is also the matter of the countdown; other times in the series, Dumbledore counts to three for shared use of a Portkey. It is unusual for him to use a countdown for Apparition.

Physical Description

At the onset of the cave scene, Dumbledore performs a "perfect breaststroke" with "the sudden agility of a much younger man." (pg. 557) This passage is wonderfully suggestive and a good set-up for the distinctive descriptors that follow, with the implication that Dumbledore is indeed a disguised Slughorn.

On page 570, "Harry hesitated, looking into the blue eyes that had turned green in the reflected light of the basin." Slughorn's eyes are described in his introduction in chapter four when "His pale gooseberry eyes had found Dumbledore's injured hand." (pg. 67) Gooseberry, as an eye-color, would be light green; however, there is room for speculation here on this point. "Gooseberry eyed" can refer to the recognizably poor quality of someone's eyesight. We are never given any other indication in the text that Slughorn has poor eyesight. The spider comparisons might be notable here, as Aragog's eyesight was also poor — but it seems that we can't rule out the distinct possibility that Rowling is letting the reader know that Slughorn is green-eyed, but that she's burying this information.

On the following page, "Dumbledore panted and then spoke in a voice that Harry did not recognize, for he had never heard Dumbledore frightened like this... Harry stared into the whitened face he knew so well, at the crooked nose and half-moon spectacles..." (pg. 571) This passage seems to hint that this person is not Dumbledore; in addition to the voice that Harry doesn't recognize, Dumbledore's face is less-recognizable, as it's objectified with the use of "the" instead of the possessive "Dumbledore's" or "his." Interestingly, the body of Dumbledore at the base of the tower is similarly objectified with the use of "the" instead of the personal pronouns "his" and "him."

Slughorn's tendency is to grow pale and sweat at the brow when he's frightened or tense. For example, "Slughorn turned paler than ever; his shiny forehead gleamed with sweat." (pg. 490) After drinking the potion, Dumbledore's face appeared "paler and damper than ever." (pg. 580) It could be attributed to the effects of the potion, but the language is identical to description of Slughorn and could indicate that there's more to it. Soon thereafter we see Slughorn again in the Headmaster's office, "who looked the most shaken, pale and sweating." (pg. 627) It is suspicious that Slughorn would appear the most shaken, if he hadn't been anywhere near the danger of the evening's events.

Speech Patterns and Lines

Often Dumbledore's dialogue sounded as if it wasn't Dumbledore saying it or had speech patterns or phrases that were idiosyncratic to Slughorn or could have been said by Slughorn. For instance, we know that Slughorn's rating system is value, and we have the following two lines that sound odd from Dumbledore: *"I am much older, much cleverer, and much less valuable,"* and, *"Your blood is worth much more than mine."* (pg. 559, 570)

In the boat, Dumbledore says, *"I do not think you will count, Harry. You are underage and unqualified. Voldemort would never have suspected a sixteen year old to reach this place: I think it unlikely that your powers will register compared to mine... Voldemort's mistake, Harry, Voldemort's mistake... Age is foolish and forgetful when it underestimates youth."* (pgs. 564-5) Dumbledore has told Harry that he performed a grown Wizard's task in HARRY POTTER AND THE GOBLET OF FIRE, and in HALF-BLOOD PRINCE, he's reminded Harry that he's exceptional and extraordinary; this seems as if he's contradicting his previous sentiments and then backpedaling. Also, Dumbledore has learned not to underestimate youth; either Slughorn or Dumbledore could be saying this with regret that he underestimated Riddle. Likewise, both professors could reasonably say, *"I taught Tom Riddle. I know his style."* (pg. 563) It's particularly resonant with Slughorn's line in the Headmaster's office later: *"Snape! I taught him! I thought I knew him!"* (pg. 627)

On page 563, Dumbledore says, *"Oho!"* This is a Slughorn catchphrase. We've heard Filch say this before, and Fudge and Vernon in Harry Potter and the Order of the Phoenix, but never previously in the series has Dumbledore said it. Several other phrases stand out as if coming from Slughorn:

"That potion... was no health drink." (pg. 580)

"...my dear boy..." (pgs. 585, 591)

"Oh, weaker resistance, slower reflexes... Old age in short... if you are lucky." (pg. 594) Compare with Slughorn's line in his first meeting with Harry: *"Can't move like I used to. Well, that's to be expected. Old age. Fatigue... The fact remains that I'm an old man, Albus. A tired old man who's earned the right to a quiet life and a few creature comforts."* (pg. 67)

Repeated words and phrases are a trademark of Slughorn's speech pattern; several show up in the cave and tower scene:

"Voldemort's mistake, Harry, Voldemort's mistake..." (pg. 564)

"You did very well, very well, Harry..." (pg. 577)

"Draco, Draco, you are not a killer." (pg. 585)

"A clever plan, a very clever plan..." (pg. 587)

"Yes, very neat... very neat..." (pg. 589)

"No, no, these are manners." (pg. 593)

The Toast

When Dumbledore toasts in the cave, it stands out in contrast to his pattern in Half-Blood Prince, during which he doesn't toast. For example, on page 265, Mrs. Cole poured them each a "generous measure" and "she drained her glass in one gulp." Dumbledore doesn't speak or raise his glass to toast. There is an instance of Dumbledore toasting in the series, in GOBLET OF FIRE. Dumbledore asks the students to "stand, and raise [their] glasses" to Cedric Diggory. (pg. 721) Otherwise, the closest thing to a toast from Dumbledore in this book was at the Dursleys' in chapter three: *"'Madame Rosmerta's finest oak-matured mead,'* said Dumbledore, raising his glass to Harry, who caught hold of his own and sipped." (pg. 48) Dumbledore again doesn't speak.

Conversely, in the cave Dumbledore raises the goblet of potion and says, *"Your good health, Harry."* (pg. 570) Compare this to Slughorn's suggestion before Aragog's burial: *"We'll drink the poor beast's — well — not health — but we'll send it off in style, anyway, once it's buried."* (pg. 481) Slughorn, in contrast to Dumbledore, toasts habitually; the only time he doesn't toast stands out against his pattern. It is in chapter four when he grudgingly offers drinks to Dumbledore and Harry, resisting Dumbledore's temptation. Otherwise, we have several instances establishing his pattern, for example: on page 485, *"To Aragog;"* on page 487, "After an hour or so... Hagrid and Slughorn began making extravagant toasts: to Hogwarts, to Dumbledore, to elf-made wine and to — 'Harry Potter,' bellowed Hagrid." Then Slughorn pockets unicorn tail hair with cries of, *"To friendship! To generosity! To*

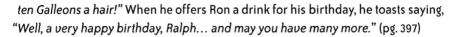

ten Galleons a hair!" When he offers Ron a drink for his birthday, he toasts saying, *"Well, a very happy birthday, Ralph... and may you have many more."* (pg. 397)

I "Forgot"

Dumbledore forgets that Harry is behind him, dripping wet and freezing: *"Harry, so sorry, I forgot."* He points his wand at Harry, and *"Harry's clothes were as warm and dry as if they had been hanging in front of a blazing fire."* (pg. 558) Slughorn warmed himself in front of a fire in his first scene. (pg. 69) Would Dumbledore forget Harry? Or is "Dumbledore's" traveling cloak actually a new-and-improved Weasleys Wizarding Wheezes Shield Cloak?

Hand Usage

Several scenes make a point of directing the reader to both of Slughorn's hands, and Dumbledore's hands figure prominently into Half-Blood Prince as well. In chapter four, it's demonstrated that Slughorn uses his wand with his left hand: "They stood back to back, the tall thin wizard and the short round one, and waved their wands in one identical sweeping motion." (pg. 65) It has just been established that Dumbledore's right hand is his wand-hand; if they were both using their right hands, then their motions wouldn't appear identical but reversed. (The image also perhaps serves as a metaphor to illuminate Dumbledore and Slughorn as equals, or at least as Wizards with comparable power: they can "back each other up" and do "identical" spellwork.) Although Slughorn plainly is using his left hand for his wand, Rowling pays close attention to both his hands, suggestive of stage magicians directing their audience to watch their hands. On page 319, Slughorn is shown with a "glass of mead in one hand and an enormous mince pie in the other;" then later, on page 369 in the memory scene, he's sitting with his feet on a velvet pouffe, glass of wine in one hand, candied pineapple in the other. Most suggestive of stage magic is when Slughorn is surreptitiously taking the venom from Aragog's body, on page 490: Slughorn "put his hand in his pocket and pulled out his wand. He put his other hand inside his cloak and took out a small, empty bottle." As noted in the introduction, Harry is watching him, and aside from the faintest clink of the vials in Slughorn's pocket, he's unable to detect Slughorn getting the venom.

By comparison, we have several mentions of both of Dumbledore's hands. Two are particularly important, as one is the moment he shows both the destroyed Horcrux and Harry to Slughorn in the same glance. On page 67, Dumbledore holds out his right hand, saying, *"You're quite right,"* then extends his left, bearing the ring, and says, *"On the other hand..."* Because we know the ring is on the left hand, and Harry must be sitting next to it to be able to see it in detail, Slughorn's attention will be drawn to both the ring and Harry at the same time. The second demonstrates exactly how badly Dumbledore's right hand is afflicted: "Dumbledore was having difficulty pulling out the stopper of the crystal bottle. His injured hand seemed stiff and painful." (pg. 199) He's holding the bottle in his left hand, trying to open it with his right. Interestingly, instead of opening it with his left hand, "Dumbledore pointed his wand at the bottle and the cork flew out." This suggests that his right hand is virtually useless and that he'd rely on his wand before relying on his left hand.

Yet in the cave, Dumbledore uses his hands differently than he has in the rest of the book, and he even uses his left-hand as his wand-hand. Furthermore, the sensitivity he appears to have in the injured hand seems contradictory to how we've seen it previously. For example, on pages 557-8 we see him using both hands equally: Still holding his wand aloft with what must be his left hand, he "approached the wall of the cave and caressed it with his blackened fingertips… touching as much of the rough rock as he could… running his fingers backward and forward… finally he stopped, his hand pressed flat against the wall." Soon thereafter, Dumbledore takes the knife from his robes with his left hand, and he then cuts his right arm with his left hand. He heals the cut using his left hand as his wand-hand. (pgs. 558-9) It's especially significant that the knife is a potions knife (as established on page 190).

Careful scrutiny reveals complex hand-usage from Dumbledore in a passage that follows, with confusion that seems to be a deliberate play by Rowling. Harry and Dumbledore are walking around the edge of the lake, on what must be the right side, because "for a moment [Harry] toppled on the edge of the dark water, and Dumbledore's uninjured hand closed tightly around his upper arm, pulling him back." (pgs. 562-3) If they were walking on the left side, Dumbledore couldn't reach him with the left hand. Soon thereafter, Dumbledore "was running his hand, not over the rocky wall, but through the thin air, as though expecting to find and grip something invisible… his hand had closed in midair upon something Harry could not see… keeping his hand clenched in midair, Dumbledore raised his wand with the other and tapped his fist with the point." Here he seems to be using his left hand to sense magic and his right for his wand again, but since Rowling mentions that he's not running his hand over the wall at his right, it could be his right hand grasping the chain. Then on page 567, Dumbledore "pushed back the sleeve of his robe over his blackened hand, and stretched out the tips of his burned fingers toward the surface of the potion." A lot of "complicated movements" and "murmuring soundlessly" from Dumbledore follow, perhaps suggesting misdirection. (pg. 568) Overall, surprising sensitivity and dexterity from a hand that was virtually useless only a few chapters before.

The Goblet and the Gasp

Several small but telling details indicate some misdirection is at play here in the cave. Aside from the curious movements and mutterings Dumbledore makes, why does Dumbledore's own goblet keep emptying every time Harry fills it with the Aguamenti spell, Harry's own water? Perhaps Dumbledore (Slughorn?) needs Harry to turn his back for some reason, and uses the water as an excuse. One possibility is that we can connect this moment to Ron's poisoning — the language used to describe his reaction to the bezoar and Dumbledore's reaction to the potion is strikingly similar. After Ron has been given the bezoar, he "gave a great shudder, a rattling gasp, and his body became limp and still." (pg. 398) Note the parallel language between this and Dumbledore on the last goblet of potion: he "drained every last drop, and then, with a great, rattling gasp, rolled over onto his face." (pg. 573)

"I am with you," the Chosen One

Dumbledore's lines *"You are with me,"* compared with *"I am with you,"* most easily can be read as an intimate moment, a metaphorical passing of the torch. (pg. 38, 578) However, there may be an inversion here; the second line gains an ironic twist, if it's indeed Slughorn, feeling safe with Harry, whom he now knows is indeed the "Chosen One." It's clear from the scene in Hagrid's hut that Slughorn didn't know until that night that Harry was the Chosen One. We have at the onset Slughorn's reluctance to give the memory to Dumbledore, plus his willingness to give it to Harry once he learns that Harry's the Chosen One and needs the information for his own personal survival. Without Harry being a prized jewel for his collection, Slughorn's reasons for returning to Hogwarts change. Perhaps his intent is to be on-hand to protect Harry from Dumbledore, who wants the memory to destroy Voldemort and may appear to Slughorn to be using Harry as bait.

Furthermore, a careful reading of the hut scene reveals that the Felix didn't influence Harry's behavior or Slughorn's choice to offer him the memory. In the Scholastic edition, Harry says, *"I don't reckon I'll need all of it, not twenty-four hours worth... Two or three hours should do it."* (pg. 476) Actually, the bottle has *"enough for twelve hours' luck,"* according to Slughorn. (pg. 188) (Bloomsbury corrects Harry's error; however, it's not clear whether Rowling intended Harry to err or to remember the amount correctly.) Harry then "raised the little bottle and took a carefully measured gulp." (pg. 477) Going by the Scholastic edition, if he's carefully measuring enough for what he believes is two to three hours, he's really only drinking enough for a maximum of ninety minutes. When he sets off for the hut, it's dusk, and when he returns to the castle, it's after midnight, giving us a time frame of approximately four to five hours. (pg. 479, 492) Even if the Bloomsbury edition is correct, three hours' worth of Felix wouldn't have seen Harry through to the conversation with Slughorn, as immediately thereafter, Harry returns to the castle, just past midnight. This would imply that when Harry on page 490 "knew he was safe: Felix was telling him that Slughorn would remember nothing of this in the morning," that he was wrong; Slughorn could quite possibly remember everything that transpired between them that evening, and likely would, since Rowling has included this passage at all. Knowing the reason why Harry needed the memory and remembering that he gave it to him would influence Slughorn's future choices, to "be brave" like Lily as Harry suggests. This is a very important character moment, not only in regards to Harry, whom we see coldly calculating of his own accord, but it establishes Slughorn's character growth and commitment to eradicating Voldemort. Even without Slughorn evolving to heroic proportions, his commitment to making a brave choice of free will is critical and evident in this scene. If there's any doubt, the scene in the Headmaster's office after the "death" should dispel it, for we see Slughorn's commitment to the safety of the students and unquestioned commitment to Hogwarts, despite Dumbledore's apparent absence.

If Dumbledore was actually Slughorn, where was Dumbledore? It seems likely that he's been faced with a dilemma: To take Harry to the cave as planned, or stay behind and defend Hogwarts now that he's learned Malfoy is poised to strike. If he can "appear to" stop off in Hogsmeade for a drink, he may also be able to appear to leave Hogwarts with Harry on the night in question, while in reality remaining behind to lend an undetectable hand to the events that unfolded. Perhaps he was functioning as an assistant in the events of the tower; perhaps another unseen assistant was at work — it seems highly likely that there was someone acting in some capacity that we couldn't see, as in stage magic.

Information

Dumbledore also seems privy to knowledge he shouldn't have. For example, how does he know *"the mead was to be my Christmas present?"* (pg. 589) This seems to further suggest he was Slughorn, who says on March 1 that he *"meant to give [the mead] to Dumbledore for Christmas... ah, well... he can't miss what he never had!"* (pg. 397) Perhaps even more information can be gleaned from the students of the Slug Club, conversations about Dumbledore's Army included: as far as we know, Dumbledore never knew that the coins were the "secret method of communication" that they used the previous year. (pg. 589)

The "AK"

Snape's look of "hatred and revulsion" when he says *"Avada Kedavra"* has launched interesting conversations among readers that it wasn't a real "AK" curse at all; since it behaves differently than AK curses we've seen previously in the series, perhaps Snape didn't "mean it" in the context Bellatrix refers to in the Ministry battle, or others have suggested it was a non-verbal spell along the same lines as Ron's *"eat slugs, Malfoy,"* which was green and non-verbal. Either suggestion seems plausible, yet it should be noted that the AK could have been real, and the recipient could have survived. If Slughorn is indeed a fictional parallel, at least in part, to the stage magician Horace Goldin, then even if this moment is an inversion of Harry's "revulsion" when feeding Dumbledore the potion, even if the AK was real, he could have had some means of blocking the AK, as we never saw Dumbledore's hand leave his chest in the events of the tower. Like the stage magicians trick, where a blank was used when Goldin "caught" a bullet with a dinner plate over his chest, the whole moment was stage magic and a real AK was never fired at all. (A fun play on words: "Slug" is slang for "bullet.") We may recall a similar scenario from ORDER OF THE PHOENIX, in the battle between Dumbledore and Voldemort in the Ministry; Dumbledore uses the statues to shield him from the spells. The victim's flight pattern (whereas no flight pattern was ever indicated in the text with a previous AK) could be explained by an unseen assistant's Levicorpus spell, or perhaps the same spell we saw Dumbledore cast non-verbally to break Harry's fall in the Quidditch match in HARRY POTTER AND THE PRISONER OF AZKABAN. The murky area around the moment Harry is unfrozen could be attributed to the spell being lifted by an alive caster. The fact that Snape doesn't drop dead on the spot because of the Unbreakable Vow is simply resolved because Draco isn't failing to kill Dumbledore, he's failing to kill Slughorn.

Dragon's Blood and the body

If there is a gun on the mantelpiece in Act I, we had better see it fired by the final curtain of the play. Similarly, we know Slughorn had a little vial of dragon's blood from chapter four, and although it was a bit dusty, he was sure he could find a use for it. We can guess that a Potions master like Slughorn wouldn't be able to use contaminated dragon's blood for any potion, but it could come in handy again for set-dressing. Once he had safely made it to the foot of the Tower, the blood from that vial would have been put on the "body" for effect; furthermore, since we've had a precedent set with Crouch Sr.'s body being Transfigured into a bone to disguise it, it seems highly likely that we'd see this again, with a twist, and that an object was Transfigured to appear to be Dumbledore's body. Also, there was no wand near the body, as there should have been, had Harry and Hagrid been the first to discover it; the inference is that Dumbledore perhaps still needs his wand. It isn't snapped at the funeral, as Hagrid and Slughorn's song about Odo suggests. This same "body" could be what we see at the funeral, under wraps and never seen, disappearing with a bang and cloud of smoke, strikingly similar to stage magic as "old as Egypt." (Edmonds, pg. 126) The suggestion of the shape of a phoenix in the cloud is perhaps Dumbledore's Patronus.

Why?

Rowling's purposes, that "the hero must go it alone," are best served by Dumbledore's death (or even "death"), but Dumbledore likely wouldn't feel it necessary or beneficial to the goal of Voldemort's eventual downfall to remove himself from the picture, if he could avoid it. And it seems that a year of forewarning should be enough time to develop a contingency plan for the Unbreakable Vow, if he does in fact know about it. Right off the bat, it seems highly implausible to accept the death on the face of it as a deliberate move on Dumbledore's part to save Snape and Draco. There is no indication from Dumbledore's character that he would choose to sacrifice himself and the greater good to allow two people to live, their souls untorn. Furthermore, his speech from HARRY POTTER AND THE ORDER OF THE PHOENIX, in which he realizes his mistake of caring for Harry more than all the "nameless and faceless people and creatures" in the "vague future" disallows him taking the same action again, as he considers it an error. (pg. 839) Clearly, if he could avoid dying, he would, in order to ensure the victory against Voldemort he's been planning for so long. And it seems that even without foreknowledge of the Unbreakable Vow that Snape made with Narcissa Malfoy, Dumbledore would realize he's only got Snape at his side for one more year, because of the curse on the Defense Against the Dark Arts position, ample time in which he can devise a means for getting inside information on Voldemort without the benefit of his double agent.

What would Dumbledore gain by faking his death? One possibility is that Dumbledore wanted Voldemort to learn of Dumbledore's death and need to verify this; through questioning of (or Legilimency on) either Harry or Snape, he'd likely discover the Horcrux hunt, and feeling that the Horcruxes were threatened, would come looking for the unknown Horcrux, unwittingly leading Dumbledore straight to it. We can surmise this in part by the Vanishing Cabinets. When he couldn't secure a position at Hogwarts, Voldemort worked at Borgin and Burkes, which provided him free access to Hogwarts via the Cabinets; later he wanted to get into Hogwarts again — Dumbledore must suspect Voldemort's motive for this and perhaps assumes there's a Horcrux there that he's got to find before Voldemort can get in to retrieve it. Thus he's doubly motivated to protect the castle against Voldemort. This plan is a gamble with time — Dumbledore giving Harry the information he needs to track down the known Horcruxes, while Voldemort is being flushed out to identify and locate the unknown one for Dumbledore to try to snap up. It's risky because if Voldemort knows they're onto the Horcruxes, they've got to be one step ahead of him all the way, which is only possible if nobody realizes that Dumbledore is alive and poised to get that Horcrux himself.

It would appear that some prior discussion between Slughorn and Dumbledore must have occurred, in which Slughorn offered to help in any way he could, and Dumbledore told him to be at the ready. Very possibly, this included a wink and a nod from Dumbledore regarding a faked death, but because he had no way of knowing when Malfoy would act, he couldn't predetermine how to proceed with this plan. Slughorn would likely be more willing to go along with it if his personal safety was assured, possibly with the added benefit of a good "slug" of Felix before departing for the cave. It does not appear, however, that Dumbledore intended for Slughorn to impersonate him for a faked death, otherwise, Slughorn mightn't have so readily accepted the challenge. More than likely, Dumbledore hadn't planned for Slughorn to face-off with Malfoy; rather, Slughorn's instructions would probably have been to take Harry to the cave, go through the enumerated steps, follow the instructions to get past the enchantments and return Harry to Hogwarts safely — with the added precaution to ask for Snape only if anything goes wrong (as Dumbledore sought out Snape when he was cursed by the ring protections). No doubt, Slughorn would be the logical choice as an accomplice, since it's been established in the text that he knows Voldemort well, knows of Voldemort's Horcruxes (as so few must be) and even the number of Horcruxes he has. Perhaps a parallel can be drawn between Dumbledore's fluency in the Dark Arts and Slughorn's, whose interest was most likely "all academic," as he allows that Wizards of a *"certain caliber have always been drawn to that aspect of magic."* (pgs. 498, 499) He may then possess some knowledge and means of how to destroy a Horcrux. Succinctly, Dumbledore knows Slughorn's strengths and weaknesses, trusts him (having known his "old friend" over fifty years), trusts his knowledge and capabilities, and knows he would probably do anything for Harry, Lily's son.

Slughorn would take a risk, then, when it came to Harry — out of remorse, or a need to alleviate his own guilt, or a desire to set some things right — and we saw evidence of that determination in the hut scene. Harry had some appeal to Slughorn that we've yet to discover: Slughorn didn't realize he was indeed "the Chosen One" until the scene in Hagrid's hut, and collecting "the Boy Who Lived" wouldn't be so desirable to Slughorn if he felt partially responsible for that boy's mother's murder, especially considering his exceptional fondness for her. Slughorn would feel he inadvertently had a hand in Lily's death, because he never made the connection until the meeting with Dumbledore (in which he provided the botched memory) that he could have prevented Tom Riddle from making Horcruxes. Dumbledore's failed attempt to secure a teacher the summer before, plus the fact Dumbledore has the botched memory in his possession by the time they meet at Budleigh Babberton, leads to the conclusion he met with Slughorn the summer prior to Order of the Phoenix, got the memory and tried to get him to come back to Hogwarts. (Interestingly, Dumbledore doesn't try to fill the open position with anyone else but Slughorn, and Hogwarts is stuck with Umbridge as a result.) Most importantly, Slughorn has since had a year to think about the ramifications of that conversation with Riddle and still wouldn't part with the memory — not until he understood that Harry was the "Chosen One" after all and there was a fighting chance at destroying Voldemort. There must be more to his interest in Harry than as the "Chosen One" or the crown jewel of his collection — Dumbledore's supposition seems to be short-sighted or perhaps a partial truth.

Summation

In the poem "CHILDE ROLAND TO THE DARK TOWER CAME" by Robert Browning, a "slug-horn" blows a battle cry at the culmination of an ill-fated quest; on the surface this is reminiscent of Harry's realization that he needs to stride into the "arena" with his head held high, regardless of his certainty that he won't survive. In the poem, Roland is on a quest to the Dark Tower, and everyone else on the quest dies by the time he reaches it; knowing that he's facing certain defeat, *"And yet, Dauntless the slug-horn to my lips I set, And blew, Childe Roland to the Dark Tower Came!"* Perhaps rather than Harry, this is more suggestive of Dumbledore, who seems to be backed into a corner with few options to remain alive and destroy Voldemort, calling upon his Slughorn despite the odds.

Without the scene in Hagrid's hut, the reader would be left with an impression of Slughorn as a flat character; but that scene between him and Harry provides us with a moment of recognition and growth, allowing Slughorn's function in the series to be more than a mouthpiece for the memory (and someone to serve as Head of Slytherin House in the final book). With this scene and her nudge in the direction of Lily's history, we're prepared to understand him as three-dimensional and purposeful to the story. And his introduction into a story that sets the precedent for stage magic, especially as a character with a historical counterpart in the magician, Horace Goldin, leads one to wonder how much misdirection and gimmick Rowling has performed. Goldin's autobiography is named, IT'S FUN TO BE FOOLED, and readers of the Potter series have been enjoying it for years.

This scenario as discussed in the pages above allows satisfaction of a number of criteria for not only HARRY POTTER AND THE HALF-BLOOD PRINCE, but the series in its entirety: for the richness of Slughorn's character that almost certainly is there; for Dumbledore to remain, in the eyes of the reader, one step ahead of the game and all the players; for Snape's actions, whether he was duped or a participant in a ruse, to likely lead to the downfall of Voldemort; for Harry to believe he's alone and summon the courage to move forward without Dumbledore; for the Wizarding World to gather their stray offshoots into one force, all around the organizing factor of Dumbledore "death;" and for Dumbledore to be ready to discover the unknown Horcrux, as it seems almost certain that he's laid a trap for Voldemort and is waiting for it to snap.

Bibliography

Browning, Robert. "CHILDE ROLAND TO THE DARKTOWER CAME."

Christopher, Milbourne. THE ILLUSTRATED HISTORY OF MAGIC. New York: Thomas Y. Cromwell Company. 1973.

Edmonds, I. G. MAGIC MAKERS: MAGIC AND THE MEN WHO MADE IT. Nashville: Thomas Nelson, Inc. 1976.

Mugglenet/Leaky Cauldron. "HBP Publication Day." July 16, 2005. Interview with J.K. Rowling, part 3. 17 Jan, 2005. http://www.the-leaky-cauldron.org/extras/aa-jointerview3.html

Rowling, J. K. HARRY POTTER AND THE HALF-BLOOD PRINCE. New York: Scholastic. 2005.

— HARRY POTTER AND THE ORDER OF THE PHOENIX. New York: Scholastic, 2003.

Steinmeyer, Jim. HIDING THE ELEPHANT: HOW MAGICIANS INVENTED THE IMPOSSIBLE AND LEARNED TO DISAPPEAR. New York: Carroll and Graf. 2003.

Daniela Teo

Daniela Teo fell in love with HARRY POTTER while working on her doctoral dissertation in French literature. She wrote informal editorials for Mugglenet, until several friendly readers encouraged her to have her own Mugglenet column, which became THE TWO-WAY MIRROR (http://mugglenet.com/editorials/thetwowaymirror/). Daniela loves the HARRY POTTER series for its good humor, healthy message, dizzying parallels and magic images. She has favorite lines on every page of HARRY POTTER, but she has seriously considered wearing a T-shirt saying: "I solemnly swear that I am up to no good!"

The Locket, the Cup, Nagini, Harry and the Mirror of Erised[1]

N THE NEWS SECTION OF HER WEB SITE,[e2] J. K. Rowling said that "So much of what happens in book six relates to book seven that I feel almost as though they are two halves of the same novel." Never before has the essence of a plot for a future Harry Potter book been delineated in the preceding installment with such precision if at all. But now, based on what we learned about Horcruxes in the HALF-BLOOD PRINCE, it appears that finding and destroying Voldemort's Horcruxes will be central to the plot of the seventh book (HBP Ch 23 "Horcruxes)".

Few will be those involved in the Horcrux quest. Dumbledore allowed Harry to share the knowledge of the Horcruxes with Ron and Hermione, but no one else is supposed to know Voldemort's secret. Harry's challenge will be to find out what the remaining Horcruxes are, where they are hidden, and how to destroy them, before taking on Voldemort himself, whom he must leave for last. This essay will attempt to trace Harry's steps before he takes them, determining the most compelling possibilities for the Horcruxes that remain to be found.

The Original Plan

Horcruxes are objects in which Voldemort has hidden parts of his soul. To make a Horcrux, one must first murder another human being, a "supreme act of evil" that rips the soul, and then attach the torn fragment of the soul to an object by performing a complex spell. This dark magic ensures that if one's body is destroyed, one cannot die, because a part of the soul "remains earthbound and undamaged" (HBP Ch 23 "Horcruxes"). Horcruxes are the dark secret to Voldemort's immortality.

What makes Voldemort even more horrible than his predecessors who have used Horcruxes is that he is the first to have made more than one, in fact, according to Dumbledore, six Horcruxes, so that he could have a seven-part soul, with the seventh part being inside his body. As Harry and Dumbledore learned from Slughorn's memory, Tom Riddle shared with Slughorn the idea of making six Horcruxes, because he considered seven "the most powerfully magical number" (HBP Ch 23).

After spending considerable time dwelling on Voldemort's past and studying his psyche, Dumbledore gained enough insight to determine that Voldemort would choose very special objects to house his "precious" soul as Horcruxes: objects of a certain grandeur, with a "powerful magical history," "objects worthy of the honor," "steeped in Hogwarts history" or that underline "the Slytherin connection" and enhance "Lord Voldemort's mystique" (HBP Ch 20 "Lord Voldemort's Request" and Ch 23 "Horcruxes"). Dumbledore suspects the items that meet these criteria best are heirlooms of the Hogwarts founders.

After diving with Harry through the Pensieve into various precious memories, Dumbledore concluded that Voldemort's six Horcruxes were to be:

1. Tom Riddle's diary (which opened the Chamber of Secrets)
2. Slytherin's ring
3. Slytherin's locket
4. Hufflepuff's cup
5. An heirloom of Gryffindor
6. An heirloom of Ravenclaw

Dumbledore doubted Voldemort ever got his hands on a Gryffindor heirloom, since he believed the only known heirloom from that founder was Gryffindor's sword, safely tucked away in his office. He did not, however, contradict Harry's succinct summary of the Horcruxes that remained to be destroyed, of which one was something of "Ravenclaw's or Gryffindor's" (HBP Ch 23). That means, he did not rule out that Voldemort may indeed have gotten his hands on something of Gryffindor's. But he told Harry he seriously doubted that Voldemort got his hands on both Ravenclaw's and Gryffindor's heirlooms, or perhaps what he meant was that he doubted Voldemort managed to make both heirlooms Horcruxes (HBP Ch 23).

The Horcruxes that Voldemort made can be divided into the known and the hypothetical. Among the known, some have already been destroyed, while others have not yet been located.

KNOWN HORCRUXES

1. The Ring: Destroyed.

Slytherin's ring was found and destroyed by Dumbledore and based on the evidence of Morfin's memory was associated with the murder of Tom Riddle's father. It was hidden inside the house of the Gaunts, Voldemort's wizard relatives, near the property of Tom Riddle Sr., Voldemort's Muggle father. Knowing with which death the ring was associated was useful information that helped the Headmaster find it. This realization may be useful in locating the remaining Horcruxes.

2. The Diary: Destroyed

Harry destroyed the diary that opened the Chamber of Secrets in his second year at Hogwarts. We can deduce from the fact that Tom Riddle Jr. killed Moaning Myrtle with the basilisk that he associated her death with the diary Horcrux, commemorating the first murder of a Muggleborn by means of the basilisk, for the purpose of carrying out "Slytherin's noble work" (of killing off all "Mudbloods"). Harry and Ron were able to find the entrance to the Chamber by talking to Myrtle, the ghost of the victim associated with that Horcrux, so that again knowing the victim was useful in finding and destroying the Horcrux.

3. The Locket: Location Unknown (but Suspected)

The locket was also a successful Horcrux, since it was already planted in the cave (and stolen by the mysterious R.A.B. who left a fake locket in its place that Harry and Dumbledore found; see Wendy B. Harte's explanation of how R.A.B. made this substitution in Chapter 2 of this book). I don't know whom Voldemort killed to make that Horcrux. I would want to bet that it was a woman. The locket was associated with Voldemort's mother, who used to wear it, and the cave was where he took two children to torture them when he was at the orphanage. It makes sense that he should associate his mother with the orphanage, since she abandoned him there. Again, there seems to be a link between the meaning of the Horcrux and its hiding place (and its victim, if it was a woman or someone connected with the orphanage).

My views on who R.A.B. is are shared by many. I think it is Regulus Black, Alphard being his uncle's name, and perhaps Regulus's middle name (OotP Ch 6 "The Noble and Most Ancient House of Black"). One would expect the middle name Alphard to show in Regulus's full name on the Black family tree, but it does not. It is, however, possible and to be expected that the Blacks removed Alphard from Regulus's full name at the same time that they completely removed Alphard's name from the tapestry, especially if Regulus was named after his uncle. (Alphard became an outcast as soon as he gave gold to Sirius, the blood traitor.) The Blacks may have chosen a more subtle form of name removal though, in order not to taint the appearance of Regulus's name. Usually burn marks reveal where there used to be a name that has been removed.

Regulus was Sirius's younger brother, whom Sirius considered too unimportant to be murdered by Voldemort himself. He became a Death Eater but then wanted to quit, which was not an option. It would be ironic for Regulus to be smarter than Sirius (and Voldemort) gave him credit to be. Slughorn seemed to think he was when he mentioned him to Harry (HBP Ch 4 "Horace Slughorn"). Wendy B. Harte, in Chapter 2 of this book, gives a good hypothesis of Regulus's motivation and opportunity for finding Voldemort's locket Horcrux. If she is right about Bellatrix also being involved, then it is indeed true that Voldemort associated a woman with the locket.

I wonder if the heavy locket that could not be opened that Harry and company found in Sirius's house might have been the Horcrux. The problem is that there was an ℑ on the locket, and the locket in Sirius's house was not described as having an ℑ on it: "a heavy locket that none of them could open" (OotP Ch 6). One would think that an ℑ would be a memorable mark and included in the description. On the side, posters in the Chamber of Secrets forums[3] have suggested that the fact that Slytherin's locket has a serpentine ℑ on it may mean that Harry will need to speak Parselmouth in order to open it.

At the end of the HALF-BLOOD PRINCE, Harry describes the fake locket as not being as "large" as the real one appeared in the Pensieve, and having no ornate ℑ (HBP Ch 28 "Flight of the Prince"). "Large" is not exactly the same thing as "heavy" (the quality of the locket at 12 Grimmauld Place) but it seems similar. Or perhaps the locket at 12 Grimmauld Place was simply one among several that Regulus considered as a replacement for the Horcrux. We see a lot of stealing going on. R.A.B. stole the locket Horcrux (HBP Ch 28). Kreacher filches Black heirlooms in the same paragraph in which the locket is described (OotP Ch 6). And Mundungus makes off with a suitcase full of Black heirlooms (HBP Ch 12 "Silver and Opals"). Stealing heirlooms is a bit of a recurring theme that in the case of the Blacks seems one of Rowling's funny ideas of hinting that the stolen Horcrux locket ended up at 12 Grimmauld Place.

4. The Cup: Unknown Location (Gringotts?)

I think we can be sure that Hufflepuff's cup was a successful Horcrux made with the death of Hepzibah Smith, Helga Hufflepuff's last descendant (HBP Ch 20 "Lord Voldemort's Request"). Would Voldemort choose Hepzibah's home to hide it? I doubt it, since he knew her family would search the house up and down looking for the heirlooms. Looking at the previous three Horcruxes, it seems that Voldemort chose to hide his Horcruxes in places that were somehow connected to him personally, but at the same time were reminiscent of the victims associated with them.

One place that might be meaningful both to Hepzibah and to Voldemort would be the shop where Voldemort worked, Borgin and Burkes. It is thus a possibility that Voldemort buried it under the shop. The four houses are associated with the four elements, fire, water, earth and air, with earth being the element of Hufflepuff (as Rowling said in an Interview with Mugglenet and the Leaky Cauldron).[1] A much more likely possibility is Gringotts bank, which also fits with Hufflepuff's earth element and the notion of burial. As Hagrid tells Harry, "— Gringotts is hundreds of miles under London, see. Deep under the Underground" (PS/SS Ch 5 "Diagon Alley"). Voldemort must know a lot about Gringotts to have been able to advise Quirrelll how to break into it in the first book, considering that it is run by "Goblins," that it is "the safest place in the world fer anything yeh want ter keep safe" and that "yeh'd be mad ter try an' rob it" (PS/SS Ch 5). Indeed, I fear Harry will have to do just that mad thing in the seventh book, without even knowing where in all that pile of locked treasure at Gringotts the cup is hidden (although his own scar may serve to guide him).

HYPOTHETICAL HORCRUXES

Now we enter the wild thickets of guesswork, as Dumbledore would say. Of the two remaining Horcruxes, we know that one was successful, and we have strong reason to believe that the other one failed. The one that failed was the one that Voldemort planned to make with the piece of soul torn after he murdered Harry. Dumbledore was sure Voldemort left the last Horcrux for Harry, since it was symbolic of his absolute victory over his enemy foreseen by the Prophecy. That means there were at least five successful Horcruxes made before Voldemort's first defeat.

5. An heirloom of "Ravenclaw or Gryffindor": Unidentified, Unknown Location

I doubt that Voldemort would reserve Ravenclaw's heirloom for Harry. It makes sense that for Harry Voldemort would have used something of Gryffindor's, since Harry's parents, James and undoubtedly Lily (who was known for her bravery) were both in Gryffindor, and the family lived in Godric's Hollow (Godric was Gryffindor's first name), not to mention that Slytherin's archenemy was his former best friend, Gryffindor.

Consequently, the hypothetical Horcrux of the five successful ones made before Voldemort went after baby Harry (not necessarily presented here in the order they were made) was most likely something of Ravenclaw's. Is it an object that we have seen before, that is right under our noses?

5.a. The Mirror of Erised: a Horcrux?

The only object I have found so far in the books that corresponds to the symbolic and magical requirements of a Horcrux is the Mirror of Erised. Harry discovered this mirror during his first nighttime wandering to the library in order to read and find out about Flamel (who alchemically created the Philosopher's

Stone, drinking the elixir from which makes one immortal).

Being nearly found out by Filch when a book started screaming, Harry ran away and hid in a classroom. At that point, he discovered the Mirror of Erised: "It was a magnificent mirror, as high as the ceiling, with an ornate gold frame, standing on two clawed feet. There was an inscription carved around the top: "ERISED STRA EHRU OYT UBE CAFRU OYT ON WOHSI" (SS/PS Ch 12 "The Mirror of Erised")

In this mirror, Harry saw his parents and his whole lost family, and for a moment thought they were still alive. But Harry learned from Dumbledore that the "immortality" the mirror showed him was not a reality, but a dangerous dream.

Immortality

The Mirror of Erised is a powerfully symbolic object. The context in which the mirror is first presented to the reader is Harry's quest for answers that involve the question of immortality: first in the library, when he is trying to read up on Flamel, and then before the mirror itself, contemplating his dead parents who seem to be alive again. A further textual connection between the mirror and immortality is the fact that Dumbledore figures out how to hide the Philosopher's Stone inside the mirror. In addition, Dumbledore's encasing of an object in the mirror seems to parallel the placing of a piece of soul inside an object.

Voldemort would have used the Philosopher's Stone to acquire a body again. Wouldn't it be ironic if the same object that housed the Stone that would give him a body also held a piece of his soul? The soul and the body might have both been in the Mirror at the same time... The Stone/body was destroyed in Book One. Maybe the soul/Mirror will be destroyed in Book Seven.

What would make the Mirror of Erised particularly appealing to Voldemort is what it would show (or showed) him if (or when) he looked into it: "Himself, all-powerful and eternal. That's what he wants," says J. K. Rowling in answer to the question.[5] The ironic twist would be even more compelling if the very object that first showed Voldemort immortal to himself served to make him so. Wouldn't Voldemort want to place, almost superstitiously, a part of his soul behind that ideal image of himself in order to animate it, at least symbolically?

Grandeur and Magic

A "magnificent mirror, as high as the ceiling, with an ornate gold frame" certainly has visual grandeur. But what really makes the grandeur of the mirror is that it has powerful magical properties. As the inscription around its upper border says, the mirror shows not the face of the person looking into it, but his or her heart's desire. And we know this is not its only property, because Dumbledore was able to use it to hide the Philosopher's Stone, so that only someone who wanted it without wanting to use it could get it. The only other objects that we know have a comparable magical versatility are the heirlooms of Hufflepuff and Slytherin as Hepzibah describes them to Tom Riddle, telling him they have all kinds of magical properties and that she hasn't figured them all out yet (HBP Ch 20 "Lord Voldemort's Request").

Ravenclaw's Heirloom

Is the Mirror of Erised an heirloom? It is beautiful and powerful enough to be one, but where is the clue pointing to a founder as its original owner? The only visual indicator that the mirror might belong to Ravenclaw is that it stands "on two clawed feet." That is not a clue to ignore, but it is not conclusive, as there are other furniture items in the books that have claws. It would also be surprising that Dumbledore should not recognize an obvious Ravenclaw heirloom. Perhaps, rather than being Rowena's heirloom, the mirror was simply designed a long time ago by someone in the Ravenclaw House. Perhaps Voldemort would settle for that.

Gryffindor's sword is all about fighting and courage; Slytherin's locket and ring are about display of personal grandeur; Hufflepuff's cup is about drinking, welcoming and enjoying life. I would expect Ravenclaw's heirloom to be suggestive of intellect. Though the Mirror of Erised reflects the heart's desire, it does seem to involve mainly the mind. It involves that which cannot be touched, like air, Ravenclaw's element. Mirrors involve reflections which are synonyms for thoughts. This mirror can thus be associated with intelligence as with aspirations and even the impossible. Also, the only person at Hogwarts who was able to give Harry the same hope about seeing his parents again as the Mirror of Erised was Luna, the seer of impossible things who belongs to the Ravenclaw House.

Whether the mirror is associated with Ravenclaw or not, it seems to belong to Hogwarts. It seemed to have already been at Hogwarts for a long time when Harry found it. Dumbledore told Harry that he discovered, like "hundreds" before him, the delights of the mirror, apparently implying that the mirror had been around for ages and witnessed the passing of entire generations (SS/PS Ch 12). The mysterious inscription around the edges of the mirror also appeared at first sight to be the writing of a different epoch, giving the mirror an aura of being steeped in history. Such qualities would have appealed to Voldemort.

Narrative Reasons

There are also literary reasons for bringing the Mirror of Erised back into the story. There would be a visual return to the beginning, a structural theme that characterizes in fact the entire series. Harry would face the Mirror again, in order to get something out of it, except this time a piece of soul rather than the Stone. He would also face his own heart again by staring once more into the mirror, and perhaps remember his greatest power. Dumbledore brought the Mirror of Erised back to the reader's attention in the HALF-BLOOD PRINCE, when he reminded Harry that the mirror showed him how to thwart Voldemort, with the power of his love, and that Voldemort should have realized what he was dealing with when he saw Harry before the mirror (HBP Ch 23). The mirror is a symbol of identity, and in facing it, Harry would confront himself as well as Voldemort.

There are a fair few mirroring objects in the novel and the theme of doubling is omnipresent. Most remarkable is the doubling phenomenon that affects Voldemort and Harry: they are both orphans who are attached to Hogwarts. Furthermore, Voldemort has marked Harry as his equal with the failed Avada Kedavra curse: through the scar they share powers and feelings. Harry and Voldemort have brother wands with cores from Fawkes the Phoenix. And thanks to the rebirthing ceremony, Voldemort and Harry now have the same blood running through their veins. The identity between the two reaches an intense climax when Harry sees himself as Voldemort in a cracked mirror on the wall in one of his dreams and when Voldemort possesses Harry in the Ministry of Magic making Harry feel what it is like to be Voldemort (GoF Ch 30 "The Pensieve," OotP Ch 36 "The Only One He Ever Feared").

Besides the doubling phenomenon, mirroring objects have also found themselves to be central to the story in each book.

1. PS/SS:

☞ The Mirror of Erised figured in the climax of the story and the Chapter "The Mirror of Erised" in which we first see it is one of Rowling's favorites.[6]

2. CoS:

☞ Mirrors were revealed to be objects that could protect against the murderous stare of the basilisk. Hermione was found carrying a mirror when she was petrified. Armed with this clue, Harry and Ron understood why none of the basilisk's victims were killed: there was always a quasi-mirror or lens protecting them. For example, the puddle of water on the floor acted as a mirror through which Mrs. Norris indirectly saw the basilisk.

☞ At the climax of the second book, a mirroring phenomenon takes place with the appearance of Tom Riddle out of the diary, a book that acts as such a powerful mirror of Voldemort that it can provide more than his reflection.

3. PoA:

 Although not as conventional a mirror, the time-turner in the third book acts strikingly as one, doubling time and those who travel through it, so that we see two sets of Harry and Hermione.

 Harry learns how to produce the most powerful Patronus thanks to the mirroring phenomenon that allows him to see himself, giving him faith in his own powers. In addition, Harry's Patronus is a mirror of his father, taking the shape of James's Animagus form.

4. GoF:

 We learn about Foe Glasses (mirrors) from Barty Crouch Jr., who, thanks to Polyjuice potion, has been mirroring Mad-Eye Moody.

 Harry's and Voldemort's wands connect creating the Priori Incantatem effect and bringing back echoes, like strong reflections, of Voldemort's victims.

5. OotP:

 Sirius offers Harry the Two-Way Mirror, an interesting object that we know from Rowling is supposed to make a come-back in the seventh book.[7] This object can be used to communicate with the person who has the other item of the pair. Harry furiously broke the two-way mirror Sirius gave him because he discovered it too late.

 In the climax of the Order of the Phoenix, a lot of glass in the Department of Mysteries was broken, shelves upon shelves of prophecies and the Ministry's entire supply of time-turners inside the glass-fronted cabinet. Both prophecies and time-turners can be considered mirroring devices. Together with the breaking of the two-way mirror, this general destruction may prefigure the breaking of another important mirror in the future.

6. HBP:

 If Dumbledore's and Harry's repeated trips into the Pensieve's memories can be considered looking into a type of mirror, a mirror that reflects the past, then mirrors were central to Harry's education in the sixth book.

 Draco's successful plot to assassinate Dumbledore involved two mirroring objects, the communicating Vanishing Cabinets.

These mirroring objects and the breaking of mirrors may prefigure a challenge Harry will face in the seventh book, to distinguish misleading reflections from reality. He may have to break or deactivate one or more mirrors, recognizing the

Mirror of Erised as a Horcrux would fit in nicely with this test, especially if Harry himself is also a Horcrux.

LOGISTICAL PROBLEMS

Hiding the Horcrux

There are a few problems that the Mirror of Erised being a Horcrux poses. One of them is, would Voldemort leave a Horcrux relatively out in the open with no protection around it? As Dumbledore says, a Horcrux must be kept "hidden and safe" in order to protect that piece of soul and assure the immortality of its owner (HBP Ch 23). Voldemort has already left out in the open one Horcrux, Tom Riddle's diary, in order to preserve that part of his history, but would he do it again?

It is possible that the protection he saw around the Mirror was of a psychological nature, and that the image that Voldemort saw of himself in the Mirror seemed to him worth the risk again. If the diary was found and destroyed (because naturally it would draw attention to itself), perhaps Voldemort still wanted at least one Horcrux to remain at Hogwarts, and he didn't imagine anyone wanting to destroy the Mirror of Erised.

Sometimes the best way to hide something is to leave it out in the open (or relatively so). It may also be that neither faculty nor students would think to steal such a huge magical object that may be powerful enough to resist transfiguration or other forms of concealment. I think it would have tickled Voldemort to place a Horcrux right under Dumbledore's nose, and to enjoy the irony of it, putting his soul in Dumbledore's protecting hands... We know now, unfortunately, that certain unthinkable things can be done under Dumbledore's nose, who has too much on his mind to keep track of everything, such as the vanishing cabinets that allowed the Death Eaters into the castle.

Making the Horcrux

Another problem is, when would Voldemort have made the Mirror a Horcrux? If he did it while still a student, and not with Myrtle's death, then whom did he kill to make the Mirror a Horcrux? Dumbledore mentions no other deaths at Hogwarts. It must have been someone from the outside.

Does an object have to be on hand to make the Horcrux spell right after (or right before) a murder is committed, or can the spell be made later, and how much later? If it can be made later, then Tom Riddle could have killed someone during a Hogsmeade weekend, say, and then got back to school and made the mirror a Horcrux. I tend to think that some time can pass between a murder and the making of a Horcrux. The soul is torn by murder, and perhaps it remains torn for quite some time, but with all the pieces inside the same body (and might begin to repair itself partially with good actions and repentance). The making of a Horcrux, on the other hand, would make the ripping of the soul irreversible, because it would be the ultimate proof that the killer has no respect whatsoever for his/her soul.

If Voldemort made the Horcrux after he left school, then he could have used Floo powder and the unguarded fireplaces to enter Hogwarts, or even the communicating pair of Vanishing Cabinets, one of which was in Borgin & Burkes since at least Harry's second year and may have been there since Tom Riddle's time. I don't think Voldemort said anything about the cabinet to Draco, but if he knew what it did, it is likely he kept an eye on its whereabouts, and that it was part of another plan of his.

Recognizing the Horcrux

Another problem with the mirror is that it seems almost impossible to accept that Dumbledore, who is so sensitive to a place that "has known magic," because "Magic always leaves traces" (HBP Ch 26 "The Cave"), did not sense the Mirror of Erised had been magically tampered with (especially when he spent time with it to figure out how to hide the Philosopher's Stone). But both in the cave and in the Gaunts' hovel, Dumbledore knew he was looking for a Horcrux and for Voldemort's magic, whereas with the mirror, he was off his guard. Dumbledore says himself that what helped was that he was "keeping an eye open for traces of magical concealment" (HBP Ch 23).

Also, perhaps the protective magic is easier to recognize than the Horcrux itself. And in addition maybe the psychological protection worked on Dumbledore. The Mirror of Erised seemed too simple, too obvious, too out in the open and safe to be suspicious. Maybe also, whatever it was that Dumbledore saw in the Mirror of Erised may have made him vulnerable and unwilling to look for reasons to destroy it. Even if Dumbledore did not consciously recognize the Mirror of Erised as a Horcrux, if his subconscious sensed Voldemort's presence, it could have given him the idea to hide the Philosopher's Stone inside the mirror in order to bring Voldemort to reflect on the route he was pursuing to achieve immortality.

Another person who doesn't seem to recognize the Horcrux is Voldemort himself, at the end of the first book. He is mum when Quirrelll needs help working the mirror, and doesn't seem to protest when Quirrelll asks himself aloud whether he should break it. This would seem to suggest that the mirror is not a Horcrux because Voldemort does not make any outward statements about the mirror's value or importance.

But I don't think Voldemort is in a hurry to reveal his Horcruxes to anyone, be they faithful followers or not. He was not likely to protest too quickly, in case he might give Quirrelll any ideas, but he did start thinking and found a solution before

Quirrelll attempted to break the mirror (and may he have stopped Quirrelll breaking it if no solution presented itself immediately). The reason Voldemort himself could not have used the mirror the way Harry did was that neither he nor Quirrelll had Harry's heart, as Dumbledore tells Harry (SS/PS Ch 17 "The Man with Two Faces").

5.b. The Sorting Hat: Not a Horcrux

The Sorting Hat was a popular idea for a Horcrux, because it was magical, intelligent, associated with all the founders, and came off Gryffindor's head, but Rowling put that rumor to rest in the Rumors section of her web site: "No, it isn't. Horcruxes do not draw attention to themselves by singing songs in front of large audiences."[8]

5.c. Tom Riddle's Award or Tom Riddle's Medal: a Horcrux?

Yet another favored hypothesis is that Tom Riddle's award for "Special Services to the School" (when he framed Hagrid for opening the Chamber of Secrets) is a Horcrux. I tend to think Riddle did not find value in that award, however. He made his own award to carry his name, which was the diary, commemorating the truth about the same events. The diary had historical value and magical powers, capable of revealing Tom Marvolo Riddle's profound identity and carrying out his attacks for him after he left. I think the diary was like a mockery of the award. It is true though that Voldemort may have wanted another object at Hogwarts to remain in the diary's stead in the event that it was destroyed, and in that case it wouldn't seem unlikely that he should have created a mirror Horcrux of the diary with his award.

A more likely Horcrux with Tom Riddle's name on it I think is his "Medal for Magical Merit." The visit that the trio makes to the trophy room reveals that there are several objects with Tom Riddle's name down there: the burnished gold shield (the award), a Medal for Magical Merit, and a list of Head Boys on which he is included (CoS Ch 13 "The Very Secret Diary"). It is possible that Rowling chose one among these objects to be a Horcrux. I would tend to think it is the medal, a glorious testimony to Voldemort's outstanding magical powers. It does seem, however, that a medal is fairly easy to steal, and one wonders why Voldemort would leave it unprotected, unless he correctly anticipated that trophies were safe at Hogwarts and unlikely to be suspected.

5.d. The Tiara(s): a Horcrux?

Many fans also think the fifth Horcrux is the Goblin-made tiara that Molly promises to let Fleur wear at her wedding. Sleuths also detected a scent when they saw another tiara mentioned in the Room of Requirement, that Harry used to mark the spot where he hid the Half-Blood Prince's book. But that tarnished tiara seems even less likely a candidate, as there is an air of cheap trinket about it. It is true that a *crown* could appeal to Voldemort as a symbol of royalty and power, of his status as the *supreme ruler* of the world. If Aunt Muriel can't find her tiara, we will have reason to be suspicious. Otherwise, it will be a crown that we have not seen yet.

I can't cover all the ideas for the fifth Horcrux that have been brought up, but I have not yet encountered other objects that seem to me interesting enough to qualify (for another Horcrux idea, see Wendy B. Harte's Chapter 2 in this book). For the present, I remain attached to the Mirror of Erised, which, although possibly not a perfect choice in terms of logistics and protection, seems the most meaningful and appealing magical object. The Medal for Magical Merit may be a possibility, also.

6.a. The Failed Horcrux (Something of Gryffindor's?): Still in Godric's Hollow?

The last intended Horcrux, meant to be associated with Harry's death, may have been another founder heirloom. I would not be surprised if it was a Gryffindor heirloom that Voldemort planned to associate with Harry's death, or at least, if he couldn't get it, a powerfully magical or historical object reminiscent of Gryffindor. If Voldemort took the object with him to Godric's Hollow the night he murdered Harry's parents, then it is possible that object is still somewhere in the ruins (unless the Ministry took care to scour and clean up the place), and Harry will find it in the seventh book.

I am very curious what the object is, because it may be useful to Harry. His visit to Godric's Hollow, while serving an emotional purpose, I am sure will be important to the plot and may even arm Harry in some way. What heirloom Godric Gryffindor left behind besides his sword is anybody's guess. I think his wand would make a neat set with his sword. The only question that remains is why Voldemort would leave Godric's wand behind if he managed somehow to retrieve his own wand from the ruins, unless Godric's wand somehow became irretrievably hidden.

There have been a couple of malfunctioning wands in the series so far that needed to be replaced: Ron's and Neville's. We know that Harry and Voldemort can't battle each other with their own brother wands, because they don't work properly against each other. Either Harry or Voldemort needs to use a different wand (or sword?).

6.b. Voldemort's Wand: a (Failed) Horcrux?

Another possibility, an idea that John Granger has developed in the chapter "Animampono Baculum" of his book UNLOCKING HARRY POTTER[9], is that Voldemort, upon finding no heirloom of Gryffindor's, decided to use his own wand as a Horcrux, an action that accidentally resulted in Harry's becoming a Horcrux.

The wand would be a symbol of Voldemort's power, and he would always have it near him, a Horcrux of whose safety he could always be sure. The core of his wand was a tail feather from Dumbledore's Phoenix, a fact that Voldemort may have known or suspected. Ollivander does not tell Harry it was Fawkes that gave the tail feathers of his and Voldemort's wands; Dumbledore does (GoF Ch 36 "The Parting of the Ways"). But Ollivander may have told the young Tom Riddle where his feather came from, although it is doubtful. Why Fawkes gave the two feathers is still a mystery and seems to be a part of one of Dumbledore's more obscure plans. All this does not exclude the connection Voldemort may have seen between his wand and Dumbledore, who after all had a pet Phoenix.

Having such a tail feather in his wand was no small matter, since Fawkes is "a Fantastic Beast who is immortal, and who is the pet of the greatest wizard living [...]" ("Animampono"). His wand would symbolize immortality and help achieve it at the same time: "What a twist, that his means of destroying the Gryffindor line will be through a wand Dumbledore gave him the money to buy as an eleven year old charity case and whose core came from the great wizard's familiar!" ("Animampono")

Gryffindor's Heir

The Phoenix, being a bird associated with fire, is naturally a Gryffindor symbol. I believe Dumbledore is related to Gryffindor, a fact that Voldemort may have discovered but which may not be common knowledge. This would reinforce the connection between Voldemort's wand and Gryffindor, containing a feather of his descendant's immortal pet. Although there is some evidence that Harry could have been the heir of Godric Gryffindor, given that his parents lived in Godric's Hollow and that Harry pulled Godric's sword out of the hat, a feat only a "true" Gryffindor could have accomplished, Rowling was sort of tricked by Melissa and Emerson into telling us that Harry is not a descendant of Gryffindor.[10]

Albus Dumbledore is thus the most likely candidate for the heir of Gryffindor (along with his brother Aberforth). There are several clues that point to his connection to the Hogwarts founder:

- Dumbledore keeps Gryffindor's sword as if he were its rightful owner after Harry brought it out of the hat.
- Dumbledore's Office and the Chamber of Secrets are presented in a parallel manner, as if their dwellers are counterparts of each other, the heir of Slytherin versus the heir of Gryffindor.
  - Harry discovers both the office and chamber in the second book.

- ❧ To enter both places, passwords must be spoken. But whereas anyone can access Dumbledore's office by speaking the right, easy to guess, candy name, Harry is the only one who can enter the Chamber of Secrets by speaking Parseltongue, Slytherin's unique gift.

- ❧ The knocker on Dumbledore's office door is a Griffin, while the metal embossing on the faucet leading to the Chamber of Secrets is a snake.

- ❧ Dumbledore has the red and gold Fawkes (associated with the Gryffindor element, fire: Harry catches him on a burning day) while Tom Riddle has the green Basilisk, (associated with the Slytherin element, water: he moves through pipes, and the entrance to the Chamber is through a sink). The two pets are matched against each other in the climactic battle.

- ☞ Dumbledore's and Gryffindor's names share a homophonous suffix, suggesting a possible family relation.

- ☞ Dumbledore is the greatest Headmaster Hogwarts ever had, and he is buried on the grounds of the school, almost like a founder.

Rowling told us that it would be profitable to investigate Dumbledore's family more, which may involve more than thinking about Aberforth. On the other hand, Rowling may have chosen not to make Harry a Gryffindor by blood in order to oppose the obsession with pure blood that Slytherin had with the idea that it is our "choices" that make us who we truly are. Harry *is* Gryffindor's true heir, but because of his heart, not blood.

Phoenix versus Horcrux

John noted that the Phoenix responds to Harry's loyalty in the climax of the second book and that the two wands with Phoenix feathers created a musical sphere when Harry dueled with Voldemort in the fourth book, giving Harry strength. Consequently, it is possible that Voldemort's wand, because of the nature of its core, reacted to Lily's sacrifice when Voldemort killed her. Voldemort's wand probably began to "shake and sing" in reaction to Lily's sacrifice, because of "resonance with sacrificial love and death" and "dissonance [...] with the wand holder" who was a murderer and traitor (if he had promised someone not to kill Lily) ("Animampono").

Faced with an out of control wand, a panicking Voldemort may have thought he could master it better by turning it into the last Horcrux immediately, using Lily's murder: "He performs the nonverbal Horcrux Animampono spell, *Animam-*

pono Baculum! (literally, Animampono = 'I place the soul,' and Baculum, its object = 'wand, staff'; taken all together, he says 'I place the soul part on the wand') ("Animampono"). John concludes: "My bet is that magically stuffing the fragment of soul the murders of James and Lily Potter ripped from him into the wand probably stilled and silenced it, at least momentarily. In that moment, the Dark Lord turned to baby Harry to kill his prophesied vanquisher with his new Horcrux wand. *Avada Kedavra!*" ("Animampono")

6.c. Harry's Scar: an (Accidental) Horcrux?

Quite a few (but not all) fans subscribe to the theory that Harry's scar was made a Horcrux the night that Voldemort went to Godric's Hollow. John Granger's scenario of Voldemort turning his own wand into a Horcrux gives a solution to a logistical problem of how Harry could accidentally have been made a Horcrux (Voldemort tried to kill him before The HALF-BLOOD PRINCE, which means he did not suspect he was one, i.e. the Horcrux was not intentional).

If no Horcrux spell was pronounced, how could a piece of Voldemort's soul end up in Harry? John suggests that something happened when Voldemort tried to kill Harry with his Horcrux wand: "Wand cores have their limits and I think they are not a match for murderer's soul fragments. Light cannot 'hold' darkness and vice versa. Phoenix-core in a state of excitement, that is, in resonance with loving sacrifice, would be especially incapable of retaining a soul fragment of Lord Voldemort's soul, misshapen and darkened" ("Animampono").

Thus, the soul fragment would have been expelled from the wand at the same time as the Avada Kedavra. According to John, it was the Horcrux that shielded Harry from the death curse: "The Horcrux is not destroyed by the curse because Avada Kedavra is not a suicide curse. To perform it correctly you have to hate the object you are cursing. Voldemort's soul, being rightly part of Voldemort and here his means to immortality, may be the only thing the Dark Lord loves" ("Animampono").

I believe, however, that it was Lily's blood that protected Harry, since her blood continues to protect Harry long after she is gone. Another solution that would take care of the same logistical problem of how a piece of Voldemort's soul would end up in Harry's scar without a Horcrux spell being pronounced, is that a piece of the murderer's soul always hits the victim with the Avada Kedavra curse, which fits with the notion of the murderer's soul being ripped by murder. In Harry's case, the piece may have gotten stuck in Harry, since he didn't die, protected by Lily's sacrifice.

Before examining more at length the clues and implications of Harry being a Horcrux, I will discuss Voldemort's (presumably) last hypothetical Horcrux, which in itself may provide proof that Harry also is one.

6.d. or 7. Nagini, a Living Horcrux: Location Unknown (With Voldemort? Lying Low in the Riddle Mansion or Cemetery? Slithering About on a Mission? Tailing the Trio?)

If Harry is a Horcrux, then it is possible that Voldemort has one Horcrux too many. That would mean that instead of having a seven-part soul, which would be the most powerful magical number, he has an eight-part soul, which might make him weaker.

Voldemort only wanted to make six Horcruxes, but something went unexpectedly wrong the night he killed the Potters. I think evidence points to the fact that Harry may be a Horcrux, but if he is, he was not intentionally made so by Voldemort. Since he had not succeeded in making his intended Horcrux with Harry's death, Voldemort believed he still had one Horcrux to go when he was finally able to use a wand again (at the earliest when he acquired the baby looking body fans like to call Babymort). Dumbledore thinks Voldemort lost no time in making that Horcrux, and used the Muggle's death (Mr. Frank Bryce, the old gardener of the Riddles) to make Nagini one. Perhaps Frank's death was considered important enough for Voldemort because he was the last person associated with that same Riddle house as his father.

We don't know with certainty that Nagini is a Horcrux, but Dumbledore thinks so, and Dumbledore's guesses are, as Rowling says, "never very far wide of the mark."[11] If Dumbledore's argument for Nagini did not seem convincing enough, I think it is because he preferred not to tell Harry exactly how he came to the conclusion. He told him that it was Voldemort's unusual control over the snake that gave him the idea, but I think he was being purposely vague, because, if my guesses about his reasoning are right, Nagini being a Horcrux implies that Harry is also a Horcrux.

Harry being a Horcrux is a conclusion of such consequence that I don't think Dumbledore would have wanted to jump to it too quickly until he was absolutely certain. Telling Harry his suspicions might have had awful consequences for Harry, so Dumbledore may have justified his silence to himself with the argument that this was not something he *knew*. Similarly, he didn't tell Harry about the Horcruxes at the end of the fifth book, because they were still only a hypothesis. I think Rowling created a loophole for herself by having Dumbledore claim to a reproachful Harry that he only promised to tell him what he *knew*. There is likely more information left to be revealed that Dumbledore suspected but didn't share.

There was a mysterious interaction between Dumbledore and one of his silver instruments in his office after Harry saw Nagini in the Ministry of Magic attack Ron's father (OotP Ch 21 "The Eye of the Snake"). Dumbledore seemed particularly interested in Harry's point of view (Harry had been inside the snake). He then tapped the instrument which showed him a snake made of smoke that seem to confirm Harry's story. I think the instrument's answer was in fact to the unspoken question of where was Voldemort, if Harry was inside the snake.

The answer was the snake. To which Dumbledore answered "Naturally, naturally [...]. But in essence divided?" (OotP Ch 22 "St. Mungo's Hospital for Magical Maladies and Injuries"). It seems most likely that Dumbledore's question refers to the fact that Voldemort could not have been all in the snake. He had to be in two places at the same time, which meant he was in essence divided. In answer to Dumbledore's hypothesis, the smoke snake divided into two snakes, as if to confirm the idea as fact. This seems to be an illustration of Voldemort's divided soul and a hint that the snake is a Horcrux (and also perhaps that Voldemort's soul has been mutilated enough to resemble that of a snake).

We learned from Snape during Occlumency lessons that Voldemort was possessing Nagini at the time that Harry was also in the snake, and it was Voldemort's presence in Nagini that made Harry's trip to the Ministry possible (OotP Ch 24 "Occlumency"). Dumbledore acted in the silver instrument scene as if he had a piece of information that was new, and that gave him a big clue, but he knew Harry had accompanied Voldemort in his dreams before, and it seems that Voldemort possessing an animal is old news. He did it during his 13 years of exile and he possessed Quirrelll, none of which gave Dumbledore any clues. What is different in this scene?

On the one hand, Voldemort now has a body of his own. It may be unusual for a wizard to be able to possess others once he has his own body. Posters in the Chamber of Secrets discussion forum[12] to my editorials countered this argument by reminding me that Voldemort said at his rebirthing party: "Only one power remained to me. I could possess the bodies of others" (GoF Ch 33 "The Death Eaters"). That seemed to suggest that he could possess before, since that power "remained" to him. At the same time, it is possible Voldemort meant that naturally without a body he would have the power of possession, the only one that remained with his condition. In case it is not possession itself once Voldemort has a body that is suspicious, was there anything else different that night?

I think spatial distance between the person possessing and the possessed being might qualify also as a new situation. Voldemort clearly possessed Nagini because he didn't want to set foot inside the Ministry. We can conclude thus that he was possessing Nagini from a distance. We learn from Snape, however, that for Legilimency spatial proximity and eye contact are very important (OotP Ch 24 "Occlumency"). Only Harry's scar has been able to defy that law. Perhaps the same spatial rules apply to possession. In that case, like Harry, Nagini has helped

Voldemort defy that limit. But while Harry has an unusual scar, there is nothing about Nagini to explain this phenomenon, unless she is a Horcrux.

Dumbledore was looking for a solution to a puzzle after learning that Harry was inside the snake. That puzzle may well have been the mystery of Voldemort's ability to possess Nagini when he was far from the serpent. It seems that Dumbledore first wanted to rule out that Voldemort was inside the Ministry. Thus he asked Harry if he had other points of view, which might have indicated that Voldemort was present: "Were you perhaps standing beside the victim, or else looking down on the scene from above?" (OotP Ch 21). This seems to describe the phenomenon of the Pensieve, when one can walk around in a memory, outside of everyone involved, without entering anyone's point of view but one's own.

In other Voldemort dreams, Harry seemed to be beside Frank Bryce when he was murdered (GoF Ch 1 "The Riddle House" and Ch 2 "The Scar") and was on the back of an owl delivering a message to Voldemort at the Riddles' home (GoF Ch 29 "The Dream"). But there are some exceptions to this rule. Harry was inside Voldemort in one dream. And it is possible he was even seeing through Frank Bryce's eyes for a moment, especially when he saw Babymort and was horrified and screamed as Babymort killed Frank. Harry seemed to share Frank's reactions, and also it is not clear if Harry could see Frank before he saw his body "fall to the ground" (GoF Ch 2). If a piece of the murderer's soul hits the victim during the Avada Kedavra curse, the point of view through Frank's eyes would be explained, if Harry is a Horcrux, as well as Harry's ability to see through Voldemort's eyes.

A good argument against Nagini being a Horcrux is that it is not an immortal being. How could Voldemort choose an animal with a limited life span to assure his immortality? It seems counter-intuitive. It may, however, be possible to remove his piece of soul from Nagini as she gets old and reinsert it into a younger serpent. And Nagini herself, like the Basilisk, may have an indefinitely long life span, if it is a magical snake.

Also, as seen with the diary, there may be advantages to using Nagini that override her possibly limited chances for endless survival. Perhaps it would be easier for Voldemort to regain a body upon destruction if a living (female) being was his Horcrux. And he may simply not trust enough any of his Death Eaters and feel the need for a living being that he control as he does Nagini. Voldemort would have made this Horcrux when he thought himself abandoned by nearly all his Death Eaters, except for the cringing Pettigrew and Barty Crouch Jr. of whose loyalty he had by then only heard. It is more than understandable, in these circumstances, that Voldemort would have wanted to create an absolute ally for himself.

How will Harry and his friends find Nagini the Horcrux? It may be, in the case of this particular Horcrux, that Harry will not have to go after it, but it will come to him. It is possible that Voldemort will send Nagini on a spying mission, tailing the trio (to assure himself of Draco's activities in that same pursuit; you always need one spy to spy on another, as with Peter and Snape). The fans' favorite for finishing off Nagini is Ginny Weasley. She would have to join the trio at some point to do that (or the quartet, if Draco will have joined the trio, having realized he can't tell Voldemort his findings about the Horcrux hunt without being murdered for knowing too much)

7. or 8. Another Horcrux after Nagini?

Fans have been hoping and speculating that Harry's Horcrux hunt will be easier than it seems, that perhaps he and Nagini are not Horcruxes, and that Harry will discover some of his work has already been done for him, such as that R.A.B. has already destroyed the locket Horcrux. But the opposite could be true, and it may be that Voldemort made more Horcruxes after his failure in Godric's Hollow than Dumbledore speculated.

As far as Voldemort knew when he was Babymort, he was one Horcrux short of his intended six, which would lend credence to Dumbledore's theory that he made Nagini (or some other object) a Horcrux. But after his rebirth, Voldemort learned one piece of fact that infuriated him: his diary Horcrux had been destroyed. Depending on what Voldemort believed would make him strongest, he may have wanted to make another Horcrux in order to make up for the destroyed Horcrux and bring the total back up to six.

A close analysis of the timing of this supposed eighth Horcrux may be able to rule out its possibility. Between the times when he found out about the diary (after his rebirth) and possessed Harry in the Ministry of Magic, I don't believe Voldemort made any Horcruxes, because he was lying low and did not commit any murders that we know of. After he possessed Harry, on the other hand, it is likely Voldemort realized Harry was his Horcrux (if he is one), and thus, upon finding out that he had the six he needed, he didn't see the need to make any more, until he decided what to do with the piece of soul lodged inside Harry.

HARRY IS A HORCRUX: CLUES AND CONSEQUENCES

Harry is a Horcrux: CLUES

Nagini

A curious aspect of the situation leading to the conclusion that Nagini was a Horcrux was that Harry was in the thick of things. To set up his silver instrument problem, Dumbledore had to look at the Nagini-Harry-Voldemort triangle. All three were in the same body at the same time, like some kind of unholy trinity. If possession from a distance indicates that a piece of Voldemort's soul is in the being that he is possessing, then the fact that Voldemort possessed Harry from a distance at the end of OotP (his body was supposedly "gone from the hall") is a clue that Harry may be a Horcrux, just as it was a clue that Nagini was a Horcrux (OotP Ch 36 "The Only One He Ever Feared").

It also seems meaningful that the dilemma of possessing from a distance is reminiscent of Dumbledore's puzzle in the CHAMBER OF SECRETS, in which, incidentally, Voldemort again possessed someone through the intermediary of a Horcrux. What Dumbledore said about Tom Riddle's diary was that the question was not who but *how*. It was Voldemort inside Hogwarts and possessing Ginny, but how in the world was he there, if his body wasn't? In answer, Harry showed Dumbledore the diary, in other words, the Horcrux. Likewise, Voldemort was possessing Nagini and Harry from a distance, but how? All three times the answer may be that Voldemort's soul was divided, and it was his Horcruxes that allowed such an unusual phenomenon to take place. These echoes may be a literary device used to prepare the revelation that Harry is also a Horcrux.

The fact that Dumbledore thinks the snake is a Horcrux also sets a precedent for Harry. It is possible for a living being to be a Horcrux, however inadvisable it may be. The step from Nagini to Harry is not as big as the step from an inanimate object to a human being would be.

If there is a connection between possessing Nagini and Harry at a distance, then not only Dumbledore realized something that night, but Voldemort did also. After the Ministry ordeal, Voldemort ceased attacking Harry, both mentally and physically. He gave special orders to his Death Eaters to leave Harry alone, that he was his to deal with. It may be that he is meditating how to deal with the unexpected situation, and how to recover his piece of soul before destroying Harry.

Harry's Scar

The most important clue that Harry is a Horcrux may be Harry's scar, which we know is a mystery that is central to the series. That is no ordinary scar. Voldemort marked him as his equal with it, as the Prophecy says, and transferred his powers to him. Harry is able to speak Parseltongue, for example. But Harry also feels contaminated by his link to Voldemort, and what greater contamination could there be than if Voldemort actually put a piece of his soul inside Harry's body?

There is also an interesting exchange between Harry and Dumbledore at the end of the CHAMBER OF SECRETS, when Dumbledore and Harry come to the conclusion that Voldemort has put "a bit of himself" inside Harry (CoS Ch 18 "Dobby's Reward").

What bit can this be? Wouldn't it be most meaningful, in the light of all that we learned in the HALF-BLOOD PRINCE, that this bit should be a piece of Voldemort's soul?

The Sorting Hat also was fooled, it seems, and wanted to put Harry in Slytherin. At the height of his doubts about his own identity and whether he was the heir of Slytherin, Harry always remembered the hesitancy of the hat (e.g. CoS Ch 11 "The Dueling Club"). Dumbledore thinks it is because Harry has some qualities that Slytherin would have prized that the hat considered Slytherin (CoS Ch 18), but isn't there more to it? What if the hat sensed Voldemort's soul, and naturally thought it was Harry's?

Another important aspect of the scar is that it has not only transferred some of Voldemort's powers to Harry, but as Voldemort has grown stronger and the connection between he and Harry has intensified, it has allowed Harry to sense Voldemort's moods, to get in touch with Voldemort's most intense feelings, be they madly ecstatic or murderous. Feelings more than anything are suggestive of a connection between Harry and Voldemort's soul.

When Harry's scar was tuned in to Voldemort's presence, intense mood swings, or acts of murder and torture, Harry felt an excruciating pain in his scar. This pain may be linked to the "mortal agony" that Voldemort feels if he possesses Harry (HBP Ch 23 "Horcruxes"). When Voldemort murders or tortures or feels, his soul is involved in the act, and perhaps at that time his other soul pieces which are usually dormant, especially the ones inside living beings, become animated. The soul piece inside Harry, upon becoming animated, feels the same unbearable pain at sensing Harry's pure soul that Voldemort himself felt upon possessing him. But because of the soul piece's proximity to Harry, it is Harry who feels the pain that should be Voldemort's.

The Return of Quirrell's Turban: "The Man with Two Faces"

Another clue that Harry's scar may be a Horcrux may be given by Voldemort's first striking appearance in the series as a disembodied face at the back of Quirrell's head. This gruesome image at the end of the obstacle course seemed to be predicted by the first obstacle of Fluffy, the three-headed dog. Quirrell hid the fact that he had Voldemort sticking out the back of his head by wearing a turban.

A rather portentous sign seems to be given to us in the HALF-BLOOD PRINCE, when Harry ends up in the hospital with a cracked skull after the game in which McLaggen hits him with the beater's bat. Harry feels his head "strangely heavy," wrapped in "a stiff turban of bandages" (HBP Ch 19 "Elf Tails"). The image of the turban is almost never mentioned in Potterverse, so that the echo between Quirrell's and Harry's turbans is strong. Harry had a disturbing and perhaps premonitory dream in the SORCERER'S/PHILOSOPHER'S STONE that he was wearing a turban like Quirrell's:

He was wearing Professor Quirrelll's turban, which kept talking to him, telling him he must transfer to Slytherin at once, because it was his destiny. Harry told the turban he didn't want to be in Slytherin; it got heavier and heavier; he tried to pull it off but it tightened painfully — and there was Malfoy, laughing at him as he struggled with it — then Malfoy turned into a hook-nosed teacher, Snape, whose laugh became high and cold — there was a burst of green light and Harry woke, sweating and shaking. (SS/PS Ch7 "The Sorting Hat")

The "heavy" turban Harry now has in the hospital, like the "heavier and heavier" one in his dream and the suspicious one that Quirrelll was wearing, may be a symbol that something as ominous is hiding under Harry's turban as under Quirrell's, a piece of Voldemort's soul. It would create a mirror image, inverted: Quirrelll had a piece of Voldemort's soul at the back of his head, and Harry has a piece of Voldemort's soul on his forehead.

The Symbolism of Disembodied Heads[13]

Besides the striking image of Voldemort's face at the back of Quirrell's head, there is a noticeable pattern of disembodied heads throughout the series that seems to prefigure a danger involving the head of one of our characters, most likely Harry. We see Harry's disembodied head when he first puts on his invisibility cloak and sees "just his head suspended in midair" (SS/PS Ch 12 "The Polyjuice Potion") and also when he scared Draco in front of the Shrieking Shack, because his invisibility cloak slipped off his head. As Snape described it, "It was your head, Potter. Floating in midair" (PoA Ch 14 "Snape's Grudge").

When the reader takes the time to notice these images, the list grows practically endless. Harry's "head" seems decapitated symbolically when he is dueling Ron, each one holding one of Fred and George's fake wands, and Ron's parrot severs the head of Harry's haddock, which droops and falls (GoF Ch 22 "The Unexpected Task"). Also, when Harry becomes the leader of "Dumbledore's Army," they have their preliminary meeting in the Hog's Head, whose picture motto is "a wild boar's severed head" (OotP Ch 16 "In the Hog's Head"). Such a sign doesn't seem to bode too well for the "head" of the organization meeting there.

Harry's destiny seems almost tied up with Buckbeak's when he is doing a reading of the crystal globe for Trelawney, who has been predicting Harry's death all year. Trelawney says hopefully, expecting a decapitation: "Does the hippogriff appear to... have its head?" and she is sorely disappointed when Harry says firmly that yes, he is alive and well and flying away. Harry predicted a future that he himself helped to bring about (PoA Ch 15 "Professor Trelawney's Prediction").

I am hoping that is a good omen for the fate of his own head. But Harry mock predicts "his own death by decapitation" in a homework assignment for Trelawney... (GoF Ch 14 "The Unforgivable Curses").

Another striking image of decapitation is conjured during Snape's description of the Dark Arts as an enemy with many heads: "Fighting them is like fighting a many-headed monster, which, each time a neck is severed, sprouts a head even fiercer and cleverer than before" (Chapter 9 "The Half-Blood Prince"). The Runespoor described by Rowling in her FANTASTIC BEASTS & WHERE TO FIND THEM is a snake with three heads, two of which often gang up on the third (the "critic") and bite it off. The animal seems to be an illustration of Snape's vision of the Dark Arts, and perhaps a metaphor for the Voldemort-Nagini-Harry trio. From Voldemort's point of view, one could say that with Harry as Horcrux, the Dark Arts have succeeded in growing a nearly indestructible head, at least in terms of the White Hats destroying this Horcrux. Who would kill Harry, when Voldemort wouldn't and he wouldn't let any of his followers touch him?

Other striking examples of disembodied heads include the strange phenomenon that happens to the Death Eater's head in the Department of Mysteries when it falls into the time jar: "A baby's head now sat grotesquely on top of the thick, muscled neck of the Death Eater [...]" (OotP Ch 35 "Beyond the Veil"). This combination of the head of a baby and the body of a Death Eater is reminiscent of Babymort, and even of Harry who was attacked by Voldemort when he was a baby. Hermione doesn't allow Harry to attack the baby-headed Death Eater, saying "you can't hurt a baby" (OotP Ch 35 "Beyond the Veil").

On the list of decapitated or otherwise metamorphosed heads one can also include the scene in which Harry "accidentally behead[s] a dead caterpillar" when he is angry with Draco (PoA Ch 17 "The Boggart in the Wardrobe"). Also, the first password we learn to the Gryffindor Tower is *Caput Draconis* meaning the head of the dragon. The Gryffindor house ghost is "Nearly Headless Nick" and in the CHAMBER OF SECRETS we meet the Headless Hunt to boot who like to play games like *Horseback Head-Juggling*, *Head Polo*, and *Head Hockey*. The walls of Sirius's Home, 12 Grimmauld Place, are horribly decorated with the severed heads of former house-elves. And Fred and George have invented Headless Hats that seem to make the head wearing them disappear. The list goes on.

One headless object that seems to be insisted upon plays a protective role towards Harry in the Ministry of Magic (MoM) fight in the ORDER OF THE PHOENIX. Bellatrix decapitated the fountain wizard: "her counterspell hit the head of the handsome wizard, which was blown off and landed twenty feet away..." (OotP Ch 36 "The Only One He Ever Feared"). Rowling keeps repeating the terms "headless wizard," "the headless golden statue," "headless statue," "headless guard," "headless statue" in that scene.

I wonder if this headless statue symbolizes someone who will help Harry though he will not know who it is (hence the missing head). Perhaps it could be Snape. Strangely, there seemed to be an ominous sign of decapitation associated even with Snape. When Harry hid his Half-Blood Prince book in the Room of Requirement, he saw a "heavy, bloodstained axe" (HBP Ch 24 "Sectumsempra"), and immediately afterwards the vanishing cabinet and the cupboard where he hid the book, with a bust on it on which he put a tiara. Snape's first name, Severus, also seems to point towards a possible "severing" of the head.

Wendy B. Harte has shared with me a compilation of interesting examples of hands in Potterverse. I can't help but think there may be a connection between these hands and the image of the disembodied head. Dumbledore's blackened hand that hardly seems to belong to his body anymore seems a counterpart of Wormtail's severed hand that has been replaced by a glowing silver replica created by Voldemort. I wonder if the confusion between the function of Harry's hand and head in the first Quidditch game in which Harry caught the snitch with his mouth (SS/PS Ch 11 "Quidditch") is meant to foreshadow that perhaps Harry's head will be as apt at helping Harry defeat Voldemort as his hand.

Horcruxes and the Prophecy

When Harry asks Dumbledore whether it is important to learn all this about Voldemort's past, and if "it's got something to do with the prophecy," Dumbledore answers that "It has everything to do with the prophecy" (HBP Ch 10 "The House of Gaunt"). This is not a self-explanatory or self-evident point. How can Horcruxes have everything to do with the Prophecy?

On the one hand, they may explain how Harry has "power the Dark Lord knows not" because he has an untarnished soul and is capable of love, a quality that someone who makes Horcruxes does not have. But I think the link may go deeper. Can knowledge about the Horcruxes explain the statement of the prophecy that "the Dark Lord will mark him as his equal"? (OotP Ch 37 "The Lost Prophecy") If Harry has a piece of Voldemort's soul inside him, he has truly been marked as Voldemort's equal. Whether that hint comes from Dumbledore or Rowling, it seems to be a clue about Harry's unusual scar.

Harry is a Horcrux: CONSEQUENCES

Perhaps the most compelling argument for Harry being a Horcrux is that it would have the most profound effect on Harry, Voldemort, and the plot of the story. Both Harry and Voldemort would be faced with extremely difficult choices. Must Harry die in order for Voldemort to be vanquished? Only if Harry is a Horcrux will this question truly pose itself. What will Voldemort choose to do with Harry, and why did he tell his Death Eaters to leave him alone in the HALF-BLOOD PRINCE? If Harry is a Horcrux, we can begin to answer these questions.

A major theme in the series has been Harry's identity, the boy who didn't know he was a wizard. Harry keeps learning about his unexpected powers and identity in each book. In the first book, he learns he is a wizard and that he is the best flier Hogwarts has seen in a long time. In the second book, he learns that being a Parselmouth connects him with Slytherin. He also destroyed the Horcrux diary in that book, just as he foiled Voldemort's plans to get the stone in the first book. Harry learned repeatedly that he could fight Voldemort. In the third book, he found that his powers can become almost infinite when he has faith in himself, as when he was able to repel a hundred Dementors with his Patronus. In the fifth book he learned about the Prophecy linking his destiny to Voldemort's.

There is always more untapped magical potential in Harry to be revealed and more mystery to his identity that connects him to Voldemort. The most staggering discovery that Harry could make in the seventh book would be that he is a Horcrux. Any other explanation for his scar wouldn't be nearly as intense, I believe. The HALF-BLOOD PRINCE has prepared the ground for this discovery, which would stun the characters in the story the most. If the Ministry discovers that Harry is a Horcrux, will they try to do him in? This scenario would have the most consequences for the story. Harry needs to reach a "soul crisis," at least symbolic, in his search for identity. Having a piece of Voldemort's soul inside him would be the most daunting challenge yet.

Even if there is some essential difference between Harry and the other Horcruxes, something that would allow Harry to live where all the other objects and Nagini would need to be destroyed, I believe that for a good while in the seventh book both Harry and Voldemort will suspect that Harry is a Horcrux.

Advantages of Harry Being a Horcrux

If Harry is a Horcrux, then he is in some mysterious way connected to all the other bits of Voldemort's soul hidden in the other Horcruxes. Although the soul is divided, the pieces are connected on some level. Otherwise, why would the soul remain "alive" when the body is destroyed just because a piece of it is attached to some object miles away?

Harry asked Dumbledore a very interesting question: can Voldemort tell when one of his Horcruxes is destroyed? Dumbledore doesn't say that Voldemort can't tell because that's not how it works. He says Voldemort can't tell because he has immersed himself so much in Dark Magic and mutilated his soul so much that he may be out of touch with some of its pieces (HBP Ch 23). We know that Voldemort has an unusual connection with Nagini, however, and also with Harry. It may be that the connection between the pieces of the soul that are inside living beings is stronger. I doubt Rowling would have had Harry ask such a question if it was not important.

Perhaps if Harry really concentrates, since he also has the power of a pure and whole soul behind him, he can sense where the other Horcruxes are simply by virtue of having a bit of Voldemort's soul inside him. Harry's scar, because it is a Horcrux, would help Harry find the other Horcruxes almost like a living map. Was Dumbledore's comment in the first book that the scar above his knee was a map of the London Underground a hint that Harry's scar could serve a similar guiding function as a sort of Horcrux divining rod?

I doubt, however, that the scar will exclusively help Harry in finding the Horcruxes. I would not be surprised if Hermione continues her digging for historical information and adds precious information to the Horcrux map. Ron, I am sure, will play his part, and I can't imagine Ginny being left out of the action. Peter Pettigrew will probably also repay his life debt, and may help destroy a Horcrux with his silver hand. I can't imagine Snape not coming in handy at some crucial point, too.

Another person that may have some kind of useful historical information is Florean Fortescue (if he is still alive and is set free), the owner of the ice-cream stand who knew a lot about witch burning. Fortescue's name is just like one of the previous Hogwarts Headmasters', also called Fortescue (although in the latter's case, it could be a first name). Rowling draws attention several times to this portrait in Dumbledore's office, placed right behind Dumbledore's desk (e.g. OotP Ch 27 "The Centaur and the Sneak"). Why would Voldemort's supporters drag off a poor ice cream stand owner, if he didn't have some kind of useful information?

Harry will not be alone. But I think his scar will be helpful also, if nothing else at least in giving him the right instincts, as it did in the climactic underground battle in the CHAMBER OF SECRETS, when without thinking, Harry instinctively knew how to destroy the diary.

On another note, if being a Horcrux is what allows Legilimency and even possession to happen at a distance, I would not be surprised if in the seventh book Harry started performing Legilimency on Voldemort and maybe even possessed him, or entered his body in some manner. As contaminating as it may sound, Harry may be left with no other choice.

Harry was not a good Occlumens, but I bet he could be a good Legilimens. I think love gives him the power to open things and that he could surpass even the "most accomplished Legilimens the world has ever seen" (HBP Ch 2 "Spinner's End"). After all, he broke through Snape's defenses during Occlumency, and

Snape is supposed to be the greatest Occlumens. Harry will need to do his own spying on Voldemort, now that Snape is gone, in order to learn where at least some of the remaining Horcruxes and Voldemort himself are hidden.

There have been hints that something like this might happen throughout the series. Harry has accompanied Voldemort in possessing Nagini and even seems to possess Voldemort in one scene, when he sees himself in the mirror as Voldemort. He also tries to perform Legilimency on a student during his O.W.L. exam, when Voldemort is attacking his mind (OotP Ch 31 "O.W.L.s"). Dumbledore said that Harry could enter Voldemort without damage to himself, but that Voldemort could not do the same, because of the purity of Harry's soul. Perhaps that was a hint of what is to come.

Harry has so far been on the defensive. Since his scar began giving signs of life, the intensity of its painful reactions to Voldemort's presence and moods grew to a near crisis in the ORDER OF THE PHOENIX when Voldemort actually possessed Harry. But then there was a turn of events. Voldemort realized Harry's power and the danger to himself of their connection, and distanced himself from him, using Occlumency. Harry no longer felt any pain in his scar. But Voldemort's being on the defensive I think prepares the field for Harry to move on the offensive. I don't know if Harry will be able in the end to move Voldemort's hand by possessing him, but I expect that at some point Harry's strong soul will be pitted in battle against Voldemort's weaker one, and he might be able to conquer the way he did in the GOBLET OF FIRE when he made Voldemort's wand regurgitate its spells.[14]

Dumbledore's Glimmer of Triumph

Perhaps if Harry's soul is to enter Voldemort's body through the scar connection, it will be immensely helpful to Harry that his own blood is running through Voldemort's veins, since Voldemort used Harry's blood to regain his body. It is as if Voldemort placed Harry's ally inside himself, an enemy within his walls, as if at chess he had hurried to take the enemy Queen (the protection of Lily's sacrifice) and hadn't seen far ahead enough that it was a trap, and that in fact he was weakening himself for the final battle. It is also possible that if Harry must die in order to destroy the Horcrux inside himself, he will be able to return to life because his blood is still running through Voldemort's veins, a magical connection that may protect him in a way similar to but better than the dark magic whereby Voldemort's Horcruxes keep his soul grounded even when his body is destroyed.

Fans have been wondering about the meaning of "the gleam of something like triumph in Dumbledore's eyes" when he learned Voldemort took Harry's blood (GoF Ch 36 "The Parting of the Ways"), and Rowling assured us that the question was excellent and that it would give too much away to answer it.[15]

It is possible that Dumbledore has been suspecting Harry might be a Horcrux since as early as the events of the CHAMBER OF SECRETS, when he learned that Harry could speak Parseltongue and had a bit of Voldemort inside him, and that the diary housed a piece of Voldemort's soul and was not the only Horcrux. It is very likely that starting with the GOBLET OF FIRE, when he saw how intense the scar connection was getting, Dumbledore's suspicions grew stronger. If the headmaster had this suspicion, he may have also instinctively looked for solutions to it, and may have gotten the flicker of an idea when he heard about Harry's blood being inside Voldemort.

Why didn't Dumbledore share any of this with Harry? Based on his previous decisions I don't think Dumbledore would have hurried to share something of this consequence unless he was very close to certain that he was right. Dumbledore also looked "as old and weary as Harry had ever seen him" after his look of triumph when he learned about the blood theft, and acknowledged that Voldemort had gotten beyond that defense of Harry's (previously he could not touch Harry because of his blood). There does not have to be a contradiction in Dumbledore's mixed reactions. At chess, if we haven't planned it, losing an important piece still hurts, even if we get a glimmer of triumph foreseeing how it could pay off further on.

Will Harry Survive Being a Horcrux?

I think that whatever happens to the Mirror of Erised and Nagini in the last book, if they are Horcruxes, could be a hint about Harry's chances for surviving the series.

Nagini is also a living Horcrux, and if she can survive the removal of Voldemort's soul piece, then another living being, such as Harry, could survive the same operation. If Nagini is killed, however, it doesn't follow that Harry will die also, but his chances will look grimmer.

The way Harry deals with the Mirror of Erised if it is a Horcrux might also be a hint about how Harry will solve his own problem, because the mirror may symbolically say something about Harry himself. If he can remove the piece of soul without destroying the Mirror, as in the case of Nagini's fate, Harry's chances at survival will look brighter. Rowling said that if Harry looked in the Mirror of Erised now, he would see "Voldemort finished, dead gone… Because he knows now that he will have no peace and no rest until this is accomplished."[16] Some also have speculated that the Mirror may prove useful in Harry's quest, possibly showing him the Horcruxes that he needs to destroy, but Rowling's answer doesn't seem to suggest it.

Conclusion

At a glance, the Horcrux laundry list is probably:

1. Tom Riddle's Diary (Destroyed)
2. Slytherin's Ring (Destroyed)
3. Slytherin's Locket (12 Grimmauld Place; Destroyed?)
4. Hufflepuff's Cup (Gringotts)
5. The Mirror of Erised (Hogwarts)
6. Nagini (Will Come to Harry)
7. Harry's Scar (Draco will Avada Kedavra Harry?)

After taking care of the Horcruxes, Harry will have to go after the piece of soul residing in Voldemort himself. To do this, he will have to be revived. Maybe it will be divine intervention, or his mother's blood, or his own blood inside Voldemort, or the fact that he was a Horcrux that will bring him back.

Voldemort having mutilated his own soul and body beyond recognition to point of resembling his former pet, the Basilisk, a murderous Serpent with an indefinitely long lifespan, the same weapon may be needed to chop off this creature's head as the one that struck the head of the Monster: Gryffindor's Sword. Harry, Gryffindor's true heir by heart, will receive Gryffindor's Sword in a will from Dumbledore, who is Gryffindor's heir by blood. The sword will display other magical properties as well, possibly serving Harry instead of a wand in the final battle against Voldemort.

Parting Thoughts

The enjoyable aspect of writing about the plot of a work that is still in the process of being written is that one doesn't come to the table with the omniscient insight of one who has seen the end, but with the stumbling anticipation of a half-blind reader trying to be writer at the same time. When studying a completed work, it is much easier to notice the clues and symbols that tie the beginning and end together, and one can forget the red-herrings that on the contrary, to the eyes that have not seen everything, seem to stand out as equally important. Looking backward is easier than looking forward. I consider myself lucky to have been able to participate in this unique and humbling experience of reading a book before it is finished and battling with millions of insightful fans for the best attempt at guessing the end.

I hope to have given some plausible answers with this speculative Horcrux hunt. Of course, none of us can be too sure of our ideas until the seventh book comes out. If still hungry for theories before Rowling says the final word, you may like reading the editorial section of Mugglenet, where you will also find my column THE TWO-WAY MIRROR, and where you can post your ideas in the discussion forums.

Writing editorials for Mugglenet has been a stimulating experience in my life as a graduate student in French literature. It is rewarding to be able to share more or less wacky ideas with an interested public fairly quickly, and to receive immediate feedback upon the posting of an editorial. This has been an informal but passionate pursuit that has been the source of much fun and edification. The presence of tens of thousands of dedicated readers of all ages who fervently discuss Harry Potter in the forums, carefully looking up quotes and references, googling or reading printed information about everything from Alchemy and Genetics to British history, Mythology and Tarot symbolism, is a phenomenon that shows that HARRY POTTER has not only stirred more youths (of all ages...) to read but has inspired them furthermore to discover the joys of scholarship.

Endnotes:

[1] The present essay is a revision and combination of several editorials that were first posted on Mugglenet in my column THE TWO-WAY MIRROR: "Double, Double... Toil and Trouble," "Harry's Dreams Part II," "Heirs and Inheritances," "The Mirror of Erised: A Horcrux," "Harry and Nagini: Voldemort's Living Horcruxes," "Harry's Scar and the Prophecy," and "Caput Draconis: Will Harry and Voldemort Keep Their Heads?" The ideas in section 6.b. and 6.c. that revolve around Voldemort's wand and the spell "Animampono Baculum" and its consequences are based on John Granger's ideas (see note 9) with some of my own contributions (in particular the arguments for Dumbledore being the heir of Gryffindor). John and I agree on major clues and consequences of Harry being a Horcrux. Note that because of variations in page numbers in the American and British hard-back and paper-back editions, instead of page numbers I provide chapter numbers for my quotes. Abbreviations are as follows: SS/PS for SORCERER'S STONE/PHILOSOPHER'S STONE, CoS for CHAMBER OF SECRETS, PoA for PRISONER OF AZKABAN, GoF for GOBLET OF FIRE, OotP for ORDER OF THE PHOENIX and HBP for HALF-BLOOD PRINCE.

[2] www.jkrowling.com, News, Monday, 15 March, 2004. I am thankful to www.madamscoop.org for locating this quote.

[3] http://cosforums.com.

[4] http://www.mugglenet.com/jkrinterview.shtml.

[5] See note 4.

[6] See J. K. Rowling's live interview on Scholastic.com, October 16, 2000.

[7] See Note 4.

[8] www.jkrowling.com, Rumours. I am thankful to www.madamscoop.org for locating this quote.

[9] John Granger, "Animampono : How Harry became a Horcrux" Chapter 6, UNLOCKING HARRY POTTER: FIVE KEYS FOR THE SERIOUS READER (Wayne, PA: Zossima Press, 2006).

[10] See Note 4.

[11] http://www.mugglenet.com/jkrinterview.shtml.

[12] See note 4.

[13] John Granger and I agree on the importance of the symbolism of disembodied heads for the significance of Harry's scar and have discussed this topic in our previous work.

[14] See also Lady Alchymia's Mugglenet editorial "The Battle for the Soul": http://www.mugglenet.com/editorials/editorials/edit-ladyalchymia01.shtml.

[15] AOL.com Chat, 19 October 2000: http://www.quick-quote-quill.org/articles/2000/1000-aol-chat.htm.

[16] See Note 4.

The World of Blogging

What is a Blog? It's a web site that people use as a journal. It's a 24/7 dynamic virtual environment that evolves as people share their ideas and experiences. Writers participate in online communities with other correspondents who share their interests, such as the dissection of the Harry Potter series. When you find people whose words intrigue you, you can reply to them. You are known by a user name (ex: HPMovieAddict) and a picture (known as an avatar) that seems to define you (ex: A big heart with "I Love Dan" in the center). You can either comment to entries under your user name or anonymously. If two writers enjoy each other, they can "friend" one another by adding their new friend's user name to a list of correspondents. Blogs can usually be established at no cost.

A Blog allows you to connect with many kindred spirits all around the world, any hour of the day or night. In these internet communities you'll find people that share your general interests (Dogs) and your narrow ones as well (Bulldog owners who like to knit). Examples of popular Blog websites include Blogspot, Live Journal, MySpace, Xanga, and Yahoo360.

Here is my first Live Journal experience: I spent months "lurking" (which means reading but not commenting) around hp_essays, a community of Harry Potter theorists on Live Journal. After Half-Blood Prince was released, I bravely volunteered to participate in a Chapter by Chapter analysis of the book. I spent weeks working on a very long dissection of Chapter 11 (Hermione's Helping Hand). Then I posted it to hp_essays, and ran out to do a quick errand, not sure what sort of comments I'd receive, but hoping they would be in the vicinity of "brilliant." Imagine my mortification to find dozens of identical e-mails all reading "LJ_Cut please!!!". Evidently I had violated etiquette by not formatting my essay such that only the first few lines were displayed on the hp_essay home page. If the introduction sounds promising users then click on the link to read the balance of the post. I was mortified, as I had managed to embarrass myself in the privacy of my own home, yet in front of hundreds of strangers. I did manage to figure out the "cut" syntax, and eventually received much feedback along the lines of "I think you read into things a bit too deeply." So I learned, to write in a Blog is to face both friendly accolades and critiques as well.

The following essay is a Blog post (used with permission) by an hp_essay writer known as "swythyv." What's wonderful about it is the original voice of the writer combined with an exciting theory into Half-Blood Prince. The author clearly understands that Harry Potter is anything but the story of a boy wizard, and that the real action is off the written page. It's a great read, and an excellent laugh. Enjoy...   — W. Harte

Swythyʋ

Swythyʋ lives in a spacious, well-lit mind furnished with lots of comfy chairs and shelves of curios and souvenirs from times when she got out more.

As a young child, she sometimes buried things in the back yard to baffle future excavators in any attempt to understand swing sets, and pondered whether dinosaurs would pose a threat to the house.

In one memorable moment that Prepared Her For Life, a frustrated professor rounded on her in the heat of a Beowulf discussion and demanded, "Swythyʋ! How do you kill a dragon!?" To which she dazedly replied, "You have to get at it where it's soft — under it's belly, or in its eye with an arrow." Upon which he turned back to the group, crying "That's right! But what did Beowulf do?" leaving her deaf to the discussion as she grappled with the shock of being asked how to handle a dragon —— Quick! — and of, apparently, knowing. Not to mention being somehow identifiable as the person to ask.

Which certainly proved the value of six hours of Liberal Arts in the business curriculum, for Life would continue to deliver these Why Has The Universe Visited Me Thus? moments throughout her career. There she regularly delivered solutions to improbable situations, often under trying conditions. She remembers fondly how charmed a favorite company was when she included the evacuation of their beloved fountain carp in the Disaster Plan.

But Swythyʋ is not sure that Life has prepared her for Ms. Rowling.

A few months after HARRY POTTER AND THE HALF BLOOD PRINCE Swythyʋ folded herself a newspaper hat, adopted her silly grin emoticon, and declared that she had no idea what was going on. She says she plans to enjoy the ride "sailing by on the banana peel of my imagination" while she tries "to figure out what it looks like when I'm not seeing something."

Her other favorite book is Roger Zelazny's DOORWAYS IN THE SAND, in which likeable career student Fred Cassidy recalls his adviser telling him "You are a living example of the absurdity of things."

"C'mon," she says, "It's fun." ꒰D

Mourning for Her Own True Love

Oh, don't you see yon turtle dove
Sitting high in a tree
Mourning for her own true love
As I will mourn for thee, as I will mourn for thee...

As HBP OPENS, NYMPHADORA TONKS MOPES. Tragically. Her hair isn't properly pink. There are all sorts of changes in her demeanor, behavior, and even her Patronus. And she never trips anymore — it's like her heart's just not in it.

Turns out she's pining for that spineless fidget, Remus Lupin.

"No, no!" quoth he: he and his aging desires are too dangerous for a fit young Auror who can legally turn into a lycanthrope-immune animal. Erm. "No, no!" quoth he: without him she shall be safer in time of War, for she may then sit upon a cushion and sew a fine seam. Erm. Right. "Look, Tonks" quoth he, "It's not you, it's me, OK?"

And then JKR associated romance with red herrings in mystery stories, during one of those interviews.

So there are truly ingenious theories that Tonks' relatives (Narcissa, Draco, maybe even Bellatrix!) have been channeling their inner Nymphadora, using Polyjuice potion. And that poor Tonks lies chained in a Malfoy dungeon, while all her pals shrug off the gaffs of her impersonator(s) as lovesickness.

Oh, don't you see yon turtle dove...

When JKR tempts me to watch the birdie, I find it's important to mind where I'm putting my feet. ¡D

Barty Crouch Jr.'s impersonation of Mad-Eye Moody worked because he was easy to imitate and "Moody" was arriving into a new place and a new role. Even so, I suspect that Barty Jr. had some previous personal contact and background information about Moody. Consider Barty's home life: Crouch Sr. was head of Magical Law Enforcement, and Moody's contemporary.

Impersonating an active, sociable Auror like Tonks would entail an enormous amount of current personal and professional background. Yet there's reasonable doubt whether her Black relations ever even *met* her.

No, Nymphadora Tonks is not a Polyjuice imposter in HBP — with the possible exception of Draco occasionally using her form to pursue his cabinet repair project. (Clever theory out there that he blocked Harry by making the Room admit only females. And I guess if Dumbledore could invoke it full of chamber pots, Draco could make it a Ladies' Room.) ; D

But *somebody* is an imposter. JKR has about staved in the big drum she's been beating about that. And her bush telegraph has also told us that Polyjuice imposters will show some behavior change, like our lovesick Tonks. So let's watch the birdie, carefully consider our assumptions, and limber up the peripheral vision. ; D

The "security questions" suggested by the Ministry of Magic in their leaflet are designed to exploit shared history. This depends on the assumption that the imposter is a stranger. But what if s/he's not a stranger, and *does* have a shared history with the target — and with you? Yikes!

Our lovesick birdie suggests that an imposter will need to explain away "behavior changes." So we assume that any "changes" are slip-ups, which the imposter will avoid or downplay. But wouldn't an imposter make some changes *on purpose?* Wouldn't s/he curtail intimacy, and avoid people who'd be harder to fool?

Really look at that birdie, for a minute. Andromeda Black Tonks furnished her daughter a strong role model: take charge, take what you want, to blazes with the social standing of your intended. And Tonks is an accomplished, extroverted, confident young woman. A lady like that builds *expectations* about her One True Love based on reality and a meeting of the minds (or more) — not *yearnings* based on some wussy unrequited crush. I reckon that Tonks and Remus Lupin had to have had a substantial relationship; and further, that this relationship was what changed her Patronus.

Now keep looking at the birdie, but think peripheral vision. What changed? Why, Remus Lupin suddenly decided that he was too old, too illegal, too dangerous, too unprepossessing, too blah, blah, blah — historically impeccable Remus Lupin cant. And he gave her the old "It's not you, it's me" speech.

If you were a Polyjuice imposter, wouldn't you?

Doggoned *first* thing, you would! It's practically a proverb that no impersonator can fool the lover. Plus she's an active *Auror* for cornsakes! And since it was likely the first thing he did, it helps us date the substitution: summer, pre HBP.

That's likely when Remus Lupin was captured while trying to convert the werewolves; which seems inevitable in hindsight. He was a known Dumbledore associate, was outed at Hogwarts as a hated *wizard*-werewolf, and had never "lived as a werewolf," whatever that entails. Fenrir Greyback had dominated that community for years; Voldemort need only tell him to put the word out. Unless some cheesed off werewolves had already turned Lupin over; Dumbledore's appeals to the downtrodden are about as effective as Hermione's, by my count. ;D

But who could know the wandering, solitary Remus Lupin well enough to impersonate him so shrewdly?

Peter Pettigrew.

The little man upon the stairs at Spinner's End, who had been assigned to a special project with Potions Master Snape... the summer before HBP. What a good thing that Dumbledore kept "Lupin" out converting those werewolves all during HBP. (Any luck yet my boy? No? Well, keep trying.)

"Remus Lupin" appears only in the 'A Very Frosty Christmas' and 'Phoenix Lament' chapters of HBP. We believed everything he said and implied, drank it all in as Received Truths. But what seemed like ordinary Remus Lupin evasions now become outrageous lies. And *what "Lupin" said* turns out to have influenced us to an amazing degree! Peter Pettigrew has a genius for this line of work. Here goes. ; D

During Christmas, as Harry importuned Arthur Weasley with his suspicions about Malfoy and Snape being up to no good, "he saw Lupin's head turn a little toward him, taking in every word," and when Harry carried on about it, "Lupin" spoke up "unexpectedly," saying "It isn't our business to know," and then repeatedly insisted that trusting Dumbledore "ought to be good enough for all of us." He deflected Harry's personal jabs about Snape, including the inscrutable statement "with a faint smile" that Harry had "inherited old prejudice" from James and Sirius. And he advised Harry to "By all means tell Dumbledore" — but not to expect Dumbledore to pay him any heed.

"Lupin" knew very well that Malfoy and Snape were up to something, though probably not *what*, hence his close attention. I found myself giggling a little at Spinner's End, substituting a voice over of "Don't listen to this Peter, it's important! *ZAP!* Go away, Peter, you can't hide and listen to us! Good thing you can't turn into something small, like a rat." Notice any, oh, *Mufflatio*-type spells being cast? No? Dearie, dearie me. A wildcard character who knows about the vow. But I digress. ; D

Was this the real Remus Lupin fecklessly mouthing the party line to Harry's rant? Or was it two pages of slyly planted "Got a problem with Malfoy and Snape, Harry? Then you've got a problem with *Dumbledore*, don't you? That's right, boy, Dumbledore's making a *fool* of you, but you'll just have to choke it down like a lemon sherbet, even though you're right. After all, you validate the lives of your father and Sirius by hating Snape."

"Lupin" then tells Harry that he couldn't write to him because he was "underground, Almost literally" among his "fellows, my equals. Werewolves." He says "Dumbledore wanted a spy and here I was… ready-made." He "sounded a little bitter" but made a quick recovery, smiling and saying, "I'm not complaining" etc.

Now to my ear, that bitter "my fellows, my equals. Werewolves" sounds like he's quoting someone — and it's not Dumbledore. I reckon it was either Voldemort or Snape, and it was a slur on Peter's school days association with Lupin. Most werewolves *are not wizards* — they're infected Muggles like Fenrir Greyback. Which helps explain why the wizarding world considers them somewhat lower than dirt. And why *they'd* hate someone who gave signs that he'd "lived among wizards."

But he really gave the game away when he said "Dumbledore wanted a spy."

Dumbledore no more sent Remus Lupin to spy on the werewolves than he sent Rubeus Hagrid and Olympe Maxime to spy on the Giants. Dumbledore sent *emissaries*. It's an important difference, and the real Remus Lupin would say it so. Besides, *spying* implies that a pack of werewolves — marginalized by both sides of the conflict — would have strategic information. "Albus! There's an urgent message from Lupin, our spy on the werewolves! I'm decoding it now… it says… *'Don't eat yellow snow!'*" ;D

The bit of history "Lupin" gives Harry (about Greyback's habits, his biting Remus, and Voldemort's using him to marshal the werewolves) is likely true. And it's well within Peter Pettigrew's ability to tell.

And then Harry remembers to ask, "Have you ever heard of someone called the Half-Blood Prince?" …and *"Lupin"* supplies the equivocations amounting to outright lies that we've relied so heavily upon in trying to make sense of the Marauders, Snape, the Levicorpus spell and the Potions book it was written in.

"Lupin" ducked the question by stating that there weren't any "Wizarding princes." *"Lupin"* insinuated that Levicorpus was not invented while the Marauders were at Hogwarts. *"Lupin"* claimed that Levicorpus "had a great vogue" and was in wide use at Hogwarts during fifth year, and *"Lupin's"* "smile was a little too understanding" when he assured Harry that James wasn't the only one using it. ["Exactly who was using it?" would have been interesting, I think.]

And *"Lupin"* cunningly asked "How old is this book, Harry?… Perhaps that will give you some clue as to when the Prince was at Hogwarts." Knowing full well that the fifty-year-old publishing date would mislead Harry, and deflect him from the truth. *Pettigrew!* He knew an awful lot about that book, including whose it was and where the spells in it got to — the little sneak.

But it gets even better. Harry later remembered another question, "and who better to ask than Lupin, the man who knew all about Patronuses?" So he asks "Lupin" what could cause the change in Tonks' Patronus. Watch:

"Lupin" "took his time chewing his turkey and swallowing, before saying slowly, 'Sometimes... a great shock... an emotional upheaval... '"

Oh, *YES!* Speak slowly to Harry at the Weasley dinner table! It's twice as good as lying. You can rely on Harry to leap to a conclusion, *and* upon the Weasleys to make a distraction. Sure enough, "Struck by a sudden thought" Harry *interrupts* "Lupin" to begin his theory that Tonks was grieving over Sirius — and then Molly leaps up to say, Look! There's ~~a squirrel~~ Percy! — and that's *that*.

"Lupin" never had to finish the list of reasons; a list that could have included "a committed love affair" as the very most common cause, for all we know. And yet no one there could ever to fault him — the rat.

We don't see "Lupin" again until 'Phoenix Lament', when Ron turned to him as the werewolf expert in the hospital wing. "Lupin" said that Bill wouldn't be a true werewolf, but that the wounds wouldn't heal fully and that he might have some traits. *Duh!* Madam Pomfrey had just told them as much, and had likely been repeating it for some time, while they were in shock. But what a lovely, timely *fakeable* "proof" that "Lupin" was their werewolf buddy.

And then Ginny told Ron that Dumbledore was dead.

"No!" Lupin looked wildly from Ginny to Harry, as though hoping the latter might contradict her, but when Harry did not, Lupin collapsed into a chair beside Bill's bed, his hands over his face. Harry had never seen Lupin lose control before; he felt as though he was intruding upon something private, indecent.

Yes, hearing of Dumbledore's death by Snape's hand was a bad moment for Peter. I won't deny the rat having a personal moment at the loss of Dumbledore, but I suspect that he was shocked and scared spitless on his own account — things hadn't worked out the way he imagined at all. He'd run straight to the infirmary with the wounded after Snape's shout of "It's over!" ...figuring Snape was a goner.

As McGonagall questioned Harry, there rose a shocked babble — including "Lupin's" harsh-voiced reminder (to himself?) that Snape was "a highly accomplished Occlumens" — all of which Harry silenced with the claim that *he knew why* Dumbledore had trusted Snape: merely because Snape had said he was really sorry.

"They all stared at him." And before they could question Harry's claim, *"Lupin"* jumped in to clinch it: *"And Dumbledore believed that?"* said Lupin incredulously. "Dumbledore believed Snape was sorry James was dead? Snape *hated* James... "

Notice the omission? It took me a really long time to catch it. Perfect manipulation, like gasoline on a fire. Harry jumped right into "Lupin's" pause with another one of his useful interruptions: "And he didn't think my mother was worth a damn, either," said Harry, "because she was Muggle-born… 'Mudblood,' he called her …"

Considering how catastrophically wrong Harry can be when interrupting people, I'm tempted to call that evidence of a friendship between Lily and Snape. "Lupin" left her name right out of it. Instead, with precision born of Scabbers' observations, "Lupin" let Harry handle it.

"Nobody asked how Harry knew this" as they all sat in shock. Then a "disoriented" McGonagall started the self-recrimination festival, and everyone was off down the "Oh woe, Dumbledore was a fool and we were fools with him!" road, never to return. Let's follow along, but watch the imposter.

It was *"Lupin"* who told Hermione that Snape "probably would have killed you and Luna" had she obstructed him. [Wow. Now I believe that *twice* as much as I did before.] ;D

"Lupin" says "A fight broke out, they scattered and we gave chase," which goes rather lightly over his own whereabouts and actions. Tonks says that they were in trouble and were losing. She mentions several people's positions and actions — *not Lupin's* — and that "It was all dark… curses flying everywhere… " She also says that "Neville ran at the blocked stair and "got thrown up into the air," having mentioned earlier that Neville "was hurt." If Neville was able to run at the stairs, I'm thinking that that's how he got hurt.

Ron picks up with "None of us could break through and that massive Death Eater was still firing off jinxes." (Note that "Lupin" hadn't tried the "cursed barrier" at this point.) Tonks continues with "And then Snape was there, and then he wasn't— " And Ginny says that she saw Snape coming, but that right then that huge Death Eater's jinx just missed her and she lost track of things…

And SO, while that huge Death Eater had *everyone else's* heads down, Snape went by and *"Lupin"* says "I saw him run straight through the cursed barrier as though it wasn't there. I tried to follow him but was thrown back just like Neville." *No one corroborated this statement.* Nor, apparently, *could* anyone.

And I doubt he did any such thing. "Lupin" would have been *thrown up in the air.* Our eyes reflexively track movement; the whole reason that Snape could be there and then be gone was *because he wasn't thrown up into the air.* And had "Lupin" been thrown back "just like Neville," he'd also have been injured "just like Neville." Then it is *"Lupin"* who claims that the falling chunk of ceiling, brought down by the big Death Eater's jinx, *also broke the curse blocking the stairs.* Curse breaking masonry, how amazing. I wonder how "Lupin" detected *that.* Did it fly up into the air? Guess everybody missed it. ;D

For he next says "We all ran forward [not *up the stairs*, not *through the former "barrier"*] — those of us who were still standing anyway — and then Snape and the boy emerged out of the dust." Cursed barrier, my Aunt Fanny. The "curse blocking the stairs" was broken when "Lupin" stopped hexing people after Snape's shout — not by falling masonry.

But there's a great moment after Molly and Fleur finish their scene over Bill.

> *"You see!" said a strained voice. Tonks was glaring at Lupin. "She still wants to marry him, even though he's been bitten! She doesn't care!"*
>
> *"It's different" said Lupin, barely moving his lips and looking suddenly tense. "Bill will not be a full werewolf. The cases are completely— "*

[Recriminations ensue]

> *"And I've told you a million times," said Lupin, refusing to meet her eyes, staring at the floor, "that I am too old for you, too poor... too dangerous... "*

Further recriminations and even feebler excuses continue — and that's the last we hear of "Lupin."

Behind the appalling theater of this exchange (frozen lips, averted eyes, big white arrow pointing at his back), I notice the implication that Tonks and Remus were engaged, just like Bill and Fleur. That miserable Polyjuiced rat broke off their engagement.

Unfortunately, everyone in Remus Lupin's acquaintance readily believed that he would do such a thing. Sorry, all you Remus fans; Tonks really wants him, so I hope he lives. But we have only the theory that putting a dead person's bits in Polyjuice is a Bad Idea — to comfort us. While Peter Pettigrew seems rather likely to have collected the entire set of the Marauders.

Like the false Mad-Eye Moody, "Lupin" has given Harry information in the persona of a D.A.D.A. expert and Order member — and that information is quite suspect. We should no more accept "Lupin's" prevarications about the HBP, the Levicorpus, and the Potions book than we should "Mad-Eye Moody's" representation of how Imperio looks and feels. And as "Lupin" was so essential to launching the "Dumbledore was nothing but a fool, and us with him!" conclusion, perhaps we should take that with a grain of salt, too. ;D

Edited To Add (ETA):

One of my correspondents reminded me that we do see "Lupin" one last time — at the funeral, apparently holding hands with Tonks whose hair is again cheerfully pink.

I miss being able to read. I really do.

Did "Lupin" decide that it was less risky to placate Tonks now, and then figure out how to scarper later? Or was the situation even worse than I had imagined, thanks to an Awful Thought that arrived overnight in my Morning Mental In-Box:

If Peter Pettigrew is so good at potions, then he can make Amortentia. Did he dose Tonks and then rebuff her advances all year? After the public scene in the hospital, he had everyone's blessing to "give in" and begin a relationship with her. And new lovers always act a little oddly...

Barbecued Rat On A Stick. That's all I've got to say. Unless it turns out to be Evil-all-along!Lupin, in which case we'll need a good taxidermist. Or maybe a bad one. ; D

The (Missing) Transcript

Yes, Virginia, there IS a full LiveJournal discussion of Swythyv's theory. Indeed two separate discussions of this essay exist in two different places on the internet. An older, public discussion of the article can be found posted in the LiveJournal hp_essays community. That discussion, however, is not this *discussion — which was, of course, intended to be transcribed for publication in this collection.*

However: we could not use it. The discussion turned out to be such a raging success, and ran so far over length that we ultimately threw up our hands in despair and each of us extracted a sample from our own posts as a teaser. The extracted samples follow in order of the poster's appearance.

There have been other edits as well. The extracts have been spell-checked and type-set in keeping with the rest of the collection. Typos (of the sort which result in legitimate words, only the wrong *words) that were spotted have been corrected. And such more sophisticated formatting as that used throughout the rest of the collection has been applied where suitable. But the grammar and content of the posts are the posters' own. Online identities have also been replaced by the authors' names as they appear throughout the rest of the collection.*

 Joyce Odell – Extracted from multiple posts

Oh, this is FUN!

Actually, the hand-holding at the funeral wouldn't be an insurmountable problem. It's been nearly a year since Tonks got anywhere close to Lupin. If he turns

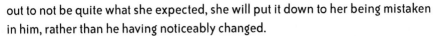

out to not be quite what she expected, she will put it down to her being mistaken in him, rather than he having noticeably changed.

«snip»

I'm beginning to wonder whether Lupin may not have been captured at the same time, and possibly in the same "sting" operation as Emmeline Vance. It would have been a perfect time to have inserted a DE agent into the Order. Even one that they did not actually see all that often (he was off with the werewolves, you know) would have been *told* what the Order was planning.

We don't know just what was intended, which resulted in Madam Vance's death. And if "Lupin" is an imposter from that point on, and was the source of the information about the matter, we cannot take his word for it. Snape was still in the north at the time, since it would have taken place right around the time that the term broke up. That he was taking credit for it a week or so later suggests that there was an operation planned that Snape was to pass information on.

Voldemort does not tell Snape everything, since he is aware of his status as a double agent, and he hedges his bets on the amount of information Snape has to barter with. This was also the point at which Snape found himself cut off from his most useful source of information, which is to say, Lucius Malfoy. Voldemort would have been perfectly capable of keeping that part of the plan from Snape, who, is still at Hogwarts.

«snip»

I reject all Evil!Lupin theories pretty much out of hand. From what Rowling has always had to say regarding Lupin they are unequivocally bogus. She hasn't written him as evil.

Throwing suspicions his way is not inappropriate, however. Lupin is NOT being straight with us, or Harry. He IS hiding things, and he learned the art of selective and incomplete truth-telling from a master. Albus *was* a master at that art.

The problem with Lupin is that he is not nearly so well put together as he appears. This is a very damaged man. His whole life has been warped out of shape by the fact that he was infected with lycanthropy as a child.

Yet on the surface, although reserved, he functions very well. He is polite, civilized, just terribly "politically correct" and rational. And he *is* a good, and a supportive teacher.

But the minute he gets upset he is apt to come out with some wildly exaggerated statement or claim which is positively ridiculous, when closely examined, or which simply makes *no sense*.

And, no, I don't think he has *ever* told us, or the kids, the unvarnished truth at any point since we have met him. But to force him to wear the traitor hat and stand in the corner is excessive. That crowd already has its representative traitor in Pettigrew. The requirements of the story do not need two of them.

Insofar as their contrasting relevance to Snape's (who is central to the entire story arc) position goes: Pettigrew is the "mirror", the one who passed in the opposite direction. Lupin is the "shadow" whose path is parallel. And Lupin *is* another of Dumbledore's spies.

Although his job is not the same *kind* of spying as Snape's. As you point out, the werewolves have no access to sensitive information. What Lupin is doing is monitoring their activities and movements. He is wearing his Jane Goodall hat, with the significant difference that he really *is* one of the creatures that he is observing. Monitoring the werewolves is a matter of periodically drifting in and out of their camp, making himself known there, and becoming accepted as a member of the group. And letting Albus know their movements and activities.

«snip»

Stop and think. Greyback was at liberty that whole period, and he was not lying low for fear of being swept up with the rest of Voldemort's supporters. For that matter, he is probably not even a Death Eater at all. He is almost certainly an ex-Muggle. And he was a bona fide *ally* of Voldemort (or possibly just Malfoy), not a follower. Voldemort was out of commission for nearly 14 years, while his organization deteriorated in his absence. Greyback spent those years *increasing* his "following". And he was just too dangerous to be left unobserved, even if he didn't know anything.

Ergo: Lupin *has* had a job all those years. Dumbledore gave him one. His shabby poverty is a part of his *cover*.

«snip»

In fact, with the Spy+Mirror+Shadow dynamic in place, I would not be surprised to learn that Albus made his initial suggestion of an alliance to both Snape AND Lupin in the aftermath of the werewolf caper.

Lupin had just gotten a *vile* demonstration of the fact that the people who did not shun him, were capable of trying to *use* him. With or without his consent. Which would have led to a discussion of how Lord Voldemort has made use of werewolves in the course of the war.

I think that was the point that Lupin was finally told the truth about the werewolf who turned him. That he was not an unfortunate sufferer who lost control of himself. But that he had stalked and bitten Lupin *deliberately*, because Lupin's father had offended him. Remus was *already* being "used". Albus would have learned the story while making the arrangements for the boy's education, and would probably have gotten the permission from the boy's parents to tell him if he felt the situation should demand it.

Lupin isn't as bright as Sirius or Snape but he is not stupid. Albus laid it out to him that Lupin was going to have severe difficulties in the wizarding world because of his condition, through no fault of his own. He would have also mentioned that there was no current way for Albus to monitor the activities of Fenrir and his pack.

I think that, as with Snape, Albus did not ask for a decision at that time. But made it understood, that if Lupin chose to turn his circumstances to account in the war effort, Albus would do everything in his power to protect and support him.

In Lupin's case I suspect the support is at least partially financial. His cover as an unemployed outcast dictates that his living expenses are necessarily low, but I suspect that the contents of his Gringotts vault are in better shape than could be otherwise accounted for.

What I suspect happened, is that, unlike Snape, who reported to Albus as soon as the DEs approached him, Lupin tried to go it alone for a year or two after finishing school. With the results that Albus had cautioned him about. Eventually he would have contacted Albus to ask what his duties would entail.

Albus would have laid it out, and warned him that it would be dirty, dangerous, and extremely unpleasant. He would need to infiltrate Fenrir's pack and gain their trust. He was not to attempt to interfere with their plans or activities, not to call attention to himself, but he was to report back so he and his allies could monitor the group. Don't make a decision right now. Think it over. Lupin did.

He's a Gryff. What do you think he decided?

«next post»

And he probably started at it before the Potters were killed, or Harry was even born. He probably didn't know about Legilimency then, or if he did he was so far out of the loop by then that he never got the chance to fill James and Sirius in on it. Or, it is possible that he felt he *needed* to keep that ability secret, even from the rest of the Order.

Which may be another reason why Sirius thought he was the spy. I've always suspected that after the werewolf caper Lupin was never able to feel quite the same about Sirius Black afterwards, and Sirius translated this extra reserve as: "up to something". But Remus was off *living* in the enemy's camp. Coming and going as if he belonged there. After all, while I suspect everything Lupin told Harry about infiltrating the werewolves was probably *true*, he never says anything which would pin down just *when* it happened, did he? It could have been all the way back when he was 19 or 20.

And he knew what he was getting into. Dumbledore would have pointed out to him what he was in for over the long haul. But Lupin *is* a Gryffindor. He would have been quite willing to turn his condition into an asset in the war.

Wendy B. Harte – Extracted from multiple posts

— I still love this essay as it understands that the real story is not the one being played out on the pages of HBP (Plus it is so damn funny)

— I agree that we are not looking at polyjuiced Tonks throughout the story. I do think that might have been Draco!Tonks during the corridor encounter as the dialogue 'clunks' (my own internal marker when I know something ELSE is going on)

— During my re-read I paid close attention to the potential P!Lupin dialogue, and it was disappointingly half clunky/but half not. I am very clear that JKR likes to PURPOSELY give us two interpretations on key scenes, so I do remain suspicious

— Lupin's physical description in Frosty Christmas is so close to Scabbers, I found it eerie

— I would include the possible 'doused her with amortentia' thought as Sluggy does say that the potion has dangerous obsessive side effects, and Tonks is clearly out of sorts

— P!Lupin's "He would have killed you" comment to Hermione clunks hard to me. It just doesn't sound like something we'd hear from Lupin

— Last, I don't think he is EVIL!Lupin, but he is a bit inadequate, handicapped by the lifetime label 'werewolf'

«snip»

JKR: There's a theory — this applies to detective novels, and then Harry, which is not really a detective novel, but it feels like one sometimes — that you should not have romantic intrigue in a detective book. Dorothy L. Sayers, who is queen of the genre said — and then broke her own rule, but said — that there is no place for romance in a detective story except that it can be useful to camouflage other people's motives. That's true; it is a very useful trick. I've used that on Percy and I've used that to a degree on Tonks in this book, as a red herring. But having said that, I disagree inasmuch as mine are very character-driven books, and it's so important, therefore, that we see these characters fall in love, which is a necessary part of life.

This is a very interesting quote. Jo seems to imply that romance is a tricky ingredient to add to a mystery soufflé. I knew that there are two Dorothy L. Sayers books on Jo's web site (www.jkrowling.com) on the "Links" page, so I looked the author up and discovered that Dorothy had a sad early love life (like us all). Her first love jerked her chain — he told Dorothy that he was against marriage and proposed they just live together. He later claimed that this stance was a 'test of her devotion', and she broke up with him. Jerk! She had much sexual passion with her next beau, but when it turned into an unwanted pregnancy, he bailed on her. The cad! She kept her condition from her parents and gave birth to a son, alone.

This son was raised by a relative, and he didn't know that Cousin Dorothy was really his mother until later in life. Third love was the charm for Dorothy and she finally married 'a nice guy', one Mac Fleming who was divorced with two kids. So Dorothy learned the valuable lesson that you need to marry someone who wants to be married. Until then, 'love' is a long senseless slog through the marshes of other people's excuses. Dorothy Sayers was a prolific detective fiction writer, and Jo clearly draws inspiration and wisdom from her work.

I find Jo's comment that the romantic element can be used to cover other people's motives most curious in the context of the Half-Blood Prince: what hidden motive could Lupin possibly posses? Is he testing Tonks to see if she really loves him? Has he slept with her and lost interest? Does it seem like Jo would write about Lupin's concealed motive as one of the vulnerable side effects of love? It seems doubtful that this angle is worthy of being labeled a red herring. The term 'red herring' is defined in Wikipedia as: a false clue which leads investigators, readers, or solvers towards an incorrect solution.

In PRISONER OF AZKABAN, Sirius Black apologizes to Lupin for suspecting him of being the Potter's betrayer. We know the true identity of that particular traitor: it was Peter Pettigrew. Right or wrong, Swythyv feels the presence of a camouflaged Lupin blended with a dose of Pettigrew. The fact that she links these two characters together is not a blind Fandom stab, but the recognition that these two particular men have solid links through Jo's purposeful prose.

Peter and Remus grew up together at Hogwarts, and both are familiar with each other's background and mannerisms. Both are aware of the ideals each expressed: disdain for Snape, admiration for Dumbledore. Both boys lived in the shadows of two friends with stronger personalities: Prince James Potter and his Knight Sirius Black.

Remus had a hidden life: he was a werewolf who transformed physically once a month. Peter had a hidden life: he was weak in his heart — a Court Jester, secretly in awe of the power possessed by others. Remus became a dark creature, but remained pure of heart. No one suspected Peter of being a dark creature, but he was a real rat.

In the two series books which seem to echo one another, we find Jo's prose reverberating with comparable physical descriptions. Peter/Scabbers becomes shabbier and more gaunt as PRISONER OF AZKABAN progresses, and in Half-Blood Prince Chapter 16, Jo similarly portrays the possible Peter/Remus pairing: "Remus Lupin, who was thinner and more ragged-looking than ever."

Is Peter undercover, working for Lord Voldemort? Is Remus Lupin being polyjuiced with the real Remus chained in some dank basement? Severus Snape does make a curious comment directly to Tonks. He tells her that her new Patronus is weak. He certainly seems to know a red herring is afoot.

Christmas Eve at the Weasleys, Chapter 16 of Half-Blood Prince, there is a song playing on the wireless radio that seems to be the voice of Tonks herself (who is not present in this scene):

Oh, my poor heart, where has it gone?
It's left me for a spell

Is it Remus or Peter reflecting on these lyrics, wondering what he has gotten himself into? Are we seeing a change of heart or a deceitful heart?

Make your own verdict on Swythyv's post above, but the theories that make the most sense to me are the ones that do not take the road that Jo tries to lead us down. The conclusions I take to heart are the interesting well-paved detours off the main highway.

«snip»

It occurred to me that it would not be unreasonable for Peter to be unmasked again keeping with your POA/Book 7 echo theory. Maybe all the time through HBP that he is masquerading as Lupin (note I'm not 100% there, but still trying it on for size), Peter sees the family life he missed (the Burrow), the school pals he left behind (Hogwarts), the love of a good woman he never had (Tonks) and this is how his change of heart comes about.

The tidbit I get hung up on is P!Lupin's tears after he finds out about Dumbledore. What are we really seeing?

«snip»

So, if Peter Pettigrew is indeed masquerading as Remus Lupin, how will he be unmasked in Book 7? One word: Crookshanks.

«snip»

John — I will say this: I have yet to go wrong by sticking with Joyce's 1/5, 2/6, and 3/7 patterning. I think of the first 3 books as the series "base", book 4 as the center of the teeter totter, and 5-6 as when Jo really set the game afire. I feel the strong presence of misdirection in HBP.

So many scenes are set up interpretation wise as A/B, A/B, A/B, that I consider A/B, but think in a new direction, focusing on COS and POA insights. Or, the scene dialog (what we hear) "klunks" for me (ex: Slughorn *"I thought I knew him!"*). Or, we get too many details provided (4-5 pages on Harry's ownership of Grimmauld Place!?) All of my insights (which yes, could be wrong) have come from attention to these incongruities. I look at all the A/B's and the prevalence of surrounding circumstances and decide: is there something funny going on? And my conclusion is frequently yes, even if I can't name it (like the potions book, I'm still stumped). The Lupin scenes are a bit funny — furtive glances, odd phrase patterns, but then suddenly, it sounds like the voice of real Lupin. So if it is not P!Lupin, I state that something funny is going on with Lupin. Sirius thought he was the turncoat in POA… but apologized. Sirius is often wrong (as is Harry), but maybe this time he was right (even thought I normally reject EVIL!Lupin theories)

And although nothing about Rosemerta's dialog reads funny or klunky, she is supposedly imperiused all through HBP. So maybe Lupin has been imperiused.

As far as Bellatrix inside of Hogwarts, it just doesn't sing to me. I need a bit more than the awkward corridor scene ("heard from the Order lately?"). It seems to me that she would be up to evil deeds and we'd hear about more strangeness within Hogwarts. Or the Black family curse would kick in and we'd see a major flub against Voldemort. Snape would tell DD, and she would be ejected.

I think they (DD and Snape) are aware that either P!Lupin or Imperius!Lupin (we will call him I!Lupin, for short) is helping Draco. So when Draco admits to being surprised by Greyback's presence, it is **true** surprise. Draco thought he was dealing with a benign Werewolf helper (either P!Lupin or I!Lupin) and, sakes alive, he gets the real thing on the Tower. Draco must have wondered how his chain got royally jerked so hard! He thought he was in control of the situation, and suddenly he gets dealt a wild were-card!!!

 John Granger – Extracted from multiple posts

…I want to get back to the thematic importance of the mistaken identity in every book except HBP. There has to be someone not being who they seem to be in each book — and it is nigh on risible that the last book would not feature two, three, or more switcheroos.

Why?

Because Ms. Rowling is writing postmodern myth. She is a philosophical realist as well, hence the morality and symbolism of the stories (no nihilistic relativism on tap here) but to neglect how much she is sympathy with the times to track the transcendent and archetypal elements of the story almost exclusively is to miss at least half of the reason these books sell so well. They resonate heroically with the spirit of our times, what is usually called postmodernism and poststructuralism.

I will get back to werewolves in a second, I promise.

In case you didn't get a full course of postmodern theory in a philosophy or critical theory survey at University, here's the bumper sticker version: "incredulity towards metanarratives" (Lyotard). What that means is that to a postmodern person, most of the world's problems are caused by people believing in big foundation stories (Grand Narratives, Metanarratives) like "original sin" and "invisible hand capitalism" or Marxist theories of economic determination. Each of these

"Founders Stories" ossifies into an ideology that is inherently and inescapably totalitarian and exclusive, dividing the world into a good core of people and a "necessary other" who by not being part of the core group are "bad," even "evil."

«snip»

…the key point is our shared skepticism about surety, our common belief that if you're certain about the world and what human beings are about or how we should behave, you're (a) stupid and (b) almost certainly dangerous, because your metanarrative is going to pigeonhole someone (and probably a lot of people as a group) as "evil" and you will go after them. Imperialism, racism, chauvinism, unrestricted capitalism, homophobia, and ardent religious belief not tempered by individualism and a touch of hedonism are the sworn enemies of the post-moderns — and you'd be silly to think the world has not become a better place in important ways because of this shared "incredulity towards metanarratives."

«snip»

Ms. Rowling as a woman of her times writing PoMo myth in large part (as does almost every film being made), is obliged to give us a Founders' Myth that is the cause of every problem at Hogwarts and the Wizarding World, namely, the Slytherin-Gryffindor battle that is the good/evil axis of the storyline, and reason to suspect that this metanarrative makes us believe what we want to believe about "what we see" rather than understand that our perspectives are laughably restricted and prone to mistakes. Prejudice is the poison consequent to acceptance of the Grand Back-story that explains the way things really are in the world.

Ms. Rowling delivers this with narrative misdirection and the theme that "things/people aren't what they appear to be." When Harry is revealed as a bone-headed idiot, as he is in every book except HBP, because he rushed to judgment, we are confronted with our own predisposition to accept metanarrative, the Sly-therine/Gryffindor axis, and condemn the innocent and embrace the evil.

Back to werewolves.

Why is P!Lupin plausible, more than credible?

Ms. Rowling's thematic meaning as a Postmodern writer requires mistaken iden-tity *and* narrative misdirection. At the end of HBP, we have Severus Snape as that fall-guy, but how surprising was that? Harry has been telling us for six books that sadist Severus is a Slytherin ace in Voldemort's hand. No, there has to be at least one good guy who is a bad guy plant — and one bad or fence sitting guy who is a white hat. P!Lupin is an excellent catch for the good guy who isn't what he seems.

I think Slughorn is the heroic white hat — and, crazy as it seems, I think Bellatrix is on deck, too, at Hogwarts through HBP. And who would be easier to drag into the Room of Requirement after Wormtail lets Bellatrix on campus through the Shrieking Shack/Whomping Willow entrance than Professor Trelawney on one of her evening bottle drops?

More on those if you like, but the important point I want to make here is that this is not a "tired" story element that is unlikely, at best, to be seen again. This is nigh on a requirement of Ms. Rowling's story-telling and moral education of her readers. "Don't believe what you see! You're not seeing anything but your preconceptions, ideas that line up with the side of the "core/other" fault line you happen to be on. The Sorting Hat is the real bad guy and the House Cup is his biggest ally!"

We need mistaken identity to drive narrative misdirection for this message. Look for a flock of these revelations in HP7 – and, especially, I think, for P!Lupin.

«snip»

I'm beginning to see the double-natured theme running through these books (of which the various switcheroos and Transfigurations are examples) as an element and important symbol of the end and aim of alchemy. This end is often represented as the Philosopher's Stone, as you know, but as often in the graphics in traditional texts and in plays with alchemy themes, the aim of the Great Work is represented as an Androgyne or Hermaphrodite, the S/He.

If I'm right that this is classic PoMo myth making that Ms. Rowling is up to, we have to see the resolution of the metanarrative's core group and necessarily evil "others." The metanarrative of the Wizarding world is the Founders Myth the Sorting Hat brings into the present by dividing every new Hogwarts student body up into partisan camps at the beginning of each year. The core polarity here is between Gryffindor and Slytherin. Who are the Hermaphrodites, the extremes meeting and melding from these groups?

Voldemort is the Slytherin Hermaphrodite. He has epitomized the Nietzschean pole of the Silver and Green house — but he has been re-formulated (ahem) with Gryffindor blood, the blood of loving sacrifice. He simply ain't the person he used to be.

Harry is another Androgyne, though the representative of the self-important Gryffindor extreme. His bipolar identity springs from the Horcrux scar he wears on his head. This and the shared blood-body he has with Voldemort is their Twining (Tom is Aramaic for twin) and twining. Consequent to Volde's rebirth, we see in Phoenix the great rise in their correspondence and connection, culminating in Voldemort's being unable to possess Harry both because of Harry's love but also because likes repel.

But the greatest S/He of the books is the conscious Alchemist, working to transform himself into the union of Gryffindor and Slytherin for the transcendence of the Grand Narrative's division, prejudice, and partisanship. Severus Snape is this bridge and it is his life on the fence that is the greater story of the books. If he succeeds, not only will Voldemort be defeated, but the Slytherin/Gryffindor enmity will be erased and the Wizarding world will have a new Myth, albeit one of Love that cannot become an ideology with a necessary "other" to marginalize and persecute.

And what does this have to do with P!Lupin or I!Lupin or Polyjuiced!Trelawney?

The last two years of the books have largely been about Voldemort litmus strip testing the S/He Snape and only incidentally about the prophecy and killing Dumbledore. The Dark Lord, as an Androgyne himself, must be beside himself that he cannot be sure of Snape's loyalties. Sending Pettigrew and Bellatrix to the castle serves two purposes in this respect. Yes, they can help insure the Vanishing Cabinet work gets done and Draco is sufficiently "encouraged" in the work (the plural part of the "other people," "better people" he claims are helping him. Yes, they can report on Dumbledore's comings and goings as much as Order members and Hogwarts faculty will know them.

 Daniela Teo – Extracted from multiple posts

«Post 1»

First, I do agree with the general idea of an enemy infiltrating us again by means of polyjuice potion. Like Swythyv pointed out… so far polyjuice has not quite struck us at the very heart. Moody was in many ways a stranger. …I am almost certain that the polyjuice phenomenon needs to be brought to a crisis, by having someone near and dear to us, someone in our very closest circle of intimate friends, turn out to be a Death Eater in disguise. However, I don't think it has happened yet.

«snip»

STRUCTURE OF THE BOOKS

…There are plenty of examples of switcheroos or shocking mistaken identity revelations in HBP. Peter/Lupin is not really necessary.

… we get an entire parade of Crabbes and Goyles metamorphosed into little blushing girls.

— Draco …how many of us expected to see his good side in the book where he takes on the evil assignment?

— The HBP book that begins by being so helpful, turns out to be savage.

— And Snape, Snape! The Order member and… D.A.D.A. teacher (like Moody, Quirrelll…), turns out to be a murderer …we can't deny that Snape is the big one, the big double identity of HBP.

— we even have a switching of objects, the Horcrux locket has been switched with the fake one! And the mysterious R.A.B., Death Eater turned ally…

This is how I read and recognize Lupin throughout HBP

LUPIN WON'T GET INVOLVED

In Snape's worst memory, Lupin is a bit between two sides, unable to take one, a bit passive, a bit disapproving of his friends when they attacked Snape but not exactly telling them off either. It makes sense that with his troubled conscience he should try to make up for the guilt he felt for not stopping his friends by actively defending Snape now. His reaction to Tonks demonstrates a type of passivity also... Lupin doesn't like to hurt people... He has a huge werewolf complex. It makes psychological sense that he should be protective of Tonks and fear to get involved.

«Post 2»

...I don't accept that Lupin has already been switched with Peter, but the Imperius curse that Joyce [and Wendy] brought up is a very interesting idea.

...I'm getting a bit of a horror chill thinking of Snape's snide remark to Tonks about the "weakness" of her Patronus; what if he knew of Lupin being under the Imperius curse, and he was deriding Lupin's weakness to Tonks?

«snip»

From the personality we have seen of Peter so far... I see it nigh impossible for him to play the following parts of Lupin's role:

LUPIN'S VOICE

HUMOR

— I don't see Peter able to "burst out laughing" when Hermione says to Lupin "You've just got a — a problem — " Lupin laughs and reminisces about James calling it his "furry little problem." Peter could have given the "furry little problem" part, but not the burst of laughter.

— Lupin is also "smiling" when Harry starts asking about the Half-Blood Prince. I find it hard for the cringing Peter to do this relaxing sort of thing. And he pokes fun in a way that I don't think Peter has the wit to do: "Is this a title you're thinking of adopting?"

«Post 3»

SENTIMENTS

— Rowling's describing Lupin's tone as "reminiscently" adds a note of fondness to his voice that I'd be shocked to see Peter adopting.

— Lupin's "smile was a little too understanding" when Harry kept asking about James. I don't see Peter achieving such a delicate reaction to Harry's desire to know about his dad.

— Lupin also says quietly about James at one point, with a touch of seriousness mixed with Marauder irony: "and I promise you, he never asked us to call him 'Prince.'" Peter could never have mustered that noble tone.

— I understand Lupin's bitter voice to Dumbledore's sending him among the werewolves; it's not bitterness against Dumbledore, but against his own condition, which he can't seem to escape. Sirius sounded as bitter about being kept at 12 Grimmauld Place.

«snip»

LUPIN AND SNAPE

On the dynamics of Lupin and Snape ...Lupin has a troubled conscience...

I think he was pushing himself hard in the "Snape is good" direction by defending Snape. When he said to Harry that perhaps he and Snape would never become "bosom buddies" because of all the past bitterness, I had to do a double take. "Bosom buddies"?

...he did it all out of guilt, towards both Dumbledore and Snape, because he deceived the former with the Marauders, and didn't defend the latter from the Marauders. It was as if he tried to make it up to both men with one action, trusting Snape, more absolutely than was required, going in fact overboard I think.

...He stretched to the max, but then the hand that was holding the sling (Snape's innocence guaranteed by Dumbledore) was taken away, and Lupin bounced back in the "Snape is evil" direction with a force equal to the one with which he had pushed himself towards "Snape is good".

...He went... even farther than the reader who sees Snape as evil, and threw his big stone stating with certainty that Snape would have killed Hermione and Luna ...Snape may have murdered Dumbledore under pressure, but I don't think he's a rampaging killing machine...

«Post 4»

LUPIN'S ROMANCE

...I think the Lupin and Tonks holding hands moment is one of the most delicate touches to HBP.

...Before the final scene of their holding hands, I don't see the situation of Tonks and Lupin as the silly unrequited crush of a teen girl. First, I don't think Tonks's love is not returned. I think it is clear that it is. Something else stands in the way, a much more adult problem, the question of the issues one individual has who can't bring himself to get involved because of them.

...What if Lupin's problem was a mental illness?

«Post 5»

LUPIN THE SPY

The reason I didn't find suspicious Lupin's listening in on Harry's conversation about Draco and Snape is that it was one heck of an interesting story ...the name of Snape in a conversation should prick the ears of any Marauder. ...Lupin's saying that Dumbledore sent him to "spy" on the werewolves doesn't necessarily contradict Dumbledore's sending Hagrid and Maxime as "emissaries" to the giants. ...Lupin says most werewolves are already on Voldemort's side. That means that Dumbledore needs more of a spy than an emissary to them.

Also, Lupin may have emphasized the "spy" aspect of his assignment because he was on his "I want Snape as my buddy" trip and perhaps felt more like a brother to Snape the spy ...And this fits perfectly with Lupin's middleman role. He is somewhere between Snape, who is pure spy (emissary to the Death Eaters???) and Hagrid and Maxime, who were pure emissaries. So here is Lupin... the man on two fences, the spy and emissary.

«snip»

I think Lupin's usefulness would be in letting Dumbledore know what the plans with the werewolves are. Soldiers are eventually informed of their mission.

«Post 6»

LUPIN'S INFORMATION

In general, I think Lupin is as informative as he can be:

— I think we learn quite a lot about Greyback from him.

— We learn from him that there are no wizard princes.

...his suggestion to Harry to look up the date of the book was sensible. On another note, I don't see Pettigrew knowing much about Snape's "private diary"

...Lupin's answers about Bill's condition, while not spectacular, are good enough (they do turn out to be true). He's giving common sense answers that anyone could perhaps guess, but that he, as a werewolf, is most qualified to give.

«snip»

Wendy, that quote from JKR is amazing. I'm not quite sure what to make of the red herring Tonks.

«snip»

To me, too, Tonks sounded out of character outside the Room of Requirement. I heard Cho. Remember when Cho and Harry were having their spat, and Cho said to him "I'll see you around, Harry"? That line has remained engraved in my mind with Cho's teary intonation all over it. Of course, it's possible that Rowling wanted to make Tonks sound a bit like Cho when her personality was beginning to resemble hers just "a little."

«snip»

I may just have to be satisfied with the mourning for Sirius versus yearning for Lupin being the red herring thing. Rowling treated Lupin's and Tonk's romance like a mystery... before the real culprit was uncovered, Lupin, the man who wouldn't get involved.

Joyce Odell

In the early 1970s, an Amateur Press Association was founded by a young science fiction fan named Mike Yampolsky. Such associations, or APAs as they are known, were very popular at that time. The world wide web, after all, was not yet even a gleam in Al Gore's eye. Such APAs are also not one-man shows; there were a half a dozen or so other fans involved. As with many, although not by any means all of such APAs, this one was founded for a particular niche interest. It was created by and for fans of children's fantasy literature. The APA is still going more than 30 years later.

In 1997 or very early in 1998, one of the couples who are members of the APA took a holiday to England, and caught the buzz regarding a new children's fantasy adventure which appeared to be a runaway success, entitled HARRY POTTER AND THE PHILOSOPHER'S STONE. *They purchased a copy and returned with the news. When the re-named* HARRY POTTER AND THE SORCERER'S STONE *hopped the pond, we were waiting.*

In October of the year 2002, I uploaded the first iteration of the Red Hen Publications web site. The essay collection was not at that time a part of it. The essay collection was an afterthought, uploaded in the spring of 2003.

Earlier versions of this essay have been posted online under the title: 'Loyaulte Me Lie'. Like all of the essays in the Red Hen Potterverse collection it is a work in development. It took a number of years to get it to this point, and this is probably not the final version. That will not be written until some time after J.K. Rowling ties off her story arc. Future developments of this, and the rest of the essays may be read online at Red Hen Publications, which may be found at:

http://www.redhen-publications.com/Potterverse.html

Welcome to My Murder: Act 1

WELL, **ROWLING HAS DONE IT AGAIN.** Last Autumn I had what I thought was a very clever theory of 'the Sorting Hat Horcrux' which finally made sense of the grossly unbalanced view of the whole Gryffindor/Slytherin issue which we have been fed over the course of the series, and she shot it down for Christmas. This Spring I belatedly jumped onto the Dumbledore-isn't-Dead bandwagon and crafted what I thought was nice, logical, *canon supported* interpretation of the events of HBP which explained the multiple screwinesses on display in "the murder of Albus Dumbledore — *not!*" as it was presented in the book, and she shot it down a few days before my birthday.

Since I'd only been riding that particular bandwagon for about 3 months, being tossed summarily onto the roadbed was injurious mostly to my dignity, but it was a shock, nevertheless. Because there is no question but that the account of that death, as presented, just plain *doesn't add up.*

This upset was all the more of an embarrassment since this collection was all but ready to go to press when she made her announcement, and sent us all scrambling to apply emergency patches. The following is a rewrite, and the original has been replaced on the web site as well. I will not be rolling it into the 7th Son collection of exploded theories.

The more so in that upon even a fairly cursory review, about 90% of the reasoning is still perfectly watertight.

This particular essay was formerly the larger portion of the essay entitled 'Loyaulte Me Lie'. It was about to bury the original subject and was still in the process of expanding, so I have spun it off into its own space.

I *will* have to admit that I sat there in stunned disbelief reading the relevant passage. Not in disbelief that Severus Snape, to all appearances, had murdered Albus Dumbledore, but that Rowling actually chose to *go* there.

Y'see, over on the behemoth Yahoo group, HPforGrownups, back toward the end of the 3-year summer, I, myself, had proposed that Severus Snape *would* be forced to murder Albus Dumbledore in order to pacify Voldemort. And that Albus might well *agree* to it! That was all the way back in 2002!

That was also some weeks, or months before my 11th-hour realization that Snape probably *had* been at the graveyard meeting in Little Hangleton (now proven to be wrong) and that nobody in charge was suspecting Snape of *anything* (now shown to be mostly correct), which eliminated any justification for such melodramatic shows of fanatic loyalty. Once I've thoroughly dismissed a possibility it's sometimes extremely difficult for me to ever take it seriously again. I'm sure the posts are still in the archives over there, but it would be a waste of your time to dig them out.

So what on earth have we got now? Apart from a royal mess.

Well: first we *did* have to ask ourselves whether Albus is really dead.

It was not all that difficult to get the interpretation that he *wasn't*. The account of that death is just… *wrong*.

Let me point out that once an element gets used in the course of this series, it is *exponentially* more likely than not to be used again. Possibly more than once.

One of the major plot elements of PoA was the discovery that Peter Pettigrew had faked his own death (twice, in fact). So, for that matter, did Barty Crouch Jr, with his parents' assistance, in GoF.

So another faked death is certainly liable to be on the menu for Book 7. Slughorn's little welcome tableau when he was overtaken by magical intruders may make a nice reprise of Scabbers's second faked death in Gryffindor Tower, but it doesn't serve to balance Pettigrew's publicly faked death back in 1981.

And we've a very short list of really viable candidates of characters who are central enough to the main issues to serve as potential subjects for such a faked death. At a glance, just Albus Dumbledore and Regulus Black. Either of whom has custody of information of which we appear to be in some need.

And just to make sure we clueless Yanks didn't overlook it; we were also handed a very heavy hint from the publishers that we really *ought* to be suspecting that a faked death, or that a death which may be believed to have been faked will figure in Book 7. Just compare the two versions of the following from the chapter of 'The Lightning-Struck Tower':

> U.K. version (page 552–553):
>
> *"No, you can't,"* said Malfoy, his wand hand shaking very badly indeed. *"Nobody can. He told me to do it or he'll kill me. I've got no choice."*
>
> *"Come over to the right side, Draco, and we can hide you more completely than you can possibly imagine. What is more, I can send members of the Order to your mother tonight to hide her likewise. Your father is safe at the moment.."*

U.S. version (page 591–592):

"No, you can't," said Malfoy, his wand hand shaking very badly indeed. "Nobody can. He told me to do it or he'll kill me. I've got no choice."

"He cannot kill you if you are already dead. Come over to the right side, Draco, and we can hide you more completely than you can possibly imagine. What is more, I can send members of the Order to your mother tonight to hide her likewise. Nobody would be surprised that you had died in your attempt to kill me — forgive me, but Lord Voldemort probably expects it. Nor would Death Eaters be surprised that we had captured and killed your mother — it is what they would do themselves, after all. Your father is safe at the moment."

Rowling is said to have authorized that addition to the U.S. edition of the work. (Although it should be noted that the addition has been excised from the U.S. *paperback* edition of the work.) If nothing else, it's a pretty strong indication that we are dealing with a milieu in which faked deaths are to be considered a hot possibility. Particularly after one already has played a major part in both Book 3, and Book 4. Especially Book 3.

Added to which, there was certainly something very *obviously* screwy about the AK which is supposed to have actually killed Dumbledore. Harry had his eyes tight shut from the pain in his scar when Cedric Diggory was murdered, but I think he might have registered the difference in the sound of a body simply dropping down from a standing position and one being tossed into the air and dropped from a great height. And he didn't.

Or did he? I'll be taking a closer look at this issue later.

With Albus, on the other hand:

"A jet of green light shot from the end of Snape's wand and hit Dumbledore squarely in the chest. Harry's scream of horror never left him; silent and unmoving, he was forced to watch as Dumbledore was blasted into the air. For a split second, he seemed to hang suspended beneath the shining skull, and then he slowly fell backward, like a great rag doll, over the battlements and out of sight."

U.S. Edition (page 596)

All things considered: that is just plain *weird*.

Still… for months after the release of HBP I thought our best candidate for the "I'm not dead yet" sweeps was Regulus Black. His death was more to the pattern set by Pettigrew's (i.e., it happened years ago). And we've got all sorts of *other* sources for discovering Albus's secrets: there's the Pensieve, into which we've seen a lot of memories placed, but very few removed. There is his Portrait, and there is Aberforth. For that matter, there are also Mad-Eye Moody, Horace

Slughorn, Flitwick and Minerva McGonagall, all of whom worked with the man for decades. There is even Griselda Marchbanks. If Reggie's true tale is to be told, he will probably have to tell it himself. Because there doesn't seem to be anyone else around to do it for him.

We *do* still need to find out whether or not he did manage to destroy the Horcrux, at least. And whether his really *was* the Locket.

So, for quite a while I suspected that a visit to Ms Doris Purkiss in Little Norton might be in order. Stubby Boardman's retirement from public life (and the popular singing group, The Hobgoblins), a convenient 15 years before the Quibbler article which "outed" him coincided nicely with the date of Reggie's purported death. (Or seemed to, before the Black family tapestry sketch was released in February 2006 and derailed that reading.)

Of course, given that Doris is claiming that he had to be innocent of the murders in '81 because he had been with her at the time, there's a good chance that she hasn't seen him in a while...

But I am no longer quite so convinced that Reggie's full tale really *does* need to be told. Nor am I still convinced that the function of the revelation of a faked death in Book 7 is to give us an additional source of *information*. Instead, I eventually came to the conclusion that the whole issue of Regulus Black is a smokescreen, and that like that street full of Muggles back in 1981, we may have watched Albus and Snape fake Albus's death right before our eyes. There was certainly something more going on atop that tower than anyone is admitting.

Well, Rowling tells us, no, he really *is* dead.

Rowling admits in her interviews that she *enjoys* the theories that fans come up with concerning her characters and the actions taking place off the radar over the course of her series. She *claims* that she only takes the trouble to shoot them down when they are leading into a blind alley. So if she is announcing to the world on national television that Albus Dumbledore is dead, then it behooves us to take that statement into strong consideration.

But for all that she has now supposedly given us the final word on this subject, she still is being mighty blooming evasive about the matter. In her statement of August, 2006 she tells us all that Dumbledore is "definitely dead". I'm sure that by August of 2006, he is. She states that he is not going to "do a Gandalf". Well, no, I don't think that he is going to show up on a white horse and lead the troops into battle either. But neither of these statements throws any light on the sheer *weirdness* that she purposely wrote into the scene of his supposed murder.

And for that matter even her supposedly clear statement of August 2006 turns out not to be anywhere near as clear as the newsbites would have us believe. The following is from a partial transcript from the LiveJournal of a fan, as to the actual wording of that statement:

Child: *How could Albus Dumbledore really be dead? Harry is so loyal to him and Dumbledore's the most powerful wizard.*

JKR (looking a little emo): *"I really can't answer that question, but… you shouldn't expect Dumbledore to do a Gandalf."*

If, even now, J.K. Rowling *still* can't come straight out and *say* that Albus is dead because Snape killed him, she's probably up to her tricks again.

"Really can't answer that", indeed.

And it does not make his death, as it was presented to us any more credible. There is something distinctly "off" about that death.

It finally registered that the real issue isn't that of whether death was "faked" or not; but that it was unquestionably *staged.*

The whole run-up to it from the Seer Overheard chapter, through the adventure of The Cave, to the Lightning-Struck Tower, and the Flight of the Prince (U.S. edition, pages 544–610) are Rowling at her most dramatic. In fact this sequence is probably the longest stretch of sustained "drama" in the series to date. And, with all due respect; drama is no more Rowling's OTG (one-true-genre) than romance is. Indeed, while competently presented, it tips well over the borders, and pitches us right into *melo*drama. In fact, a rather *cheesy* melodrama.

The series as a whole is not really a *melodrama.* Is it?

I finally have to step back and consider that if this was a conspiracy to falsify the circumstances of Albus Dumbledore's death, then we have to admit to the possibility that for at least part of the time, everyone actually engaged in the conspiracy was *acting.*

Which raises a lot of questions and drags in all sorts of related matters. Such as:

We not only needed to ask whether or not Albus is really dead — and we *did* need to at least *ask* that — but whether, and by just how much was he taken by surprise by the events that overtook him the night of his death. And by which ones, exactly? How much of that performance was under his own control?

Just where does that overheard argument with Snape, that Hagrid reported fit into the picture? That wasn't a part of the public performance. What were they arguing *about?*

For that matter where does the Unbreakable Vow fit into this? How much was Snape taken by surprise by the terms of that? Or *was* he taken by surprise at all? And did he *really* know what Draco's mission was, or did he just pretend to, in order to lure the sisters into being indiscrete? But, if so, why didn't he even let them *discuss* it!

And just what exactly *was* Malfoy's mission and what did *his* conduct contribute to the equation? Because the mission, and the Vow, and the murder are all so closely interrelated that you can hardly discuss any one of them without having to discuss all the others as well.

And where does the sea cave adventure come into it? Because the sea cave junket is also intrinsic to the puzzle. That wasn't just an irrelevant side trip, either.

We also need to consider the likelihood of there being at least a "third man" (to deal with the body) involved in any conspiracy regarding the murder of Albus Dumbledore, because Snape and Albus couldn't have managed that end of it between only the two of them. In fact there may have been *more* than one additional conspirator.

And we first need to ask just why they did it at all? Why not just keep dodging that particular bullet as long as they could?

Well, once again we need to remind ourselves of one of our main axioms.

Remember: the *villain* is the *story*.

We lost track of one of our main players over the course of HBP. We were so wrapped up in following the trajectory of young Tom Riddle that we completely lost sight of the present day Lord Voldemort. What was he up to after he dropped Malfoy into the soup at the opening of the book, and boogied off?

We don't know, do we?

Was there any purpose, any purpose *at all*, to that stream of reports in the DAILY PROPHET of DE raids, Imperius attacks, Dementor attacks, and random violence? Beyond the obvious purpose of keeping people frightened, that is?

It sure doesn't look like it from where I'm standing. That was all just keeping the pot well stirred.

And, for that matter, after his presumably public ultimatum to Fudge at the beginning of July, and his suspected "personal" murder of Amelia Bones around the same time, was there any report of anyone having caught even a *glimpse* of him all year long?

Not that I noticed.

At a guess, I'd say he's got another one of his Byzantine plots in the pipeline. Probably a big one, too. And it wasn't ready to be launched yet over the course of HBP.

And, at a guess: first, he needs a lot more Dementors.

Second: Albus Dumbledore needs to be out of the way. This doesn't need to happen right this moment, because the main operation has any number of other components that are going to take time to develop, and it's going to take several months to a year to get his ducks in a row before he can launch whatever it is. But it needs to happen. And it needs to happen by the end of this academic year.

That sudden shift of attention from Potter to Dumbledore is the kind of thing that ought to make Albus and Severus sit up and take notice. Which it did.

In the first place this is a warning that Tom may have figured out that the kid is his final Horcrux. At the very least, it is a heavy hint that he *really might* have eavesdropped on Harry's debriefing after the raid on the DoM, and now knows that he has to kill the boy himself. In the meantime, he has returned to Plan A. Kill Dumbledore. In fact he has bumped that item to the head of his list.

Lord Voldemort wants Albus Dumbledore dead. Within the coming year.

This forces Snape and Albus to consider their options. On matters like the life or death of an individual wizard, Lord Voldemort generally *does* get what he wants. Eventually. This throws an unacceptable level of uncertainty into their long-range goals. They know that sooner or later Tom Riddle is going to succeed in removing Albus from his path.

For that matter, it is entirely possible that by the time the Black sisters showed up on his doorstep, Snape was *already* under orders regarding the Headmaster's death. He had certainly been told to stand aside and let young Malfoy have a go, first.

Snape was probably not told the details of Malfoy's orders, but he certainly knew his own. He claims to be one of the few who knows of the plan (very little of it, I suspect, at least officially). And his statement that "He intends me to do it in the end, I think" may be no less than the truth. So even before the Unbreakable Vow entered the equation, Snape may have already been cast as Second Murderer. And he would have reported as much to Albus.

So. Is it likely to be a bigger risk to openly thwart Lord Voldemort for as long as they are able, or to let him think he's got what he wants?

Or to *give* him what he wants? Hold that thought.

Are they more likely to be able to *benefit* from openly thwarting him for as long as they are able, or from letting him think he's got what he wants?

Have they *also* got something to gain from the death of Albus Dumbledore?

Whatever it is that Riddle has planned — and it is *most* unlikely that Snape has any *details* on whatever is planned — are they going to be in a stronger position to derail whatever it is, by trying to keep Riddle delaying the launching of it by openly thwarting him (and *will* that even put the launching of his plan off, and how long is Snape's cover going to hold under *those* circumstances?) or to let him think that he is the one in control, opposed by only a headless Order and an ineffectual Ministry — with Albus off the radar, lurking in reserve, and Snape in a position to perform sabotage from deep cover?

In the two or three weeks since Voldemort was forced into the open, the progress of the war has drastically changed. Snape can now do Voldemort more damage from inside the DEs than he can from the periphery at Hogwarts. Voldemort is down to about 3 dozen human followers and one saboteur can make a big difference in a group of that size. Albus was in a position to watch that take place over the first year of his Order, with Pettigrew.

This is probably one of the main reasons that Albus finally *gave* Snape the D.A.D.A. position; so Snape would *have* to leave the school before the year was out and Voldemort would not be in any position to raise objections, since he set that situation up himself by cursing the post in the first place.

Albus used Voldemort's demand for his own death as a way to facilitate Snape's removal from the school; abandoning his post before the jinx got out of control and bit him in some undetermined manner — for now that we know the jinx *is* real we have to take its possible actions into account in any of our calculations.

Unless Albus finally took the opportunity to *lift* the jinx, and get it out of their way. So that Snape's flight only *looked* like the jinx leaping into action. And what kind of a backlash might lifting that jinx have produced? We know that it has killed at least one man already. Could *that* be what *really* finally doomed Albus?

For that matter; *was* Snape really the D.A.D.A. instructor that year at all? Or did Albus officially appoint *himself* as the instructor of record that year. With Snape deputized to actually teach the main *classes*. You could make a passable argument that Albus *was* teaching D.A.D.A. that year, even if only to one student, and the announcement at the opening feast was that Snape was to be "taking over" the position of D.A.D.A. teacher. He's substituted as D.A.D.A. instructor before without ill effect.

Once considered, Snape and Albus may have had a *lot* to gain by letting Albus "die" on his *own* terms, and at *his* date of choosing rather than Voldemort's. There is more going on in this war than just a hunt for Tom Riddle's Horcruxes, after all.

Speaking of which, Harry is going to need to be assigned his mission a year early. Because Dumbledore isn't going to be around to do it next year.

And, even at the end of Year 6, Harry is *still* missing crucial information concerning that mission. Information that I suspect Albus has been too cagey to share with anyone else, and now there isn't *time*. Albus has no choice but to retire to the sidelines and work indirectly. (Would Albus *really* have withheld information likely to be so vital as that, *yes* Harry, you *can* trust Snape, and here is *why*, unless he was confident of being able to get the information to the boy by the time he really *needed* it?)

And, besides, if Potter does take his mission up now, and does *not* return to Hogwarts for his final year, Albus will not be in the best position to protect him from the vantage point of his position as Headmaster. Any way you slice it, it is time for Albus to leave his nice tower office in the fastness of Hogwarts Castle and do the job he has been putting off ever since Tom Riddle returned from his first exile and started kicking up larks.

Harry is also going to need to have Voldemort's attention diverted from him, and Albus knows he will probably be able to do so a better job of that from behind the scenes, NOT hampered by his high-profile position or his duties as Headmaster of a school. That's what Albus has *really* sacrificed; his position as Headmaster. And it WAS a sacrifice. He *loved* that job.

And, besides, *he* doesn't know that he is a fictional character in a series that has only one more book to run. *He* doesn't know that there is only one more year until the conclusion of this war. He has all of his eggs in one basket with Harry Potter's name on it and he needs to be in a position to protect his investment.

He can no longer do it directly. He's got to distract Voldemort's attention to somewhere else and let Harry get on with it. He can't micro-manage the hunt for the Horcruxes. Between him and Snape they probably hope to keep Voldemort busy and distracted and if they can manage to encourage dissension in the DE's ranks and whittle down those ranks a bit further that will be all to the good. (Snape will at least be in a position to learn some of the remaining DE's names that aren't already known, which will come in handy in the final mop-up stage after Voldemort falls.)

But *we're* not going to be in the best position to witness this.

Because, I think that regardless of whether Albus Dumbledore is alive or dead, so long as we are viewing the action through the Harry filter, he is going to stay quite thoroughly off the radar. We are not going to come face to face with him again, as himself, in *any* form, until after the threat of Voldemort is settled.

Rowling is quite right when she speaks of the requirements of the sort of story she is telling us. The old wizard with the long white beard is never going to settle the central problem on the young hero's behalf in the tale of a coming-of-age quest. That is something the young hero has got to do for himself. But the old man can do any number of things behind the scenes to smooth the way.

Young heroes on a coming-of-age quest, just about always have to go the last stretch on their own. But traditional heroes in every fairy tale you care to mention *always* are given help that they have earned by means of kindness or courtesy. Harry will be eligible to receive help and advice for quite a while yet along his Hero's Journey.

There is also the faint, rather unpleasant possibility that Albus could not see any way for Harry to get out of this tangle alive. I think he was very much aware that the boy may be Tom's 6th Horcrux. And Albus may not know of any certain manner in which it may be disarmed without killing Harry. His exhortations on Death being no more than the next great adventure, his repeated affirmations that Harry's greatest strength is his ability to love others, and that he is forever marked by his mother's loving sacrifice, and even the demonstration of his own murder may be in the way of forcing the concept of a possible self-sacrifice into Harry's head, should such a thing prove necessary.

But the *Order* knows that Albus *is* still with them. He sent his message out at his funeral. He still has his organization, and the organization knows it still has its Leader.

Albus was not immortal, nor did he wish to be. To die, or to depart peacefully after seeing his "great work" accomplished, and to pass the torch to others would be perfectly in keeping with tradition. But his great work is *not* yet accomplished.

Still, IF Snape and Albus engaged in a conspiracy to make an all-star production out of Albus's murder, they certainly did not do it on the spur of the moment. They took all year to set it up. Nor would they have left anything more to chance than they had to. They had to have gone over every new detail, as it came up, to see how it could be turned to their advantage.

Nor is an elaborate set-up leading to a staged death beyond Dumbledore's capabilities. It isn't even slightly out of character. In the course of the series as it stands we have watched Albus Dumbledore orchestrate two elaborate year-long scams which ran over the entire course of both Book 1 *and* Book 5. It is not too much to consider that he may have done so over the course of Book 6 as well, even if this was not a reflection of anything that we had encountered back in Book 2. And, for that matter, there may be another one running behind the scenes in Book 7.

In HBP Dumbledore was giving out statements all year that he is *old*, he is slowing down, he is *expendable*. His request all the way back in Chapter 3, that the Dursleys continue to give Harry house room for as long as the protection on him lasts has all the ring of a "last request". He has put his affairs in order. His exit this year, genuine or otherwise, is *planned*.

Act I of this set-up period took place during the hectic first couple of weeks of the summer. Off Harry's radar.

And just how hectic was it? Well, read on. This chronology has gotten some recent adjustment and I think that I may finally have most of the events accounted for, in pretty much the proper order. It looks like the interval of time between Harry's raid on the DoM and his arrival at the Burrow was one of the busiest periods in the whole series for the rest of the wizarding world.

It also looks like the first thing Scrimgeour did when he got the post of Minister for Magic was to hold that fruitless meeting with Dumbledore, which must have taken place only 2–3 days before his meeting with the Muggle Prime Minister. We only saw the first couple of paragraphs of the article reporting the meeting in the Prophet, but there was no mention made of Dumbledore having a blasted hand in what we could see of the Prophet's report, and I suspect that there was none in the rest of the article either, or Snape would have hardly needed to feed that information to the two sisters when they showed up at Spinner's End.

The events which we *know* to have taken place during this interval are:

PHASE I: taking place after conclusion of the O.W.L.s in mid-June:

1. The raids on the DoM /Ministry admits Voldemort has returned /VoldWar II officially begins.
2. Final two weeks or so of school /recovery of those injured in the raid / school breaks up for the summer/ calls for Fudge' resignation begin.

PHASE II: first week of July, approximate:

3. Voldemort's public ultimatum that Fudge step aside in his favor /Fudge's refusal.
4. Murder of Amelia Bones /bridge collapse /Giant attack in West Country /attempt made to put Muggle Junior Minister under Imperius /murder of Emmeline Vance in vicinity of Muggle PM's office.
5. Fudge's resignation; Scrimgeour's appointment as Minister /meeting between Scrimgeour and Dumbledore /Kingsley Shacklebolt goes undercover in Muggle PM's office /mass Dementor attacks.
6. Scrimgeour's meeting with Muggle Prime Minister.
7. Albus vs. Horcrux — alleged Snape intervention /Malfoy is assigned his mission /Spinner's End meeting.
8. Two weeks after end of term; Albus collects Harry from the Dursleys' /visit to Horace Slughorn /Harry arrives at the Burrow for the summer.

One could wish that Rowling, who is remarkably good at plotting, were a little more dependable for timelines. Her shaky grasp of numbers erodes our confidence, even when there are no obvious contradictions. Snape and Albus's presumed actions are tucked in around the edges of the above to the point that it is almost as difficult to trace them as it is to trace Hagrid's and Harry's movements during the famously "missing" 24 hours.

We also do not know just what actually happened to Emmeline Vance. Given that the first chapter of HBP opens to discover the Muggle PM reflecting on the week past which had seen the bridge collapse, the "'hurricane" in the West Country, the peculiar behavior of a Junior Minister, and two highly publicized murders, and we later are told that Fudge was replaced as Minister for Magic only three days before he shows up in the PM's office, the whole of the list of events under item #4 seem to have taken place over the course of no more than about four days.

Fudge also tells us that his own constituency had been howling for his replacement for the previous fortnight. Presumably as part of the fallout from the raid on the DoM, which took place immediately following the O.W.L.s in mid-June, and the wizardng public's discovery that the Ministry had been falsely denying Voldemort's return, which was reported in the DAILY PROPHET a week or two before Voldemort delivered his ultimatum.

And, indeed, it is clear that the DEs were very active in the vicinity of the Muggle government offices over that week. From the general level of DE activity, and Kingsley Shacklebolt's current assignment, is seems likely that not only the Ministry's Aurors, but the Order of the Phoenix as well was involved in a concerted effort to engage with the DEs. Since we know nothing of Madam Vance but her name it is uncertain whether her involvement in the events of that week were due to her membership in the Order of the Phoenix, or as a result of some capacity as a Ministry employee. But the location that her death took place, (around the corner from the PM's office) strongly suggests that she was probably engaged in some official activity to do with the war. Madam Vance was one of the original Members of the Order. Most of the original Order members were people who were known to have escaped DE attentions at least three times. She was already on the "most wanted dead" list.

What seems most likely, if we agree that Snape is a White Hat, is that Snape had indeed passed information to the DEs. Information that the Order probably knew that he had passed, or had even *designed* for him to pass as a part of setting up an operation. Madam Vance was unlucky enough to have been captured and killed in the confrontation. We do not know whether the DEs also took losses.

Snape, who was probably still in the north at the time, took what advantage he could of the situation by claiming credit for the information leading to her capture.

One might expect that Snape would have had to have still been at Hogwarts when Albus made his raid on the Horcrux. But seems not to have been the case. Dumbledore summoned Snape to Hogwarts upon his return, after destroying or capturing, the Peveril Ring. Since Snape is known by the DEs to be a double-agent, it would not compromise his cover to receive and respond to such a summons.

We do not know what Voldemort was told of the injury, but, even if Snape knows about the Horcruxes (which I do suspect), he does not "officially" know of them, so all Voldemort was told is that Dumbledore has tangled with something that he could not counter, and has sustained permanent injury to his wand hand.

Snape is unquestionably in his own home at Spinner's End on the day Draco was actually *assigned* his mission. At some point before that date Snape has been in contact with Voldemort and got a kernel of information which at the very least enabled him to make his claim of having known what Malfoy was ordered to do, and incidentally to find himself lumbered with Pettigrew in his own household. He was clearly not at the meeting in which Voldemort actually *gave* Malfoy his assignment, which is likely to have been earlier the same day that Narcissa and Bellatrix showed up on Snape's doorstep, after dusk. I can not imagine that upon learning of this assignment, that Narcissa — in the state she was in — would have waited even one day before attempting to enlist help and protection for her son.

So, following the Snape thread in all this:

Snape finishes his duties at Hogwarts, perhaps a day or so after the students leave and returns to Spinner's End. He reports to Voldemort, accounts for his actions regarding the raid on the DoM (probably claims to have been off in the forbidden forest searching for Umbridge, Granger and Potter who were all missing), and gets debriefed regarding his dealings with Dolores, and Dumbledore's return to the school.

And, it has only *finally*, in the week of August 14-20, 2006 dawned on me that I have managed to lose track of the villain again. This is always a mistake. In this case it deflected me from recognizing the probable event that drove just about the whole action of the ensuing book!

But, really, I can't see that I was alone in that error. I've not seen the matter posted anywhere else online either. And the conclusion really *is* all but unconceivable.

But it really does seem to be boiling down to the likelihood that *nobody* — nobody *at all* — over the previous two years — ever *told* Voldemort about the loss of the Basilisk and the Diary!

Yes, I know. How could he NOT know?

But, he didn't. He just *didn't*.

Look at his actions and behavior, and — more to the point — look at *Lucius Malfoy's* actions and behavior over the course of OotP, after Voldemort had already returned and was back in command. Is it even *remotely* plausible that Malfoy would have been walking about loose if Voldemort knew that Lucius had managed to get his Diary taken out of the equation? Particularly now that we know what that Diary *was*?

Particularly when you register his utter fury and the *extraordinary* level of his determination to wipe the Malfoy line out, root and branch, by the opening of HBP. This is *not* about the failure to retrieve the Prophecy record. Bellatrix *also* was a part of that failure to retrieve the Prophecy record, and he is merely "not speaking" to *her*.

It is all too easy for the reader to assume that whatever the Diary revenant knew or learned is something that Voldemort knows as well. But it *isn't*. There was never an open connection between the Diary revenant and Vapormort.

I now think that what happened was that once the term broke up and Snape reported for his debriefing, now that Lucius had been packed off to Azkaban Voldemort demanded that Snape, in his character as a Malfoy family friend, fetch his Diary back. He hadn't entrusted it to *Narcissa*, after all. And Draco was just a kid.

And I think that he *may* have intended to deploy it over Year 6 *himself*, and raise some hell on Albus's turf at long-distance, without any personal risk.

Having to explain what happened to it must have been the worst spot Snape had found himself in since he had to explain to Albus why he had arranged for Barty Crouch Jr to be Kissed before his testimony could become official the year before.

And the resulting explosion *did* get reported to Albus. Albus confirms it.

That's *how* Albus could say with such confidence that when Voldemort learned of the destruction of the Diary his anger was "terrible to behold". He had been given an eyewitness account. Indeed I wouldn't be astonished to learn that it threw Voldemort into such a rage that the whole hideous 4 days that the Muggle PM and Fudge were mulling over in Chapter 1 were the product of a Tom Riddle tantrum.

Because when you go back and examine the narrative; where the Diary revenant had to *ask* why Harry survived the curse, the reborn Voldemort was never in any doubt of the matter *whatsoever*, and while he related the failure of the QuirrellMort experiment he said *not one word* about the Year of the Basilisk.

And who would have dared to volunteer that information? Particularly if he wasn't *asking* for it? For that matter, who *could* have volunteered the information?

The student body was never told the details. They knew only that the monster had been killed, but not what *kind* of monster it had been — and Hermione had torn the page out of the library's copy of the book that referenced it. I *don't* think they were ever told that one of their fellow students had been taken over by Lord Voldemort either — and they *certainly* knew nothing about the Diary. So, wild tales from school wouldn't have seemed relevant enough for any DE daddies to be passing on. Particularly not tales from a couple of years earlier.

The only adults present when Harry related the story were Minerva, Albus, Molly and Arthur — and Lockhart who was completely out of it. The conversation wasn't about *him* after all. The Staff seems to have been filled in on the basics later, since Minerva was able to refer back to the matter at the end of HBP without feeling the need to give an explanation, but the staff was hardly going to tell the story to Voldemort. Nor were Harry and his friends. (Although they had a lucky escape in Year 5 when Ginny threw the subject in Harry's teeth at Christmas. It is a good thing Voldemort wasn't hitching a ride in Harry's head at the time.)

Which leaves Lucius himself. Fat chance of *him* speaking up. Narcissa *may* have known something as well. Dobby did claim to have heard Lucius *discussing* the matter with somebody. But Narcissa, along with Bellatrix, *does* seem to think that the Dark Lord's rage *is* all due to the failure of retrieving the Prophecy record, so I doubt she has been approached regarding the matter herself. And Snape would have been ordered not to discuss it with her.

Snape would have been forced to tap dance is way out of knowing about Lucius deploying the Diary without "officially" knowing about the Diary itself. If Voldemort mentioned the *Chamber of Secrets* or the *Basilisk*, Snape would have had an opening and could have gone; "But Master, the school was under attack by a Basilisk two years ago. Potter killed it. There was something about a cursed book, but I was never able to discover the details." But he himself never actually *saw* the ruined Diary. Harry had given it back to Lucius before Albus could show it to Snape.

And… Peter Pettigrew.

Peter certainly *could* have told him. He has to have heard the story when Ron and Harry filled Hermione in on what she had missed while petrified. After all, where *else* did he get the information that Voldemort was haunting a forest in Albania? And he could certainly back up Snape's story once anyone thought to *ask* him. But he was totally out of the loop where anything to do with the Horcruxes was concerned. *He* was never one of the Dark Lord's lieutenants during the first war.

And, besides, when you stop and consider it, Peter is a veritable black hole where it comes to information. You can never be altogether sure just what *has* gotten into his head, but it never comes back out. Not unless harvesting that *particular* crop of information has been represented to him as his *job*. Anything beyond what he has already *agreed* to tell you has to be forced out of him. So, no, on reflection, I *don't* think that Peter would have told Lord Voldemort about what happened to his Diary. After all, if he waited long enough somebody *else* would do *that*.

So Snape returns to Spinner's End lumbered with Pettigrew. (An enraged Voldemort may have even ordered both of them out of his sight.) Snape cannot help but smell some kind of a trap at this development. And for that matter he cannot help but know that Voldemort's rage is about to descend upon the Malfoys. Which certainly explains how Snape could claim to know about Malfoy's assignment by the same day Malfoy was actually given it. Even if he wasn't there.

With Pettigrew underfoot, communications between Snape and Albus must have been a bit strained. At the very least, Pettigrew would have recognized a Patronus Messenger for what it was, so they needed to be sparing of any such communications. But I think that this matter was important enough that Snape managed somehow to get the message out. And that may have been what made Albus decide to finally take the Ring (and the Locket?) out of the picture.

With such results and repercussions that resulted in the whole production to stage his own death at the end of the year.

Or, in short: we have just been handed yet another Book 6 = Book 2 parallel. The entire central issue of the book was precipitated by Lucius Malfoy having deployed the Riddle Diary without permission.

By the time Scrimgeour was having his interview with the PM — with whom he spoke a couple of days after his altercation with Dumbledore — Dumbledore has dealt with the Ring, which he had almost certainly located earlier, but left in place in case Voldemort decided to check on it after his return. Dumbledore may also have intended to finally deal with the Locket from #12, and only now discovered that it had been discarded on Sirius Black's authority.

In any case: Dumbledore makes his raid on the Ring, and allegedly is gravely injured. He manages to return to Hogwarts and summon Snape. Even if Peter saw Albus's Patronus at this point, the summons was something that could be explained by Snape's function as a double-agent.

Snape responds to the summons, manages to save Dumbledore's life — assuming there really *was* a deadly curse on the Ring. If we are dealing with falsified information, we need to keep in mind the possibility of intentional misdirection on the part of the conspirators. But it is likely the Ring *was* cursed.

However, if there was no conspiracy before this date, this could be the point at which the issue came up. They may have had to adjust their plans for the upcoming year in consideration of the possibility that Dumbledore is now on borrowed time. If Albus had only a year or so to live *anyway*, it is time to take some risks.

And in light of Voldemort's new demands, to ultimately give Tom *exactly* what he asks for is no longer all that much of a hardship. Albus has certainly more in the long run to gain from his own murder than he has from peacefully dying in his own bed.

Snape had probably already have been given warning that he is being called off the ever-pending job of assassinating Dumbledore. Such a reassignment will certainly go to Draco Malfoy (who else, after all, is likely to be at the school and in a position to do it?). Snape definitely was warned off at some point.

It is possible that an earlier plan to fake Albus's death in 1981 (which I suspect is why Snape was sent into Hogwarts in the first place; to assassinate Dumbledore on Voldemort's signal) are re-examined and revised. By the end of the year Albus will be dead.

It is possible that the plan to recall Slughorn and finally give Snape the D.A.D.A. position is also discussed at this point, but Albus may have made this decision on his own and not told Snape about it until after he had gotten Slughorn's agreement. Snape certainly gives every appearance of being unaware of it the evening the Black sisters showed up on his doorstep. Although that in itself is hardly conclusive.

If he wasn't able to do so before, Snape also fills Albus in on the fact that he now has Pettigrew underfoot and expects some form of "test" to be thrown his way.

Snape returns to Spinner's End; reports Dumbledore's injury, probably by Floo in Pettigrew's hearing. He may even exaggerate its extent. He can truthfully say that he does not know the cause, beyond the fact that Albus tangled with a curse that he could not fully counter. It should be noted that the news of Dumbledore's injury is also *deliberately* fed to Narcissa, Bellatrix and the DEs. It is later put on public display at the Start-of-Term feast as well. Snape & Albus *want* the DEs to believe that Albus has been weakened.

If he has *not* done so already, Voldemort officially suspends Snape's standing orders to be prepared to assassinate Dumbledore on his signal at this point. He may even tell him to keep out of Malfoy's way and to not interfere, although I rather suspect he did not think to do that. That may have been one of those small details of the sort which Riddle tends to overlook. Particularly when he is in a rage. In fact, the news of Dumbledore's injury may not be altogether welcome, and distracted him. He does not intend for Malfoy to *succeed*, after all.

When Narcissa turns up on his doorstep, perhaps the following evening, Snape knows that the job has indeed been reassigned, whether Voldemort has directly informed him of this or not. He also realizes that her visit explains the reason for Pettigrew's presence in his house.

Before we get any further ahead of ourselves, however:

We need to take a step back at this point and reconsider a few details which we have been taking a bit too much for granted. We ought to take a second look at one of those contributing factors which is routinely brought up whenever we postulate that Albus's death was genuine, but voluntary.

Namely, the blasted hand. I am going to have to admit that I am still not *at all* satisfied regarding that blasted hand. Albus never gave us a satisfactory answer regarding what happened to his hand, and the explanation that he finally did give us was very much in keeping with some of his other "likely stories".

Plus, for all that it must have *looked* terrible, after the first evening we never really got the feeling that he had a problem with *using* it. It was his *wand* hand, for heaven's sake! If he had blasted it beyond recovery, you would think that it might have slowed him down at least a *little*. Instead, apart from one comment to Harry in Chapter 3 that it was "a little fragile", and some clumsiness opening a bottle the same evening, the injury didn't seem to inconvenience him at all. And back in

Chapter 3 the injury would have still been quite fresh, and not fully healed.

I do tend to think that it is more likely than not that he *did* have a curse blow up in his face when he destroyed (or got hold of) the Ring (or lifted the jinx on the D.A.D.A. post) than that he injured his own hand on purpose — although given the way that once an element has been used in the series it generally gets used again, we can't automatically dismiss the possibility. *Pettigrew* certainly injured *his* hand on purpose (twice).

IF the injury was sustained acquiring or destroying the Horcrux, Albus may even have come very close to dying from it. And it may have only *been* Snape's timely intervention which saved his life at that juncture. But I am not convinced that his injuries were *permanent*.

And he certainly seems to have intended that the news of his "disabling injury" be circulated within the DE circles as quickly and as widely as possible.

In retrospect, IF we are dealing with a staged death here, and several months of intermittent acting, By the start of the school term, the blasted hand may have been suffering from not much more than purely cosmetic damage. It may, in fact, have been a piece of "performance art".

I have come around to accepting that some variant of the "Stoppered Death" theory which has been floating around the fandom for several months may well be in play. At this point the basics of that particular theory seems to fit all of the requirements. And Albus's tower statement of; *"Well, I certainly did have a drink… and I came back… after a fashion,"* is an anvil-sized hint that Rowling has just handed us a clue to *something*. Although we can't be altogether certain just what.

I am now inclined to think that Albus was well aware that he was already dying before he left the castle that last evening. For that matter, he had already arranged *everything* about the timing of his exit.

To that point, his death *had been* "stoppered". It wasn't any longer.

But it wasn't Snape who had stoppered it.

It was his late partner, Nicholas Flamel.

We were told that Flamel and his wife had enough of the Elixir of Life stocked to put their affairs in order before they died, and Rowling stated in one of her interviews that the Flamels are dead now. But c'mon, they'd been without the Stone since the previous summer, and it had been sitting in their Gringotts vault before that, not in their own keeping when they agreed to let Albus use it for bait. How often do you need to take the stuff?

They must have made sure to have had a considerable stock of the stuff put away before they turned the Stone over to Albus. And at that, there was always the risk that Voldemort *would* somehow manage to steal it. So they couldn't have been *absolutely* certain of getting it back. I think that the Flamels must have done a lot of thinking over the year that the Stone was at Hogwarts. I think that perhaps they came to the conclusion that their lives had devolved into a matter of *habit*, and that perhaps two-thirds of a millennium was long enough. I think their affairs were *already* in order when Albus finally went to convince them to permit it to be destroyed. And *they* may have been the ones to bring that particular solution to the problem up. *They* didn't use their final batch up to the last drop themselves. They left it to Albus, to be used in case of an emergency.

If Albus was being straight with us about the curse on the Ring, then Snape undoubtedly slowed the progress of the curse long enough (as he did later, with Katie Bell) for Albus to be able to take his first dose of the Elixir. And from that moment, Albus was on borrowed time. Once you start drinking the Elixir of Life, if you ever stop, you die. And with the Stone gone, there was never going to be any more of the stuff once the Flamels' stash was gone.

Rowling even makes a point of bringing the Elixir back up *in this very book* and having Albus *explain* how it works and what the disadvantages of using it are. The connection was just sitting there waiting to be made. But no one seems to have done it until she assured us Albus was dead.

I also really do tend to think that the fans may be making rather more of the *phrase* "stoppered death" than the reference really warrants.

Snape is *not* a blowhard who has a track record of making empty boasts.

If he tells his First years that *he can teach them* to "put a stopper in death", then it stands to reason that something which complies to this description is a part of the standard Hogwarts curriculum. Even if only once they get to NEWT-level ("— *if you aren't as big a bunch of dunderheads as I usually have to teach.*")

Brewing fame and bottling glory can probably also be stretched to apply to some of the more advanced potions taught as well. Again, we only seem to have gotten a glimmer at that sort of thing once we reached NEWT-level. But then I think that teaching teenagers the art and science of brewing fame and bottling glory would be right up Slughorn's alley, as much as Snape's. More even.

So what is one of the first things that 6th year potions students find themselves learning to brew?

Antidotes.

We didn't come up against anything like antidotes in the lower grades. Or certainly not with the kind of *complexity* that Golpalott's Law on antidotes seems to dictate. I am not at all convinced that by claiming that he could teach them to "put a stopper in death" Snape was not referring to *exactly* this specific skill.

So the really ornate theories of "stoppered death" (and some of them get *very* baroque) are probably superfluous to the requirements of Rowling's story. The *concept* looks pretty sound, but the details need scaling back.

Albus's behavior, and his statements over the course of Book 6 were a perpetual reminder to *everyone* of his own mortality, and I have finally settled into the camp which believes that his death had been "stoppered" by some means, at least temporarily. And he *knew* that it was temporary.

Which makes the theorizing over the staging of his actual death rather simpler upon the whole. In particular, it removes the necessity for Snape to have been working blind in order to circumvent his Vow, which in itself was an awkward kludge of a work-around, and I'm just as glad to be able to jettison it. It also makes the whole issue of timing over the year a lot less random, since it was more under Albus's control. In fact the timing of the event was *entirely* under Albus's control.

Yes. HIS control. Entirely. Or at any rate there are enough links (or potential links) in place to read it that way. Just watch:

By this point in the series we are pretty much obligated to cut our cloak to fit the cloth, and to strictly work with what Rowling has given us over the course of the series. It's 3200 pages, so that ought to be no hardship.

Even the certain knowledge that she *has* deliberately held back crucial pieces of information for Book 7 is no longer sufficient justification to theorize magic that has not already been explained, or at least introduced to us.

There are a limited number of methods of forestalling death that have been explained in the series to date:

There is the drinking of unicorn blood, which will preserve the life of the body at the cost of harm to an innocent, and of cursing the life so saved ever after. I think we can all agree that Dumbledore would have found this an unacceptable solution.

There is the creation of a Horcrux, which prevents a true death, even though it does not preserve the body itself. It does this at the cost of the death of an innocent and the mutilation of the immortal soul. Dumbledore would have found this solution even less acceptable.

And, finally, there is the Elixir of Life which will extend one's physical life and well-being indefinitely, for as long as you continue to drink it. The cost here is the monumental effort of acquiring the wealth of knowledge, and the purification of spirit which one must undergo in order to create the Philosopher's Stone from which the Elixir is generated, and moreover a dependency upon the Elixir itself once one begins to drink it. For once you start to do so, when you stop, you die.

Of the three methods, this is the only one which Albus would have considered an acceptable method for delaying his impending death.

Which means that he and Snape *did* deliberately plan for Snape to be the one to actually kill him. The Unbreakable Vow *was* almost certainly an intrinsic part of the plan. Snape *did* lead Narcissa to demand it, and he would have done it *anyway*. The Plan required that Albus be *murdered*. You cannot time something like the Elixir to the *minute*. Whoever killed Albus had to be prepared to cover the possibility that their timing might be off, and he would die *too soon*.

It also means that even though he could not time his demise to the exact day, from the beginning of July he had a ballpark figure of about how much time he had left.

And he messed with Draco's mission to ensure that the invasion would take place on *his* signal, and not one minute before.

Oh. Yes.

He also knew that facilitating an invasion was part of Malfoy's assignment.

The next item to crop up in the chronology is Malfoy being assigned his mission. And this particular item requires a considerable digression. Please forgive the delay; we will be working our way back around to Snape and his part in the matter, eventually. (I know that's all some of you are really interested in.)

Snape was clearly not present when this assignment was handed out to Malfoy. For that matter we do not know for certain whether Narcissa was actually present, either. Draco may have been privately escorted to the Dark Lord by his aunt Bellatrix. Voldemort is bound to be in hiding somewhere. His "striking" appearance must limit his movements considerably, and Malfoy cannot Apparate on his own yet. Plus, we *still* do not yet know for certain whether Narcissa is officially a Death Eater *herself*, or whether she is only a supporter and the wife of a Death Eater.

Which raises the question of whether Draco, himself, is officially a Death Eater.

It is certainly possible that Voldemort made an exception in his case. The whole business of Malfoy and his mission is exceptional. But Harry tends to see Death Eaters under the bed whenever he is dealing with people he dislikes. And I'm not sure we can take his reading of the matter at face value.

My own suspicion is that over the course of HBP Malfoy is *not* officially a Death Eater yet, and that he may not ever be forced into/given the opportunity to become one. Voldemort understands the uses of carrots as well as sticks. And, besides; why should he go to the trouble of marking the kid, when a mark would make it easier to expose him and see him safely off to Azkaban before he manages to get anything accomplished?

In addition; Voldemort expects the kid to *fail*. Indeed he *intends* the kid to fail. Why mark him? The mark is a *summoning* device. This kid hasn't even learned to Apparate yet. And he won't be old enough to get an Apparition licence until next June. If Voldemort has anything to say in the matter Malfoy isn't going to live long enough to get an Apparition license.

Even the supposed Dark mark-reading barrier that the DEs allegedly put on the staircase to the top of the Astronomy Tower during the battle in the corridor is inconclusive evidence. Malfoy got to the top of the stairs well before the barrier went up, and it had presumably been demolished by a stray curse before Snape bustled everyone back down that staircase.

And, for the record, I think the "received interpretation" of that barrier on the staircase is a complete red herring and that what was going on there was something else entirely.

No; I think that the mission was presented to Malfoy as his *initiation assignment*. If he pulled it off, Voldemort would induct him into the circle a year early. He felt he was being *honored*. But if he *failed*, he, and his mother, would be killed.

Which raises the question of just what Malfoy was showing Borgin in order to get his cooperation in the matter of the cabinets. I do *not* think he was flashing a Dark mark. (And I certainly do not think he was flashing a werewolf bite.)

We already have a couple of possibilities. A message from the former sales associate, Tom Riddle might certainly do it. Tom has long-term connections with Borgin & Burkes. And he has reached a position where you simply *do not* refuse his requests. Regardless of whether you are a Death Eater or not. It's just so very bad for business. To say nothing of your health.

A far more interesting line of inquiry, however, are those lacquer cabinets.

They are a "paired set".

One of them is at Hogwarts.

It has evidently been there for quite some time. In fact, it was presumably undamaged and still fully operable until Harry's 2nd year, when Peeves smashed it at Nearly-Headless Nick's urging in order to get Harry out of a detention.

The other is in London.

I rather suspect that those cabinets were originally Headmaster Phineas Nigellus Black's emergency route home to Grimmauld Place.

Phineas's daughter Belvina married a Herbert Burke. Caractacus Burke of Borgin & Burkes might have been her father-in-law, brother-in-law, or — at a considerable stretch — her son (the "little old man" of the Pensieve wasn't being questioned until some time after 1947, but it is most likely he was *not* her son). I think that after her father died (and probably her Aunt Elladora as well), Belvina laid a claim on the London cabinet and her brother Sirius, now head of the family, let her take it.

Belvina lived until 1962, if the date on the tapestry sketch can be accepted without question. We do not know how long the London cabinet has been in the shop. 1962 is well after the period that Tom Riddle worked there. He may not have even known about it or its abilities if no one has ever thought to volunteer that information. And, apparently it has not been in use for decades, or you would think that either Dippet or Dumbledore might have done something about such a potential security breech.

But my contention is that those cabinets probably figured in some Black family anecdote, which Draco may have learned from his mother, or even great-aunt Walburga, whom he might have met when he was a small child, or from the former head of the Black family, his great-uncle/distant cousin, old Arcturus Black, who was alive until the year that Draco started Hogwarts, and was certanly old enough to remember his own grandfather Phineas Nigellus. In any case, Malfoy *already* knew about such paired cabinets when he heard Montegue's story. That's *why* Montegue's story rang a bell for him in the first place.

And Narcissa or Aunt Bellatrix was able to confirm that yes, there *was* a family story of great-great(-great)-grandfather Phineas Nigellus having once had a pair of such cabinets when he was Headmaster of Hogwarts.

The very fact that Malfoy was visiting Borgin to secure cooperation regarding the London cabinet well before the school year started is proof enough that getting a group of Death Eaters into the castle was an intrinsic part of his mission.

What he was showing Borgin to secure that cooperation was probably something to invoke his family connection to the cabinet, and to make it clear that he knew the secret of the cabinets' intended function. He was clearly questioning Borgin about the damage the Hogwarts cabinet had sustained and asking for advice as to how to repair it. After all, neither cabinet is of value as anything more than furniture if they do not work as advertised. Such cooperation is to Borgin's material benefit.

Which brings us to the agenda item in all of this that I have a real *problem* with: Voldemort's demand that Malfoy get a squad of DEs into the castle.

Why? *Why* send a pack of outsiders into the castle? This was clearly a part of the original plan, or Malfoy would not have been slipping off to Borgin to give instructions regarding the London cabinet before the school year even started. But what was the *point*?

If the mission was really a legitimate test of the kid's mettle, Voldemort would have told him to do it entirely by *himself* and that if he ended up needing to make a run for it, to go to Snape who was already in place. Never mind bringing in outsiders. They'd only complicate things. Instead, one of the major snags and delays of complying with the assignment was arranging for a way to bring the outsiders *in*.

I really don't think that they were sent in to "help" Draco. They really weren't all that much *help*, were they?

Draco could have gotten up to the top of the tower to wait for Dumbledore's return after *any* of his frequent absences much more easily on his own. The Headmaster was not being particularly secretive about those absences, and he cultivated a *predictable* practice of returning to the castle by always flying in to the top of the Astronomy Tower — a *known* favorite haunt of the *Slytherin House* ghost. The Baron isn't nearly as chatty as Sir Nick, but that particular bit of information regarding Dumbledore's habits doesn't need to travel very far to be of assistance to Malfoy, does it?

Draco no doubt *believed* that the Death Eaters were sent as his back-up, and to cover his retreat. But if he had managed to lie in ambush and kill Dumbledore without witnesses he could have just gone back to the Slytherin dorm and if it later looked like there were suspicions flying, tried to slip out to Hogsmeade and used Rosemerta's Floo the next day. He knew about Snape's Unbreakable Vow to protect him by Christmas. Snape would have been *obligated* to cover his retreat — if a retreat was called for.

For that matter; *when* over the entire preceding 5 books has Malfoy *ever* refused Snape's praise, support, or assistance? And if he is suddenly doing it now, doesn't that suggest that he has been given a compelling *reason*?

I'm beginning to suspect that the invasion component of that assignment was set up as a potential double-cross.

I think that, yes the DEs *were* sent to serve as witnesses to the success of the mission. But they were also expected to be prepared to finish off Dumbledore, *and* to execute Malfoy then and there, if he failed.

And, quite probably, to execute him even if he had *not* failed. That crew were assigned by Voldemort himself. They were not sent by Malfoy's mother. Narcissa would never have sent him *Greyback*. I don't even think that *Bellatrix* would have sent him Greyback, unless she was *told* to. And you will notice that *she* was not sent *herself*.

That crew were not Voldemort's most loyal followers. They were not his most competent followers. They were his most *vicious* followers. With Greyback invited along (or, hanging around Borgin's and inviting himself along) just for the fun of it.

Voldemort expected Malfoy to fail. He *wanted* Malfoy to fail. It is not beyond what we know about the former Tom Riddle for him to have taken steps to ensure that it should be assumed by everyone that Malfoy *had* failed. So he could send that message back to Malfoy's father. This is another vote against the reading that Malfoy had already been formally inducted into the circle when he was given that mission.

But how was it that *Albus* learned about the planned invasion?

Well we've got a couple of hot possibilities to consider:

Harry's trip to Diagon Alley to get that year's school supplies took place very early in August. Harry was yattering on about Malfoy being "up to no good" from that point forward.

By that time Albus had already tangled with whatever blasted his hand. Snape had already helped him to "stopper" his death, and they had made their plans.

Albus also would have already been filled in on the fact that Snape has been ordered to step down and let Malfoy have a go at assassinating him. He would have taken Harry's information very seriously indeed. Once he heard it.

So the first task is to fill in the gap on *how* he got the information. Because considering the number of parties involved in the matter, it is a bit much to assume that he never did.

My favorite (although far from the only) candidate for this particular leak is Fleur. She was actually living at the Burrow over the relevant time, and she isn't so much older than Harry that she would dismiss his theories on the grounds that he is just a kid. Remember; she's *seen* Harry in action.

I suspect that she would have passed Harry's observations/suspicions on to Bill. Bill is far enough removed from his parents' household that he probably doesn't take Harry's observations for granted either. He might very well have mentioned the matter to Moody, or Shacklebolt, or Tonks, or *somebody*. From there it would have been relayed to Albus. A sure thing? Hardly. But perfectly plausible within fairly simple parameters.

So. Okay; on to somewhat shakier possibilities. We are approaching the realm of "extreme theories" with this one. This is the single gap in my current interpretations which lacks an obvious canon link.

What do we *really* know about Borgin & Burkes?

It appears to be a somewhat dodgy curiosity shop, perhaps one of the more reputable businesses in a highly unsavory district. And it's been in operation for at least the past 70 years, probably longer. It specializes in Dark Arts artifacts and it draws a customer base from a broad spectrum of wizarding society. All the way from very shady characters indeed, to serious collectors from prominent families.

So, given that kind of a customer base, can we *really* anticipate the proprietors' own political views? Apart from Dark Arts sympathies, that is? I don't think we can. B&B have a vested interest in telling each and every customer *exactly* what the customer wants to hear. We've watched the current proprietor, Borgin, do precisely that.

And Tom Riddle was once employed there. Indeed, he was a favored and highly *valued* associate — and he grossly abused his employers' trust; murdering one of their most valuable customers and absconding with the two most precious items in her collection. Admittedly the murder could not be proved, but he was unquestionably revealed as a thief. And he undoubtedly knew many of their business secrets. This cannot have been a welcome or a *comfortable* discovery for his former employers.

Soon afterward, Albus Dumbledore, almost certainly already a member of the Wizengamot (although probably not yet Chief Warlock) shows up investigating the death of Hepzibah Smith, and the movements and history of Tom Riddle in an attempt to trace the missing artifacts. He speaks with the proprietor of the period, one Carractacus Burke. We were shown only the barest fragment of that interview. Only the portion concerning Burke's acquisition of the Slytherin Locket.

We do not know what *else* they may have discussed.

It has only belatedly occurred to me that B&B could hardly be expected to be enthusiastic *supporters* of Tom Riddle, in either of his identities in the face of this early discovery. And that even before he became Headmaster, or Chief Warlock of the Wizengamot, Albus Dumbledore was a force in the wizarding world to be reckoned with.

And a shop in Knockturn Alley, particularly one with such a *broad* customer base, would be a very desirable source of information concerning the activities of various… *elements*… in wizarding society. Even before the advent of Lord Voldemort.

And neither Caractacus Burke, nor Mr Borgin are any more shady a customer than, say, Mundungus Fletcher — who may have served as some sort of go-between, much as Hagrid served as courier between the Dumbledore brothers at Hogwarts Castle, and the Hog's Head. Indeed B&B is certainly no *more* dicey a possible outpost for Albus' informers than the Hog's Head. Quite comparable, in fact.

Albus may not have *needed* Harry's story to be on top of the Draco affair.

But, in the event that B&B was NOT already one of Albus's sources, once Albus did hear of Harry's suspicions he would have sent someone to Knockturn Alley to investigate. Indeed, he may have gone himself and made another opportunity to flash that blasted hand about where people could be trusted to note it and carry tales.

And who should he or his agent discover in Knockturn Alley but Fenrir Greyback, tricked out in borrowed wizard's robes loitering in the vicinity of the shop and making sure that Borgin *sees* him, in accordance with Malfoy's threat.

Is it really so much of a stretch to wonder whether Albus may have managed to get the story out of Borgin in return for a promise of protection?

And even if not, he may have recognized that the lacquer cabinet in the shop was a match to the one at Hogwarts. The Hogwarts cabinet had figured in a very notable and disturbing incident right at the start of the previous term. If Snape is a White Hat, he would have hardly have failed to fill Albus in on the matter, as soon as he could. Which was only a matter of a month earlier. The information would have been fresh in his mind.

After all, just because Harry and his friends said nothing about the twins having stuffed Montegue *into* the cabinet, it really is a bit much to assume that Snape didn't get *something* of the story out of the boy before he clammed up. He was the boy's Head of House, after all. And he was clearly trying to *help* him after his ordeal. There was ample reason for some degree of *trust* there.

Snape may have even been the one to advise Montegue *not* to spread the story around. Although it sounds like the boy found it just too good to resist passing on to his housemates.

Completely off Harry's radar, of course. Which, when you think about it, would be all of a piece with everything else that was going on over the course of OotP.

And if the cabinet rang a bell, a brief stop by #12 to look at the tapestry would have confirmed that Phineas's daughter Belvina had married Herbert Burke. And Phineas could have confirmed that the cabinets were paired.

Furthermore, if the cabinet had not already been moved into the Room of Hidden Things, then Malfoy and his goons must have done it themselves, after curfew one night, in full sight of the Hogwarts art collection — since I doubt that leading Crabbe and Goyle by the hand, with them lumbered with a full-sized cabinet (even with a weight-reduction charm on it) under the cover of Peruvian darkness powder, with the aid of the Hand of Glory would really have been on.

And if the cabinet *had* already been moved, to get it out of the way of further mischief, well, there is a painting of trolls in tutus and a wizard attempting to teach them ballet prominently on display opposite the door, to serve as a sentry — and to overhear what the petitioners were asking of the Room as well, if they had no better sense than to ask for it aloud, even if under their breath.

Once it had been reported that Malfoy and the cabinet had taken up residence in the Room, all the cards were in Albus's hands. After any evening that Malfoy had been reported spending time in the Room, Albus would visit that night and undo what Malfoy had done, stringing the whole project out for as long as the Flamels' stash of Elixir lasted. And then when he had taken his final shot of it, he went and repaired the cabinet himself — all but a simple detail or two — and waited for Malfoy to enter the room again and discover it.

Once Malfoy was reported entering the room, he sent for Harry.

And Malfoy was sent a hand-picked backup team that he would absolutely *not* have been able to fight off alone, or to escape, once the main objective of the mission was accomplished. If they managed to get that far.

Nobody seems to have anticipated that they would run into defenders patrolling the halls, and that they would need to fight their way out of the castle. If they had, you would have thought that they would have at least brought along their *masks*. Every one of the DEs went into that mission *bare-faced*.

But where the DEs were coming from, Malfoy was toast.

However, Voldemort wasn't *quite* prepared to dispense with Snape as well. Or, at any rate, not just *yet*.

Which brings us to the Unbreakable Vow. I suspect that Voldemort wasn't a bit pleased about that Vow. But that we heard of no fallout regarding it suggests that it wasn't a major issue for him. Voldemort may have realized that he had not made himself sufficiently clear that Snape was not merely to stand down and leave the way clear, but that he was to *stay out* of the matter *altogether*. He certainly had not let Snape in on the fact that the mission was a planned double-cross.

Still, he wasn't altogether *dis*pleased to learn that his currently most-favored follower was committed enough to what he knew of his Master's objectives that he was willing to put his life on the line to see that those objectives were carried out. Even if that wasn't at all what his Master had intended.

Therefore, Snape had to be kept out of it, so he wouldn't be zapped by the 2nd clause of his Vow. And Bellatrix through innuendo, misrepresentation, and outright lies, made sure that Draco tried as hard as he possibly could to *keep* Snape out of it. If McGonagall hadn't sent Flitwick to alert Snape it might have all gone pear-shaped. It almost did, anyway, thanks to Greyback.

I also think the DEs had their orders not to interfere with Snape, IF he turned up.

He was to be kept OUT of it. They were NOT to confide in him. They were NOT to contact him. But *if* he showed his face, they were to let him take charge. *Regardless* of whether the boy had completed his mission or not.

So. About that Unbreakable Vow:

The Unbreakable Vow is not the biggest fly in this particular pot of ointment. The Vow only made it obligatory that Snape take the role of the villain who would be "known" to have murdered Albus Dumbledore. And that bit of casting was already built into his and Albus's plan. If the death was staged, *who else* was there that Albus would have been able to trust to *kill* him? In fact, they had to do whatever they could to ensure that the job *would* fall to Snape, and that the others would stand aside and let him *do* it. No. from where I am standing, the big, black, buzzing bug is our not having any idea *why* the gratuitously weird details about the actual murder were stuck in there at all. They don't appear to be *necessary*.

And at this point, and on that issue, I have no clear answers

The more carefully you read the Spinner's End chapter the more convincing is the suggestion that rather than being tricked into the Vow by Narcissa, Snape *led* Narcissa into asking him to take that Vow. He was clearly leading that whole conversation and playing both those women like hooked trout.

This is the old "where your loyalties lie" confrontation all over again. What is going on here is not just what is dancing about on the surface.

That whole chapter really begins to read rather like deliberate entrapment. And it isn't Snape who is being trapped. "Won't you step into my parlor?" Said the cunning spider to the flies… Complete with a sting.

But the real issue is probably a bit more complex than that. I suspect that Snape's throw-away line to the two sisters that Pettigrew "has taken to listening at doors", was not just a caution that their visit might be reported, but a back-handed statement to Pettigrew that Snape knew perfectly well that Pettigrew *would* be listening, and would report any conversations to Voldemort. It may even have been a hint to Pettigrew that Snape would be amplifying Pettigrew's report with one of his own, so he'd best not make any flights of fancy in that report. Snape certainly had no qualms about openly talking about that Vow to Malfoy later. There was clearly nothing secret about the Vow in DE circles by Christmas.

But I suspect that the attempted "entrapment" at Spinner's End was not on Snape's part. Neither was it primarily directed *at him*. When Snape opened the door to the Black sisters, he recognized that this was the test he had been expecting ever since Voldemort sent Pettigrew home with him. But he also recognized that *he* wasn't the one who was being tested.

And I really do think that forcing Peter to come out and show his face, and that little throw-away line to alert the sisters that Pettigrew may be listening wasn't there by accident. No, not at all. It was damage control.

I've suspected all along that once it entered the equation, Snape and Albus were depending on the news of that Vow getting back to the DEs through Bellatrix, and I rather think that they were depending upon Pettigrew reporting it to Voldemort as well. We heard Pettigrew go up the stairs after Snape zapped him. But the man is an *Animagus*. He would have stomped up the stairs, transformed, raced back down through the walls and been listening to the whole conversation at a mouse hole.

Sneering at him and zapping him for good measure would have put his back up. And what does a Gryffindor do when you get his back up? Particularly an underhanded Gryffindor? Besides, why would the Dark Lord have sent Pettigrew home with Snape if *not* to report Snape's contacts and conversations? He's not going to stop listening on Snape's say-so.

The warning that Pettigrew will be listening kept Narcissa from asking for anything that could be construed as *disloyal*. Two of the three clauses of the Vow appear to be directly related to the successful completion of the mission. The other was just a predictable mother's request to watch over and protect her son.

Snape later even makes a point of directly *telling* Malfoy that he has sworn an Unbreakable Vow to Malfoy's mother. This was not accidental either. Snape was *using* the Vow to call attention to himself as the default assassin in the event that Draco was not able to carry out the task. And this was *absolutely* deliberate.

In the first place, it sent an unequivocal message to the Death Eaters as to whose side Snape was on. They may have disliked him, been jealous of him, and tried to keep him out of it. But he was a *rival*, not an *enemy*. They were all confident that he was on *their* side. This is not a minor issue. And it will pay dividends later on.

In the second place, being solidly cast in the role of Second Murderer might lower the chance of someone like the Carrows or "Brutal-face" jumping in and queering the deal by trying to finish off Albus — who has spent a year establishing that he is vulnerable and *helpless* — themselves, if it became clear that Draco couldn't do it. No one took Greyback into account. I doubt that it occurred to either Snape *or* Albus that anyone would send the Big Bad Wolf on a mission into a school full of *children*. Snape got there just in the nick of time.

In the third place, it set the DEs up to see what they *expected* to see. They expected to see "Snape the Assassin" and that is exactly what they did see. Even if there were anomalies in his performance (and there were), these will probably not have registered. From where the DEs were standing, Snape was already cast as the murderer of Albus Dumbledore before he even got to the top of the tower.

I also suspect that Snape and Dumbledore had agreed that, if at all possible, Snape should try to insinuate himself into Malfoy's plans in order to try to apply damage control from the inside.

Of course Malfoy managed to make a hash of that. I'd say that he did it without half trying, but it's clear that he *was* trying, and trying very hard indeed. If he'd cooperated with Snape, rather than Bellatrix, he could have agreed to fake his death and gone into hiding, and no-one would have been any wiser. With the Vow in play, both he AND Dumbledore would probably have to "die" (Dumbledore's death being the *point* of all this effort, after all) and there would have been some plausible reason lying about for why Snape *could not* have assisted Malfoy, and so managed to escape being zapped by the backlash of the Vow. But, it just didn't happen like that.

While the Vow must have been an inconvenient and intractable element to have to juggle over the year leading up to the final performance, it was not there by accident, and Snape was not tricked into making it. He volunteered. We saw him do it, and even if it was a spur-of-the-moment improvisation Dumbledore no doubt agreed that he hadn't really any other choice, considering what was at stake.

And, once it was in play, they could certainly turn it to their own use. I have come round to the view that even if it *wasn't* their idea (and I really do think it was), the Vow rapidly became an intrinsic part of their setting the stage.

And awkward as it might have been to maneuver around, it really is beginning to look like they managed to gain a great deal more by the use of that Vow than they lost by it. If Malfoy had just been a bit more cooperative, there would have been everything to gain.

Providing yet another indication that including a Malfoy in your plans is just asking for trouble. (Molly: *"That whole family is trouble!"*) Or, given Wendy B. Harte's views on the matter, maybe that should be rephrased as the inherent problems with depending on a Black in any complex operation.

And, at that, it may not have been *that* awkward, really. An Unbreakable Vow is not a piece of obscure Dark magic that nobody knows anything about. If a pair of country-bred, home-schooled, geographically and socially isolated 7-year-olds know what an Unbreakable Vow is and how to set one up, it can't exactly be considered *obscure*. It is probably some creakingly obsolete bit of contractual magic that turns up regularly in wizarding folktales. And it has probably been superseded in everyday use by something far more manageable and effective in modern wizarding business practices where any form of contractual magic is required. Although some very old traditional contracts probably still draw on it. When you stop and consider the matter, the Unbreakable Vow bears a more than slight family resemblance to the "magical contract" to compete that locked Harry into the TriWizard Tournament back in Year 4.

Watching out for and protecting the boy is something Snape would have done as a matter of course, and it was imperative that if anyone was going to throw an AK at Albus, it had bloody well *better* be Snape!

But none of this was the primary reason that Snape was all but openly suggesting that Narcissa ask him to swear an Unbreakable Vow.

He really has been associated with the Malfoys for a long time. He has *benefited* from the association. And, nasty piece of work though he may sometimes be, rank ingratitude does not really seem to be one of Snape's failings. He has known the Malfoys long enough to have some genuine concern for their welfare.

Narcissa had figured out the double-cross.

That "double-cross" theory is another one right up there with Snape-loved-Lily. Once it finally occurs to you, it takes hold and you just cannot look away. Unlike Snape-loved-Lily, the double-cross has some canon support. The very fact that whoever sent the DEs into Hogwarts chose such a group and included *Greyback* suggests that whatever his objective was, it wasn't just to ensure that *Dumbledore* died.

And if Narcissa had figured it out, it would explain the level of her hysteria, which otherwise seems over-the-top and even positively unbalanced. Bellatrix acts as if she is totally clueless, and she may well be. But the probability is that she just doesn't care. So far as she is concerned the kid is a Malfoy, not a Black. And whatever the Dark Lord wants is good enough for her.

But when you factor in the certainty of both of them being aware of a double-cross in the background, the subtext of the dialogue between Narcissa and Snape in Spinner's End now comes across as something like:

"He's given Draco a mission that he cannot survive. My son is going to DIE!"

"Yes."(subtext: got it — message received and understood.)

"You are his most valued advisor, his favorite —"

"I can't talk him out of it."

"But you could help Draco!"

"Yes. MAKE me help him."

And the penny finally dropped as to just *why* Pettigrew was sent to Spinner's End in advance. He wasn't sent there permanently, and he wasn't sent *just* to report on Snape's movements. Voldemort knew perfectly well that if she figured it out Narcissa would go running straight to Snape. Snape has been associated with the Malfoys for yonks. Snape is sharp. Just sending Pettigrew home with him would be warning enough for Snape to know to back off and keep his nose clean. But Pettigrew's real assignment at Spinner's End was to spy and report back *on Narcissa.*

Voldemort was just itching for an excuse to execute her for disloyalty. Draco's mission may even have been intended to serve as bait, tempting her to say something damning before witnesses. That *would* have been another nice message that he hoped to be able to send to Lucius. Bellatrix may have actually had an inkling of that one. She didn't give a damn about the Malfoys, father *or* son, but she *would* try to keep her own sister from doing something that would get her killed.

It was a very close call. They dodged that bullet. Between them, Snape and Narcissa managed to make an end run around the Dark Lord's plans and save Draco's life. And Narcissa's as well. Dumbledore could have had no objection.

And, between them, Snape and Narcissa even lucked out and managed to make it sound rather as if Snape *only* swore the Vow at all because Bellatrix got up his nose and mocked him for not agreeing to swear it immediately! Bella gets the blame.

Of course, the fact that the Vow came bundled with all sorts of value-added benefits for the "Murder of Albus Dumbledore" extravaganza was just so much gravy.

And I really doubt that the Vow is still an issue by this time.

Snape wasn't swearing a Vow to the great judge of hereafter. He was swearing a Vow to *Narcissa*. Subject to Bellatrix's judgment as to whether he had fulfilled the requirements. And I think that he fulfilled his oath in a manner which would completely satisfy both Narcissa *and* Bellatrix (well maybe "satisfy" and "Bellatrix" don't really belong in the same sentence, but I doubt she would be able to make any objections she might have stick).

Which right there is a clue as to how an Unbreakable Vow works. You bind your *own* magic to your promise to fulfill the actions required by the petitioner. Essentially this is; "Cross my heart and hope to die" made literal. There is no impartial judge overseeing the matter, just your own knowledge of whether you have made an honest attempt to comply with the demand. If you cannot convince yourself that you *have* made an honest effort, your own magic will *kill* you.

If Voldemort tries to read Snape by Legilimency, Snape can show him exactly what happened on the tower without a qualm.

From where the DEs are standing, the mission is complete. (Mission accomplished!) The DEs are certainly not going to go back to try again.

So I think that by now Snape is safely off the hook regarding that Vow. If any clause was still in effect by the next morning, it is the 2nd clause, the one to protect Draco to the utmost of his ability. But neither Snape nor Albus are likely to object to that.

Voldemort, however, almost certainly *does*.

Voldemort very likely did tell Snape to step aside and give the kid a chance, in a manner that Snape might have claimed to have been left with the understanding that he was to complete the mission himself if the kid didn't. Indeed those might well have *been* his orders. His *original* orders, that is. Malfoy was to fail his assignment, and then, after things cooled off a bit, Snape was to murder Albus. And don't waste your breath trying to convince me that *Snape* would have been ordered to facilitate any invasion of the castle, because I won't believe you. That's how it was *supposed* to go. Or at least until Snape and Narcissa put a spoke into the wheel by throwing an Unbreakable Vow into the equation.

And afterwards, he was being kept out of the loop, remember? He didn't "officially" know about any intended double-cross in order to know not to *interfere* with it.

But having his most effective lieutenant sworn to protect Malfoy in perpetuity is inconvenient to the Dark Lord's future plans. Especially any future plans for *Malfoy*.

For as long as the Vow served as an additional fall-back to ensure that Malfoy's mission (which was *essential* to Voldemort's other future plans) was successfully completed, he would let it stand. But it was already very much in the way, and he wasn't likely to let it stand one minute longer than it needed to.

Particularly given that the kid did turn out to be too squeamish to complete the assignment. I rather think that Voldemort ordered Bellatrix and Narcissa to release Snape from the Vow as soon as he managed to get all three of them in one place together. Such Vows cannot be broken, but I will bet you almost anything that the Bonder can release you from one, or why would the Vow *need* a Bonder?

Consequently; by this time, I don't really think the Vow is any kind of an issue any more.

Which now brings us to the overheard quarrel. Frankly, I am not altogether satisfied on what that was all about, either.

I'm not convinced that Snape had gotten cold feet about the staged death itself. He may have had reasonable doubts regarding the *performance*, but they were both already committed to the plan and he would hardly ask Albus to go back to the drawing board and start over. But he might have been being shirty about some of the details. He could even have been quibbling about the need to stun whatever messenger (apart from Harry) might be sent to fetch him, or — more likely — over some other part of the advance prep work.

I do think that he hated the necessity of having to be the one to throw that AK. I could be wrong, and he may *have* been arguing that the murder itself wasn't really *necessary*. That if Albus was dying anyway, they probably could arrange for some kind of a finesse that would allow him to die in peace. If Albus was *already* dead, Snape probably *wouldn't* be zapped by the Vow's 3rd clause, and Malfoy might be given another chance.

If that was the case, Albus wasn't having any. If he was dying *anyway*, he wanted to *use* his death to buy them all something worth *having*.

It's also possible that the quarrel may have been about some future action related to Snape's mission the following year, once he was in deep cover. Probably something to do with supporting Potter. Not everything we encounter in a given book is about what is going on the current book, after all. But if this is the case, it's a shoe that won't fall until Book 7 is out.

Or; given that the quarrel took place very shortly before Ron Weasley managed to be poisoned by mistake. Snape may have been proposing to haul back on Malfoy's leash, or sit on him, rather than to continue to stand back and let the kid make random murder attempts without interference, as previously agreed.

Quite possibly, the complication with Malfoy was giving Snape more and more cause for concern as the year went on. Because, while the first botched attempt (in fact both botched attempts) to curse or poison Dumbledore might have been initiated by Malfoy on his own, they *knew* that Malfoy was engaged in an invasion plan *as well*, and was claiming to have help from someone outside the school. Snape may have been worried that it wasn't just his mother and aunt. Snape was being deliberately kept out of the loop. Which would have galled him. Snape *likes* knowing everyone's secrets.

He may even have been arguing over following Albus's lead and leaving poor Madam Rosemerta under the Imperius curse, so as not to tip Malfoy off that they were aware of his having put her under his control.

Or he may have been objecting to being told to stay in his quarters until called, and have to run all the way from the dungeons to the top of the highest tower before he could intervene, and possibly arrive too late to perform his role.

Or, and this is something that only just surfaced on one of my discussion boards; Hagrid may have been mistaken over what Albus meant when he advised Snape to make investigations in his House. Hagrid is convinced that this was something related to all the House Heads being instructed to try to find out about who cursed Katie Bell.

However, *we* already know that Snape has a house of his own. *How* do we know for sure that Albus *wasn't* referring to the house in Spinner's End?

And if he was, what might Snape have been engaged in at Spinner's End that he wanted to get clear of? There is just no shortage of possibilities for that quarrel.

But, I have to agree that the most straightforward answer to the problem was that Snape was beginning to balk over the murder being necessary at all, and wanted off the hook of being the one to have to kill Albus, even if this defection risked his own life. And Albus flatly refused to permit him to risk his life in such a manner.

But, otherwise I think I'm just going to have to pass on that overheard quarrel.

Which brings us to our next major digression;

The Adventure of the Dark Lord's Sea Cave.

That expedition can't have been altogether irrelevant either, you know.

I suspect it was an intrinsic part of the staging of Dumbledore's exit.

Act Three, Scene Two, in fact.

We need to back up a bit again at this point, however. We've another curiosity to clear up first. Harry Potter was unable to find or to enter the unknowable, unplottable Room of Hidden Things when Malfoy needed it to be inaccessible. When Malfoy was in residence it was literally off the map.

We do not know what limits applied to Albus. (Or to Trelawney?)

Albus's office is around on the other side of the castle from the Room of

Requirement, as Harry pointed out to Tonks when she encountered him near the RoR one evening, claiming to be looking for Dumbledore.

But Dumbledore's *private* quarters are near enough to the Room that he managed to blunder into it one night, looking for the loo. And if you were in a position of stewardship to that castle, and you know that the castle contains a room which is so ripe for misuse, if not downright disaster, wouldn't *you* have set up some form of surveillance in it? Indeed, mightn't you *inherit* some form of surveillance in it? At the very least, the painting opposite the door might stand duty as a sentry.

So let's take another look at what we know about the timetable for that evening.

Act Three, Scene One

Just before curfew, which, since it was approaching the summer solstice, was at sunset, Harry was summoned by Dumbledore to come to his office at once. Hurrying along the 7th floor corridor, he hears a shriek and a crash and finds Trelawney with her sherry bottles sprawled on the floor. She engages him with an account of having walked into the Room of Hidden Things to hear someone start celebrating, piles on a querulous complaint about being afflicted by sudden darkness and rudely ejected from the room, maunders on about her inner eye and the Lightning-Struck Tower, and finishes up (no doubt thanks to free-association) with her account of the night Albus hired her and Snape had been ejected from the Hog's Head. We do not know how long she delayed Harry, but it was at least a few minutes. Whoever was in the room is still there. Harry gets rid of her.

Harry dashes to the Headmaster's office, and finds him on the point of departure. They discuss Malfoy celebrating in the Room of Requirement, Trelawney's story of Snape having fitted up Harry's parents, and whose side Snape is on, anyway. Albus recounts the "likely story" of Snape's remorse and his own forgiveness back in 1981. He clearly considers telling Harry something more, possibly the truth, but resists the temptation. Malfoy, meanwhile probably sneaks out of the Room and returns to Slytherin House.

Dumbledore invites Harry to accompany him on a raid for one of the Horcruxes. Makes him promise to obey orders. Then he sends Harry off to "get his cloak" — actually to alert his friends, give them the rest of the "lucky potion" and urge them to patrol. He and Dumbledore meet in the entrance hall and depart for Hogsmeade.

Dumbledore has left arrangements for the castle to be patrolled by both staff and Order members. Snape is not included in these orders. He presumably remains in his own quarters, away from all sources of information. But although it is now after curfew, he does not prepare for bed.

Indeed, Albus sends Harry off to "get his cloak", despite the fact that he had *already* instructed Harry to keep it with him at all times at the beginning of the year. This is our first clear instance over the course of the evening where Harry has been distracted or deliberately gotten out of the way for a critical few minutes.

Regarding Albus's somewhat curious behavior over the rest of the evening; what I currently think is that in Albus we are getting an outside view of what Harry's behavior must have looked like to Ron and Hermione the night he was under the influence of the Felix Felicis potion.

We know that Slughorn had a batch of Felix with him when he showed up at the beginning of the year. The bottle of it that he awarded Harry only held one ounce of the stuff. What happened to the rest of it?

For that matter, once we discovered that the stuff takes six months to brew, we realize that Slughorn must have started that batch by the previous Spring — during the period he was supposedly squatting a week at a time in vacant Muggle houses. And Sluggy tells us that the stuff is fiendishly tricky to brew and disastrous to get wrong. I'd say that there is more to Albus and Horace's association than we've been told.

I think that Albus *commissioned* that batch of Felix Felicis from Slughorn, and we haven't seen the last of it.

And if heading out of the castle on the night you and your confederates intend to stage your own murder doesn't constitute an appropriate opportunity to maximize your luck, I don't know what does.

It has been noted by a number of people that Albus seemed to be "feeling his way" through the sea cave. I'd have to say that the reading that he was watching the possibilities unfold and waiting for Felix to point out the best one, certainly works for me.

If Albus has been monitoring Malfoy's progress with the cabinet, once Malfoy was reported as having entered the Room after Albus had repaired the cabinet for him, he took his dose of Felix and sent for Harry. While waiting, he alerted the Staff, called in the Order members and set up the additional protections on the perimeter.

For that matter: how do we know that some form of surveillance was not at the other end of the connection, in Borgin & Burkes, as well? We *know* that Dumbledore had *some* kind of dealings with old Caractacus Burke — after Burke's trusted assistant Riddle proved to be a thief and quite possibly a murderer. I don't get the impression that Borgin would refuse an offer of protection from the Chief Warlock of the Wizengamot at the price of allowing a spy eye of some sort to be installed in the shop. Not with the kind of hell that has been breaking loose all year.

While we are at it: how did *Trelawney* get into the Room, when, after weeks of attempts, Harry never managed it? Did she have the fools' luck to blunder in during the few moments that Malfoy *wasn't there?* When he was off in London *testing* the cabinet? He has to have briefly left the Room to do that. He'd hardly be whooping in celebration until he knew for sure that it *worked*.

Albus had already realized that he needed a good excuse to haul Harry out of the castle when the planned invasion was ready to go off. He had finally learned his lesson the year before. If Potter was left at liberty in the castle during the invasion, he would *mess* with it, and that would be likely to prove fatal for somebody other than just Albus. The invasion and the staged murder was much too delicate a balancing act to risk Potter mixing into it. Taking him out of the castle to hunt a Horcrux while the rest of the cast assembled, would be a much safer option. They might even manage to get one more of them settled before Albus made his exit, and that would leave the boy with only three to find and neutralize.

You *will* notice that just about *everything* Albus did that evening was calculated to keep Harry from getting actively involved in the evening's main event.

Dumbledore next makes a point of being seen (apparently alone, Harry is under his cloak on Dumbledore's orders) in Hogsmeade by Madam Rosemerta, before he and Harry Apparate to the coast. Malfoy is unlikely to set his trap until he knows that Albus is out of the castle. So Albus has just ensured that Malfoy will believe the way is fortuitously clear. Before the DEs have the time to make any better plans than the ones they can throw together on the spur of the moment.

Malfoy passes the word by some as yet unknown means to one of his confederates outside the castle (not Madam Rosemerta, I think. Not for this) and the invasion team is called up on something like an hour's notice.

For that matter, can you say, *for certain*, that Albus *hadn't* already figured out Madam Rosemerta's coerced involvement in Malfoy's plotting?

I suspect that he *had* figured it out *at least* by the time he heard about the bottle of poisoned mead. His pretending to only realize it during the conversation with Malfoy passed that information to Harry, thereby tying off a loose end, and ensuring that the situation would be rectified after he was gone.

And then there is the trip into the cave itself.

If Albus Dumbledore had a hand in the "murder" of Regulus Black he knew perfectly well that there was no Horcrux in that cave. But we do not know yet whether Albus ever had any dealings with Reggie Black.

His statements and much of his behavior are calculated to give us the impression that he has never been there himself, although he clearly knows the Inferi are stashed there. In fact, he knows a suspiciously large amount about what he and Harry find in that cave for a man who supposedly has never been there before.

I really suspect that he *had* been there before. Once, at least, and quite recently.

On John Granger's HogPro discussion board the question was posted as to how Dumbledore learned of the cave in the first place.

I think that Albus "found" that cave in his own memories. He told us all the way back in GoF that he was in the habit of off-loading and re-examining memories in a Pensieve, which made it easier to organize what he knew.

When he revisited his own memory of delivering Tom Riddle's Hogwarts letter before sharing it with Harry, Mrs Cole's account of the two children who went off with Riddle at the seaside and never were the same again set off all sorts of warning bells. I think he spent the next several weeks determining just what part of the seacoast that orphanage had taken the children to for their summer outings back in the late 1930s and investigating the surrounding cliffs. Not all solutions to wizards' problems are to be found in the wizarding world, after all.

We already know that Riddle likes to revisit the scenes of his earlier triumphs. Albus knows it too. And terrorizing two of the other children to the point of permanently damaging them Riddle would have certainly accounted a triumph. Riddle also has a habit of *acquiring* such properties if he can. I am pretty sure that he himself is the "absent, rich" owner of the Riddle house. And he probably owns the old Gaunt property as well, even if only by means of fiddling the land records in his uncle Morfin's absence. He has certainly taken possession of the cave.

I am convinced that the inner chamber of that cave, the lake, and the fountain are all far older than Riddle, although he may have tampered with any of them. I think that when Riddle returned to the cave as an adult he realized, as Albus did, that the place had "known magic" And searched until he found the entrance.

When Albus got there nearly sixty years later the same principle still applied.

Actually now that we come right down to it, I think that some of Albus's behavior on our trip there with Harry must have also been performance art. He had already gotten into that cave once before. That's how he knew about the Inferi. And he *obviously* already knew about the Inferi. He also obviously knew about the fountain, although he probably hadn't made any serious attempt to drain it on his first trip, just ran some diagnostics on the problem. He evidently decided that getting whatever was hidden there *out* of the fountain would be a nice project in which to involve Harry. And he knew he *needed* such a project.

So. Just what *is* the potion in the Birdbath of Doom, anyway?

Well; it's green.

And it glows.

And it sounds altogether *nasty*.

And if what we all witnessed there was another piece of "performance art", we haven't a clue as to what it actually *does*.

Apart from keeping anyone from touching it, that is. Or getting to anything that may be in the basin with it. We do not know whether it works the way the barrier charm supposedly cast on the staircase does and only keeps out persons who are not wearing a Dark mark. But it is far more likely that it was designed to keep out *everybody*. Although Tom himself may have some handy way of getting past it.

And we can't necessarily believe a word of what Albus told us about it, either. Particularly when even what he *did* tell us was presented as a lot of gosh-and-guesswork.

I'm not convinced that Dumbledore wasn't speculating completely without evidence on the potion's effects. Mostly to play down the risk, so Harry would follow through on his orders. I would certainly not take the accuracy of any his statements regarding it for granted. He couldn't really *know*. He *suspected* that the drinker wouldn't be able to drain the basin on their own initiative, and he was pretty sure that the drinker wouldn't immediately drop down dead. But that is about all he could really count on. Even Felix couldn't show him much more than that.

Of course depending upon just *when* the Horcrux was supposedly put into the cave there is the off-chance that Snape might have been able to fill him in on that potion. But we can't count on that, either. The potion may have been a feature of that cave decades before the Horcrux was. Although it would be hard to account for *why*.

Dumbledore no doubt had sufficient reason to suspect that the potion wouldn't kill him instantly (or possibly at all, although it might make him pretty sick). But, yes, I do think he may have been spinning theories to order to try to put Harry at his ease and make the task more doable, even if not easy, for Harry to go on feeding him the potion, despite its effects.

Or it's *apparent* effects. That could have been acting. Or at least exaggeration.

Of course, one rather ugly suggestion is that the green potion may be an intrinsic part of what *creates* Inferi.

The way that everything on that island is set up, the potion seems to be calibrated to be vile enough to prevent anyone from finishing it off AND to drive its drinker to the lake for water. And no other water source seems to be permitted on that island. Unless Albus was being twisty and vanishing the water Harry summoned himself. But I doubt it, I don't think he would have done anything that would lead Harry to mess with the lake. Touching the water of the lake clearly signals the Inferi to drag you under and drown you.

So one would have to say that the green potion *seems* to be an intrinsic component of a trap. It is possible that the potion is calibrated to work in concert with the lake water to produce an Inferius.

What appears to be missing from this trap, however, is the *bait*. The faintly glimmering green light in the center of the cave might very well draw the curious to check it out. But there is nothing which we were shown about that set-up which would tempt a trespasser to *drink* that potion. (It's *glowing* for heaven's sake!)

And the fact that the boat only takes one wizard at a time makes it unlikely that a prisoner would be brought to the island, forced to drink the potion and shoved in to be drowned. Unless everybody got on and off the island in relays.

Harry could not see the Horcrux lying in the bottom of the basin through the potion. My first reading was that the potion must evidently be opaque. But this may not, in fact, be the case. The potion may, in addition to being luminous, be reflective. *Highly* reflective. So reflective that if the trespasser has any light source of his own — such as a wand casting Lumos, the light so generated will reflect off the surface of the potion and prevent him from seeing into the basin.

In order to see into the basin, the trespasser would need to douse his own light and wait for his eyes to adjust to the dimness until the potion's own luminescence is enough to reveal what is concealed within. Albus and Harry did not do this on their trip into the cave. It is unknown whether Albus did it on his own trip there, alone. If so, he might have seen that the locket in the basin was not the one that disappeared from Hepzibah Smith's collection. But this is not likely to be information that we are going to be filled in on. Or not soon.

But under normal circumstances, there seems to be no reason why anyone who did not already know that something was hidden in the bottom of that basin would risk drinking the potion to get to it.

So, unless there is (as Swythyv put it) some goofy legend about a fountain of youth, or arcane wisdom, or specific knowledge (or unpleasant truths), attached to that Cave and that Fountain, then either wizards are even more feckless than they are usually presented, or there was some *compulsion* involved (although it did not seem to work on Harry, but then, neither does Imperius).

Or Albus was making up "likely stories" on the spur of the moment.

What seems most likely is that Voldemort was gambling on the probability that any trespassers finding a basin of glowing green ook which they could not even touch would eventually just give up and go away. If the Inferi didn't get them first. Which they probably would.

Because, really, the idea of keeping the drinker alive long enough to be questioned only works if security on the place is set up to ensure that any drinker will BE questioned.

And it isn't. There is no monitoring on the cave to alert Voldemort that he has an intruder there. So questioning intruders can't really be the *purpose* of that potion. No one is going to be summoned to question *anybody* in that cave. Voldemort obviously *doesn't care* if the Inferi drown intruders without learning how they got there.

What I think was going on was that, if he didn't have inside information on it already (which, depending upon when the Horcrux was supposed to have been put into the cave, he just might have), Albus was prepared to gamble that a person *could* drink the potion and survive — at least for a while — if he could manage not to be dragged underwater and drowned by the Inferi in the attempt.

Following this script, Albus might even have swallowed a bezoar before departing from the castle with Harry (although that might have interfered with the Felix, so maybe not), or while Harry's back was turned to get him some water after he staged his first "collapse". (Incident #2 of Harry's attention having been deliberately diverted for a critical few moments.) He might have possibly had a vial of Phoenix tears about him, or some other antidote. Possibly even a *specific* antidote, if he was able to bring a sample of the potion out of the cave the first time. Just *something* to keep him going until he kept his appointment on top of the Astronomy tower.

I have also begun to wonder whether the sea cave adventure may not have been another Madam Rosemerta-style *message*. Albus *pretended* to "suddenly realize" that Madam Rosemerta was under Imperius, expecting Harry to take it from there and pass the word to someone in authority. He may have *deliberately* shown Harry where Voldemort's army of Inferi are kept hidden for very much the same reason. And that's a blow that can be struck against the Dark Lord without much risk. All Harry has to do is *tell* somebody. Let's hope the kid figures that out and lets someone know about it *before* Voldemort moves them out of there and puts them into play.

If Albus already *knew* that the Locket was the Horcrux that was *supposed* to be in the sea cave, then to drink the potion must have been one of Dumbledore's purposes for making the trip there. He suspected that he would need somebody's help to do it. He also needed to give Harry a plausible reason which would account for why he later did not, or "could not," defend himself when the DEs cornered him. There had to be a plausible reason to account for the fact that he neither attempted to escape, nor to fight back. At least one that would play for the time being.

He might have set up the required scene establishing his "helplessness" in some other way, but if he *did* know about Reggie, then he probably also knew about the Locket at #12, and that Locket has now gone walkabout. He may have wanted to retrieve the fake in order to introduce the R.A.B. complication to Harry.

Because the real Locket *has* gone missing, and despite following various leads on it all year, he has not been able to relocate it. And now his time for that job has run out. He *has* to pass the torch to Harry.

And, of course, from a meta standpoint Albus had to introduce the great, whopping, red herring of R.A.B. and the adventure of the sea cave Horcrux to the reader in order to distract and confuse us all, so we won't just *automatically* assume that "of course" Albus faked his death; who else is there who might have done so?

But, really, just as with the blasted hand; for all that drinking the potion appeared to leave him staggering, reeling, and falling down in a faint every 20 minutes, it didn't really seem to keep him from *doing* anything, not even some pretty *impressive* things, whenever he actually *needed* to, did it?

Incident #3 of attempting to divert Harry's attention took place on their arrival in Hogsmeade and Albus's second "collapse". This attempt was derailed by Madam Rosemerta. Knowing what we do now, she was undoubtedly instructed to watch from her window for sight of Dumbledore, and to point the Dark mark out to him to draw him back to the castle, and into ambush.

Which brings us right up to the Grand Climax. The private performance on top of the "Lightning-Struck" Tower.

As well as incident #4 of attempting to divert Harry's attention: Dumbledore *appears* to have intended to send Harry to summon Snape to the tower before the invaders got there. We don't know how that particular script was supposed to go. There was probably some alternate plan to immobilize Harry so he wouldn't meddle, if his own prudence didn't dictate discretion.

(Thank heavens for Minerva and Flitwick, otherwise the message might not have gotten through in time.)

And, if the murder was *staged*; the "Severus, please..." pleas were a part of the *performance*. They need no further explanation.

At this point, Rowling diverts our own attention with her statement that one of the first things she settled upon when she set her world up is that dead is dead. Nobody comes back after having passed through true death. I doubt that even "momentarily dead" would pass muster. Not if "dead" is *dead*. This isn't Star Trek.

But she also set up the possibility of *faking* a death, and has already even given us faked deaths as major plot elements in two of the five earlier books. Most spectacularly in the book which is being positioned as containing the underlying pattern for the anticipated Book 7.

And the whole issue of "dead is *dead*" is begging the question *anyway*, since when Rowling set up the Potterverse up she made quite sure that it amply supports the possibility of a *very active* participation from *ghosts*.

Just because most ghosts *don't* actively participate in Potterverse events, doesn't mean they *can't*. And Albus Dumbledore has always made his own rules. Perhaps we ought to take another look at Nearly-Headless Nick's little speech on just why *he* became a ghost at the end of OotP. We *knew* when we first read that speech that it had to be relevant to *something*.

Nick claims that he became a ghost because he was afraid to move on, and that this is a *typical* reason for wizards who manifest as ghosts.

But it's not the *only* reason. We've also been given the example of Professor Binns who simply doesn't seem to realize that he is dead. That's one of the standard *traditional* reasons for manifesting as a ghost.

But the absolutely #1 reason in all literature for manifesting as a ghost is that of having *unfinished business*.

And in any event, in the Potterverse, you *do* evidently get a *choice*.

So for the moment anyway, I am provisionally going to assume that Albus *is* dead. But he is not *gone*.

And Riddle certainly isn't in a position to go whining to the Ministry to have a ghostly Albus Dumbledore confined to Hogwarts, the way Olive Hornsby did to Myrtle (who seems to have lingered out of spite, and spent *her* first few years as a ghost haunting the girls who had teased her, in revenge). Nor does it take a whole lot of imagination to think of any number of ways in which a ghostly Albus Dumbledore could prove to be *much* more of a nuisance to Tom Riddle and his aspirations than a live one *ever* would be. (Be careful what you ask for, Tom.)

I agree that Nick's reasons wouldn't faze Albus. And Albus is much too aware not to realize that he is dead. But that third reason? Oh, yeah. I could see it. I could even see Albus sacrificing his hope of eternal rest in favor of being "neither here nor there" if there was a chance of atoning for the "hugest" mistake he ever made, putting things right, and seeing the former Tom Riddle (whose soul ironically is no longer intact enough to manifest as a ghost) permanently taken out of the world forever.

We've also been hearing about the Draft of Living Death ever since Harry's very first Potions lesson all the way back in Book 1. We've even brewed the stuff now. The references to it could all be set-dressing, or they could be actual hints.

So far there has been no indication that DoLD has played any part in the story to date. But when the author keeps bringing the subject up you can't exactly ignore it.

Until, of course she informed us that Albus really *is* dead. I guess we can dismiss further consideration of it from this particular essay, anyway.

The weak point in any theory is the point at which you feel you have to invent magic which is not already known to be in canon. The minute you have to do that, your theory is probably hosed. Particularly this late in the series.

I seem to have managed to dodge that particular bullet regarding the "modified AK" that I extrapolated back in the original iteration of the Changeling hypothesis in 2003. The spell I extrapolated almost certainly does exist in canon. It's even been refered to. But it isn't a variety of AK. I got the name wrong. Maybe the mechanics, as well. I can live with that. I didn't properly anticipate the name "Horcrux" either

— or the number of them — but I nailed the concept correctly.

Let me say that I am aware that I may not have all of the relevant details correct in the matter of Dumbledore's murder, either. But I think I have some of them, and all of the ones I postulate are at least *plausible*, even if they later turn out to be incorrect.

This reading also complies with the underlying rule that the better theories need to be simple. Just not obvious. Any conspiracy regarding the staging of Albus Dumbledore's murder was pretty elaborate, but the concept is simple enough. And the complicated parts of it are strictly in the mechanics. There are a lot of different threads in this bundle, and they all have to be accounted for.

And it would be a big mistake to try to extrapolate unknown magic here.

Besides, we don't need to.

Rowling has already given us all the pieces we really need in order to account for what we saw. We just have to hunt through the rest of the series to find them.

None of this gives us any explanation as to just why we were *shown* it, of course.

Snape hit Albus squarely in the chest with an AK. By this time Harry has already seen a number of AKs thrown at Albus Dumbledore in the course of the duel in the Atrium a year earlier. He's had a few thrown at himself as well. This one looked just the same. I believe it was absolutely genuine. It had to be. Otherwise Snape was flirting with the 3rd clause of that Vow.

But we have never before seen an AK throw it's victim up in the air.

It didn't do that with the spider. It didn't do that with Frank Bryce. We don't know for sure about Cedric Diggory, since Harry had his eyes tight shut and didn't watch.

But there is NO SUPPORT in canon for the notion that you can invoke one spell and perform another. Snape did NOT say *Avada Kedavra* and mean Levicorpus. He cast an AK. He might have followed it up with a nonverbal levitation spell, but he cast an AK *first*. And we saw it hit Albus squarely in the chest.

We already know that the "unblockability" of an AK basically means that there is no counter-curse, and that no sort of magical shield spells will stop one. Solid inanimate objects will stop one just fine. We've watched them do it.

Inanimate objects take *damage* from spells, since nearly all magic designed to attack living creatures seems to translate into crude physical force when it hits something that isn't alive, but they do keep the spell from getting past.

So, by the time the AK actually hit him, was Albus *already* an inanimate object? Did the green potion foul their timing up by reacting badly with the Elixir of Life (or the Felix, which I really do still think was a factor). Did Snape barely get his AK in *on time* for it to have *read* as a murder?

And when the magic of Snape's AK translated into physical force upon hitting an *inanimate* object, was the force of the *blow* what actually knocked Albus off of the tower.

Is my *original* interpretation of what happened on top of that tower the correct one after all? That Albus died of the *potion*? That it was *Harry* who actually killed him?

Or did the green Potion unravel such immortality as was granted by the Elixir of Life until the curse that blasted his hand reactivated, resumed its progress and it was *Tom Riddle* who killed him after all?

I don't think we are going to find out for certain until Book 7 is out.

But, as soon as you look at that whole sequence from the viewpoint of "what happened is what was *meant* to happen" then the fall from the tower must have been a part of the plan as well. For some reason, it was considered necessary for them to get the body out of sight for a crucial few minutes. And the way they did it was fishy as all get-out.

And if the fall from the tower was a part of the plan, then whatever intensity of AK Snape hit Albus with had to have enough magical force behind it to translate into sufficient physical force to knock Albus off his feet, and off the tower as well. Albus may have even cast a weight reduction charm upon himself during the flight back to the castle to more easily facilitate it.

From rereading the order in which Albus's murder and the fall from the tower took place, above; the AK — which was genuine, even if not "powerful" — blasted Dumbledore into the air, (which was required) and then Snape (or someone) caught him non-*verbally* — which was that split second when he seemed to hang suspended under the Dark mark — and then nonverbally cast *another* spell to slow the fall so that he seemed to "fall slowly" past the battlements. We've already encountered a "slow falling" charm available for their use. Albus cast it on Harry when he fell off his broom in a Quidditch match. The match where Harry passed out from the Dementors swarming the stadium in PoA, in fact.

And we have *no* idea why they must have felt that this was *necessary*.

Or do we? Was getting the body out of the way to make sure that there would be no witnesses when the hoped-for ghost managed to manifest? They couldn't have known how much control they would have over *that*.

Was making him "fall slowly" a mark of *respect*?

While we are at it, when Malfoy disarmed Dumbledore Harry saw Albus's wand fly over the battlements. Ergo: if the death *had* been faked, it was on the ground at the foot of the tower, waiting for him. But, of course Rowling assures us that the death was *not* faked. Or, rather, she assures us that Albus is most sincerely dead.

It's small wonder Dumbledore petrified Harry so he would witness the murder (they needed a witness who would remain at the castle) but couldn't mix in. That would probably have been disastrous.

And while we are on the subject: Snape was also probably the one to remove the Petrificus from Harry once he saw it was safe to do so.

Petrificus Totalus *doesn't* have to be lifted by the person who cast it! Petrificus Totalus is something you learn in First year. It responds to a simple Finite Incantatem — as well as any number of other canceling charms. Harry was barking up entirely the wrong tree when he convinced himself that only the death of Albus Dumbledore could have freed him from the Petrificus. We know better than that — and so does he.

And besides Albus's death demonstrably *didn't* free him.

AK kills *instantly*.

We *saw* it kill the spider. We *know* it killed Cedric as soon as it hit him. Cedric was not "dying" when Harry finally managed to open his eyes. He was dead.

Snape's AK hit Albus Dumbledore squarely in the chest, and blasted his *corpse* into the air and over the battlements to fall to the bottom of the tower.

And Harry was still petrified. He could not move. He could not *scream*. He had to stand there silent and immobile and watch it happen.

He only unfroze once Snape had disappeared into the stairwell. At which point he suddenly realized that he could move again.

Harry isn't thinking at all clearly. And just in case we missed the point, Tonks had *already* released Harry from *Draco's* Petrificus back on the Hogwarts Express at the beginning of the school year. The cancelling spell Tonks used produced a flash of red light. She used something other than the standard Finite Incantatem, probably because Harry couldn't tell her what he was supposed to be canceling. A plain-vanilla Finite Incantatem does not produce pyrotechnic effects, but it will cancel a Petrificus.

The caster's death, however, didn't.

Not *this* time anyway. Maybe it's *supposed* to.

So, why ever might it not have *worked*...?

Well there was one moment; when Snape first burst onto the top of the tower, wand in hand, and did a sweep of the whole area, before one of the DEs spoke up and Albus made his first plea, that Snape could have probably added a 2nd, nonverbal petrificus on top of Albus's. That way when Albus's petrificus was dispersed by his death, Snape's would have held until it was safe to lift it. But Snape would need to be able to see through an invisibility cloak, or at least know where the boy *was* to do that. We have some indication that *Albus* could see through Harry's cloak, or at least see the cloak, even if not who is inside it, but no such suggestions regarding Snape. Is this something that can be taught?

However, we *have* already watched Snape perform a general "area" cancellation charm which nullified all of the spells within a given radius. He used it back in the chapter on the dueling club in CoS. He wouldn't have even needed to know Harry's exact location in order to *release* him. He only needed to know that Harry was *there*.

And if this was a staged performance, then he certainly knew that Harry was there. Albus would have told him that he was taking Harry out of the castle with him.

What we seem to have in operation here is a variant of the device known as the "unreliable narrator". The tight focus on Harry's PoV can make for some very unreliable narration — when Rowling needs it to. And, for the record, I also contend that this is a deliberate piece of authorial misdirection, not a new piece of information about how magic works. Rowling has already shown us how *this particular* type of magic works. *Not* the way Harry is trying to convince us (and himself) that it does.

And then Snape had to chivvy the DEs out of the castle.

Small wonder he was overwrought by the time Harry caught up to him down at the main gates and tried to fight him. And for Potter to be trying to fight him was just the icing on the cake.

Snape must have been on tenterhooks as to whether or not their plan had really worked as intended until Albus's message reached him the day of the funeral, and put his mind at rest. I mean, really! If you accept the premise that it was a conspiracy to stage a *murder*, and you can't stay to find out whether or not it went as planned… it's small wonder a control freak like Snape was in such a state.

It has also been pointed out, over on the TEA AT SPINNER'S END board, that just about all of the thugs that Malfoy smuggled into the Castle who were at liberty to do so, had a go at attacking Harry during the escape-and-pursuit down to the main gates. Fenrir tackled him, knocked him down, and would have savaged him. The Carrows hexed him from behind. The "Big Blond" (probably either the elder Crabbe or Goyle, who were identified as the largest of the DEs at the graveyard assembly two years before, if you remember) even hit him with Crucio. And Snape put a stop to it all with the exhortation to remember their orders that Potter belonged to the Dark Lord. Before he Apparated away, pursued by a hippogriff.

After first giving the boy a last dueling lesson, and then turning him over to Hagrid.

And, right about now, maybe we ought to go back and question whether it really was Neville who petrified Greyback after all.

Neville was certainly the only one of the defenders who was in a position to do it. Everyone else was engaged in one-on-one battles by the time Harry scrambled out from under Greyback's petrified body, and they weren't likely to have been in any position to have been watching out for Harry a moment earlier. Particularly since from their point of view the battle had been ongoing for some time and their enemies had just gotten reinforcements. Neville was down, having been injured earlier in the melee, but he was still armed and still conscious.

The order in which the raiding party started down from the tower was: Malfoy, Greyback, the brother-sister act (who by this time put one strongly in mind of a pair of overexcited pugs), Snape, and Brutal-Face.

The defenders let Malfoy and Snape through. Harry had already petrified Brutal-Face. As soon as he emerged from the stairwell, he caught a glimpse of Snape whipping around the corner at the end of the hall when Greyback broke away from another fight and tackled him. Somebody petrified Greyback and Harry scrambled up to find that everyone but Neville was engaged in a one-on-one battle. He mixed in and once three of the invaders broke away and the hall cleared a bit, he pursued them.

So. Okay. Harry *heard* the "Petrificus Totalus!" which got Greyback. It was cast verbally. Which argues in favor of it having indeed been Neville who cast it.

On the other hand, if Snape and Albus were in cahoots since before Harry's birth (Which is gone into in some detail in other essays posted on the Red Hen web site), Snape knows *exactly* how important Harry is to the ongoing mission to take out Voldemort, and he knows that Harry is right behind him, about to run straight into a clutch of Voldemort's most vicious fighters.

Tonks says she heard Snape shout something although she couldn't be sure of what. It could have just been the "It's over!" announcement. Or possibly not.

It would have looked highly suspicious for Snape to hold back in his "retreat" while he was still in the hallway among the castle defenders, but, how do we know that he did not whip around the corner, urge Malfoy on, and, in his character as "Leader", take one last look, and, just maybe, fire off one last hex?

After all, we *know* what Snape thinks of werewolves.

But, I think the only way we are going to find out the truth will be if Harry tries to discover who saved him in order to thank them, and none of the defenders will admit to it. Given the frequency with which we've heard Harry actually express his gratitude to the people who keep saving his bacon, I'd give the subject about a 30% chance of coming up at all.

Snape definitely *did* put a stop to the Big Blond's Crucio with the exhortation that Potter belonged to the Dark Lord. Snape had certainly not mentioned any orders to the effect of Potter "belonging" to the Dark Lord the summer before at Spinner's End, and Bellatrix would have regarded such a justification inarguable.

So either this was a more recent order which was given since the face-off in Snape's sitting room, (quite possible, since that was nearly a year earlier) or Snape improvised, on the spur of the moment, knowing that it would almost certainly be accepted — since it chimed in tune with the orders from the previous year, when everyone was to leave Potter alone until Voldemort had heard the whole Prophecy. He was taking a risk that none of these clowns will mention that "reminder" in Voldemort's hearing, but I think he may have second-guessed the Dark Lord's wishes in any case. Or, that may have *been* their orders. Or, at least, *his* orders.

And there is always Obliviate.

And Fawkes, who could Apparate to London on a nanosecond's notice to eat an AK on Dumbledore's behalf last year, *this* year can't be arsed to haul his tail feathers to the top of a tower of the same castle? Oh puh-*leeze*. This event was just SO *planned*…

Which brings us to those "silent partner(s)" in the conspiracy.

If any.

I'm pretty sure that there was at least *one* more person involved, even though not one who was fully *informed*.

I, for one, am not *at all* convinced that the DEs put a barrier on the staircase. Nor have we ever heard of magical barriers which can be demolished by a stray hex. Magical barriers are designed to *repel* hexes. And falling masonry, too.

And just whose purpose did that barrier *really* serve? Would the DEs have *cared* if the battle followed them up to the top of the tower?

But *Albus* would care.

The *last* thing he would want would be for his staff or the Order to start messing with the staging of his murder. Particularly not with Harry invisible and immobilized and unable to get out of the way of a melee.

I think we've got another Book 6 = Book 2 moment.

After all, we watched Dobby pull *exactly* the same "throw him through the air" number on Lucius Malfoy at the end of CoS, didn't we? On a *staircase*, too, thank you very much. Dobby snuck in and played a very *active* part in the resolution of book 2. I think he may have done it again.

And the mark of a good House Elf is that he *isn't seen*, unless he *chooses* to be.

I think Albus sent Harry off to "get his cloak", and then he summoned Dobby and asked him to monitor the staircase.

Dobby wasn't really a party to the events going on up on the top of the tower. He was just standing guard on the staircase and keeping the staff, the kids, and the Order members from getting up the stairs. Albus absolutely did NOT want them messing with his murder. And I don't think he'd have left that kind of thing to chance if he didn't have to. And he *didn't* have to. Dobby *trusts* the Headmaster.

So Dobby had his orders: let Malfoy and the DEs go up to the top of the tower. Keep everyone else out until Professor Snape comes and takes the DEs away. And Dobby would have happily spent all night keeping people out if it had been necessary.

So much for curse-breaking masonry. Once Snape went up the stairs, and started herding the DEs back down, Dobby's job was done and he went back to his quarters.

There has to have been at least one more member of the cast, however. Unless Albus has his staff so well trained that he could leave them to wrap the matter up without direction. Albus was dead and Snape was gone. *Somebody* was going to have to wrap the business up in a tidy bow, and to arrange for a nice gaudy, *conspicuous* funeral so Voldemort will be certain to get the message that he has won this round.

Minerva is the most likely suspect, of course. She had the authority to make all of the arrangements. And she was also the one who sent Flitwick to fetch Snape — and was able to tell Flitwick exactly where to find him, too. But Minerva's reaction when she learned of Dumbledore's death (or, more specifically, that Snape had *murdered* him) would have been hard to fake, and she hasn't been set up as being any kind of an actress. She nearly fainted.

And *could* Snape and Albus *really* have kept Hagrid out of it? I really, truly doubt it. This was a "Dumbledore's men" production all the way. With Snape (as usual) cast as the villain, Harry as witness, and Hagrid as chief mourner.

And Hagrid is the one — the only one — who seems to have actually dealt with the body. Carried it into the castle and laid it out, probably in Dumbledore's own rooms. And later carried the corpse, wrapped in its pall to the place of internment.

And of course no one could possibly have cast any doubts upon the "genuine-ness" of the matter, in the face of such profound grief as Hagrid's, could they? Hagrid is virtually incapable of dissembling, isn't he?

Well, yes. I'm sure that everyone involved in the plot was counting on that widespread assumption.

But, contrary to most appearances, Hagrid *can* keep a secret. He sometimes blurts what is at the top of his mind, but he only blurts among people he trusts, those he is confident are all on the same side. He has never, not even once, *what-ever* the provocation, let anything indiscrete slip out in the presence of, say, Malfoy. He's a bit like Snape, in that regard. I very much doubt that Snape has ever thrown one of his tantrums among his fellow Death Eaters.

For example: what would you be willing to wager against the probability that Hagrid has known the identity of the barman at the Hog's Head ever since Aberforth Dumbledore took up his post there? And in what must be at least 40 years, if not longer, he has never even dropped a *hint*?

Of course Hagrid is *aware* that he tends to blurt. And he trusts Dumbledore absolutely. He would not have insisted upon knowing the full details of the plot. What he knew — if anything — is that Voldemort wants Dumbledore dead, and that Dumbledore is going to do something.

Hagrid doesn't know what, he doesn't know how, he doesn't know when, and he certainly does not know that Snape is going to be the one to *kill* him.

But when you step back and take a hard look, it seems rather interesting to reflect that whereas in PoA Hagrid was fulminating over the perfidious Sirius Black and growling that if he got his hands on him he would rip him limb from limb, he makes no such vengeful statements directed at Severus Snape. Indeed that statement of his that Dumbledore "must have told Snape to go with them Death Eaters" now sounds suspiciously like one of our regulation Hagridian blurts.

And, even later, when all voices are raised in vilification of Severus Snape, we notice that Hagrid's voice (and Flitwick's for that matter) is conspicuously absent from the chorus. Indeed I cannot think of any point in the entire six books where Hagrid has *ever* uttered a single word against Severus Snape.

And by the time he shows up in the hospital wing he is in such a flood of tears that it deflects any impulse to *question* him. He remains behind this barrier of tears all through the funeral as well.

And we may have one more backstage helper in this production as well.

With this one I am less certain. The matter *could* be exactly what it appears.

But it really does seem just a *bit* much to expect us all assume that after micromanaging the affair practically all the way to the final curtain call, that the conspirators should then just sit back and leave it to *chance* to get the false Horcrux out of Albus's pocket and pass it on it to Harry.

I mean, a fat lot of good it would have done anybody left in Albus's pocket for Hagrid — or Minerva — to find! But isn't it a bit late in the evening to be introducing a *totally random* element to the proceedings?

However, if *that* was stage-managed as well, then we may have some reason to believe that Albus *knew* that the locket in the cave was a fake.

So what is the situation: Harry and Hagrid approach the crowd gathering around something at the base of the tower. There is a gap for them to get through. And there they find Albus lying on the ground, spread-eagle, his glasses askew, a trickle of blood from his mouth. Harry does not actually see the locket at all. He only discovers it a moment later because he managed to kneel on it.

Somehow, my attention manages to snag on what must surely be the most irrelevant detail in that whole description.

Why blood?

Corpses don't *bleed*, properly speaking. Their hearts are no longer pumping blood at high enough pressure for it to leak out through a break in the circulatory system. Not unless it is a *large* break. Or it is getting some help from the force of gravity. But Albus was lying face *up*. And he had fallen *slowly*. He wouldn't have hit the ground at full force. And any damage would have been to his *back*, not an artistic little trickle from his mouth.

Neither an AK *nor* the green potion are likely to have made him *bleed*.

Yet we have seen blood used "artistically" in this manner before, haven't we?

Dragon's blood. A little dusty now, but possibly still "useful".

It isn't particularly difficult to draft out a script wherein Slughorn (death-scenes tableaux on a 2-minute notice, a specialty) was waiting at the base of the tower to catch the body as it fell. He would have set the scene, arranged the body, (welcomed the ghost, if it manifested) made sure the robes were decently covering Albus's skinny old legs, and taken the false Horcrux out of the pocket and gotten it open. Then he would have lurked until the crowd showed up (pretending to be a bush?), mingled in, and when Harry approached the body he would have conjured the locket into position for him to kneel on.

No, not difficult at all. I'm just not totally convinced it *happened*.

I do know that if it *did* happen the Props Manager *would* have been Slughorn. He would have been glad to do it too. It would have given him a perfect reason to be out of the castle while the DEs were invading it.

Horace Slughorn is an incorrigible old showman. But I think that Albus *appreciated* a good show. And they worked *very* well together. Horace had *already* passed the Potions's book, *another* critically important item, to Harry. Which I'm sure was Albus's plan. And apart from Snape, Slughorn *is* the only member of the staff who has some knowledge of their Horcrux problem. So it is not all that much of a *stretch*.

Although I do think he overplayed his hand a bit with that trickle of blood.

I really do expect the school to remain closed for the coming year. Or at least for the Autumn term. But it will not be empty. At the very least, Hagrid, who is remaining at Hogwarts anyway, will have to move indoors, since his hut is uninhabitable. The castle is Trelawney's home as well. And the House Elves'.

And by the time the students board the Hogwarts Express to return to London (which hasn't happened yet in canon, actually), the rest of the Order of the Phoenix also would have known that Albus is still around.

Albus was in attendance at his own funeral. One way or another. He had an important message to send out, after all.

Albus Dumbledore's grand public send-off was a fine bit of communication all round. It sent a loud, obvious message of the end of an era to the Ministry and to the Wizarding world in general.

It sent a loud and clear message to Lord Voldemort, as well.

It also sent another, not so loud, somewhat different message to the members of his Order. Nearly all of whom, even his brother Aberforth, were in attendance at it.

We know that the members of the Order of the Phoenix communicate with each other by means of their Patroni.

Patroni, as we know, are silver-white. And each one's form is unique.

Albus Dumbledore's Patronus always took the form of a Phoenix.

Harry was sure for a moment that he saw the form of a Phoenix rising joyfully from the white smoke and the (bright, white) funeral fires.

Which disappeared into the blue, no doubt bearing its message to one particular Order member who was *not* at the funeral.

Was this Albus's Patronus? I'm sure we will find out eventually.

And the Order all now knows that he may be dead, but he is not gone.

And, now for the $64,000 question:

Why?

Why should Rowling go out of her way to inject such a monumental level of ambiguity into the question of the death of Albus Dumbledore?

Because she clearly put a lot of *work* into making the whole thing such a masterpiece of confusion and contradiction.

She's the author: she *could* have written the murder of Albus Dumbledore simply, powerfully and effectively, and instead she has chosen to make it flashy, melodramatic, and confusing. I doubt this was either by accident or through any lack of confidence as a writer.

As somebody over at Spinner's End pointed out, the whole thing is practically seamless. Every single questionable detail supports two just about equally valid interpretations. One of these supports the reading that Dumbledore is dead, and the other, just as convincingly supports the reading that he isn't. But if she *wanted* us to suspect that the death may have been faked, why did she go out of her way to deny it a year later?

Of course the very fact that there *is* such a stacking order of ambiguous details is in itself highly suspicious. Because if Rowling had *wanted* the matter to be clear, there would be no question about it. The AK would have hit him and he would have fallen down dead and there would be *no question*. He's dead, Jim. Move on.

Instead, we have the present morass of confusion and contradictions. This end result simply did not happen by accident. Ms Rowling is one tricky customer, and she clearly *intends* for us to be confused. Something is fishy here, and there is more of a twist to this tale than we are picking up. We simply don't have the proper context for something that really *matters*.

But then, flashy, melodramatic and confusing isn't exactly an *unfamiliar* combination with Rowling, is it? I don't think you can *get* much more confusing than the climax of OotP (which she wouldn't even let us *watch*).

But I think our real parallel here is the last few chapters of GoF. In fact the climax of GoF and the climax of HBP can practically serve as a pair of bookends wherein first Voldemort, and then Dumbledore see to it that Harry he is rendered immobile and silent and then forced to watch as one's servant mutilates himself in order to facilitate the one's return, and then the other's servant mutilates his soul to facilitate the other's departure. (One wonders whether the mysterious overheard quarrel is supposed to be a companion piece to the discussion in the opening chapter of GoF wherein Pettigrew offers to find some *other* wizard to serve as a blood donor for Voldemort's return, rather than Harry Potter, and is overborne.)

Nor is that the only possible GoF parallel. There is also the nagging issue as to whether AK throws its victim into the air.

It doesn't do that in an enclosed space, anyway. Both the spider and Frank Bryce were murdered indoors and they fell where they stood. We *were* shown that much. But it turns out that we've got another very screwy account over the murder of Cedric Diggory, which we weren't permitted to actually witness.

At the point of the confrontation leading to that death, Wormtail had been approaching the two boys in the graveyard. He is stated to have paused next to a towering grave marker "only six feet away" from them and the three of them stare at one another. Then Voldemort gave his order to kill the spare, Harry was hit by a headache, shut his eyes, heard the swish of the wand and Pettigrew's Avada Kedavra, followed by a heavy thump next to him.

He pried his eyes open to see Cedric lying on the ground, dead. Wormtail grabbed him, forced him over to that towering grave marker (still only 6 feet away) turned him around shoved him up against the stone, bound him to it and gagged him.

It then states that Harry saw Cedric's body lying "some 20 feet away," with Harry's own wand lying at his feet, and the TriWizard Cup beyond.

Where is a continuity editor when you need one?

Preferably one who can *count.*

Point: Harry heard Cedric fall *next* to him. Not some 14 feet away.

Point: he seems to have *dropped* his own wand when the pain of the Voldemort-induced headache blindsided him. He did not toss it across the graveyard.

Point: the wand is still lying *next* to Cedric's body.

This is just plain sloppy writing, and I am not convinced it means *anything* except that some editor wasn't on the ball. We certainly cannot draw any safe conclusions from such a mess of internally inconsistent data as that.

I am inclined to think that the deliberate confusion of the climax of HBP is intimately linked to another bit of deliberate confusion, namely, the "grand contradiction" between Albus and Sybill's conflicting accounts of what happened the night of the first Prophecy. The first of these incidents marks the beginning of Harry's part in this story arc. The second incident refers back to that beginning and moves us into position for the beginning of the end of the series.

Which, if Rowling holds to the established pattern that she has set up; wherein the first three books of the series are being echoed by the last three; we will have already seen enacted in proxy form in the climax and conclusion of Book 3: HARRY POTTER AND THE PRISONER OF AZKABAN.

Which in comparison with the last three books was a masterpiece of clarity.

For that matter PS/SS and CoS had nice, clear resolutions as well, comparatively speaking. Even though there was a great deal going on in all of them. Rowling *can* write a satisfactory climax if she *wants* to.

The official climax of PoA was the race back through time to save Sirius Black and Buckbeak. In the course of it we got the mass Dementor attack in which Harry discovers his true "Patron," his protector, and it turns out to be himself.

But the part of the book that really connects with the reader, the part that sticks in the mind long after finishing it, isn't so much Harry's epiphany by the lake, but the confrontation and revelations in the Shrieking Shack.

The whole course of action over the progress of PoA was structured to lead up to that confrontation in the Shack. Pettigrew's escape and the rescue of Sirius Black (and Buckbeak) feel almost like an afterthought.

If Book 7 is a reflection of PoA there is no way that Rowling is not going to give us a redux of the confrontation in the Shack. It's just too major an element to omit.

But this time it is possible that she may hold it back to the very end of the story, *after* the threat of Voldemort has been settled.

I think that all through HBP she was "moving furniture" to get her stage set up to throw us all back into the same frame of mind that we were in at the opening of PoA.

She had a much easier job of setting the scene in PoA. She could arbitrarily introduce Sirius Black, who we'd only heard mentioned once before in the whole series, as the enemy without a jot of background. Absolutely nobody questioned the implication that Sirius Black was Harry's enemy from page 1. Any background information she fed to us later, in the course of the book.

Sirius Black was the enemy; the first time Harry saw Sirius's picture, Harry thought that he looked *exactly* like a vampire; he was Voldemort's second-in-command; he had betrayed Harry and his parents, he had murdered Peter Pettigrew (the Potters' *true* friend) — along with a dozen Muggles in front of a whole street of witnesses, and now he was stalking Harry. And by the time the two came face to face Harry "hated him more than he hated Lord Voldemort."

Sound *familiar*, much?

If this is what she is up to — and I am confident that it is — it's a much more tricky balancing act than she had back in PoA.

Back in PoA we hadn't anything but the apparent flip-flop of Sirius Black having suddenly gone from being James Potter's "inseparable" best friend to the official Ministry viewpoint of his being Voldemort's 2nd-in-command, without *anyone* ever having suspected a change in his allegiance, to make us suspicious. I mean, really, looked at logically, this story made absolutely *no sense*, and not everyone in the wizarding world bought it (Rosemerta didn't, for one). But none of *us* ever questioned it over the course of the book. We were nowhere near as aware of just how tricky Rowling is back in 1999.

But this time she has built up six whole books of apparent familiarity with the character that she is now shoving into the Sirius Black role, and while she might misdirect us all over the place she cannot altogether make us forget that we've been watching Snape for several years now. She has hedged her bets by holding back all sorts of information about him, and not really giving us much to work from when trying to interpret him. But we know even less about Remus Lupin (to say nothing of Peter Pettigrew — which is what *she* usually does), and yet have far fewer suspicions of there being any great mystery about *him* to solve.

If we are building towards another Shrieking Shack revelation/reversal, then what she did over the course of HBP was to deliberately weight the scales in the opposite direction in order to tear down the confidence that the reader had built up in the character of Severus Snape over the previous 5 books. By this time, we are *supposed* to hate Snape as much as Harry does.

And I suspect that over the course of Book 7 we will be given even more apparent reasons to do so.

We will learn more of Snape's history through the lens of any number of 3rd-parties' current biases — now that they believe him to be a traitor, and a murderer, and Lord Voldemort's second-in-command — and the surface reading of this information will not show in Snape's favor.

We will almost certainly get some sort of equivalent to the Three Broomsticks eavesdropping scene complete with information that will sound very bad indeed, but like that discussion in the Three Broomsticks, will ultimately prove nothing but that people are determined to interpret what they see according to their biases. I suspect that whatever interaction Snape may have had with Lily Evans (if any) could come out during this sequence. It will *not* do Snape any credit.

But, just to make a tentative prediction: I think that despite Voldemort (who may be flitting in and out of sight as much as the Grim did in PoA — something of ill-omen will be anyway) and the hunt for the Horcruxes, and the probability that the story is going to be wall-to-wall with Dementors, I am pretty much convinced that Snape's role as a fugitive in Book 7 is going to take a fairly central position. Book 7 is going to be as much about Severus Snape as PoA was about Sirius Black

And just what did we finally *learn* in the Shrieking Shack, *last* time?

We learned that the enemy we've been dodging all through the book *isn't* the enemy. He *isn't* the traitor. He *wasn't* the one who betrayed Harry's parents. Or certainly not *intentionally* — although his actions contributed to that betrayal. And he has been trying to *protect* Harry, not kill him.

The *real* traitor was someone else entirely, someone *nobody* ever suspected. Someone whom *everyone* had trusted. Someone everyone believed to have been foully murdered — by Sirius, before multiple witnesses. And it was *that* murder, not the betrayal of the Potters, which has made him a fugitive.

Sound familiar?

Which means that we older fans who for some years have been convinced that somehow Peter Pettigrew was going to prove to be monumentally significant to the resolution of the series may have been a bit off-target.

Oh, sure, Peter will no doubt be awarded his little Gryffindor moment, and probably will go out in a teensy blaze of glory. In any event, he's toast. But it isn't Peter Pettigrew himself which is going to prove significant, it is his former *role*.

And in the final reckoning, Albus Dumbledore will be playing that role.

Let me explain myself.

I am trying to project the final conclusion of the story arc according to what I interpret as an underlying pattern to the series as it has already played out to this point. And Snape being "Dumbledore's man" fits that pattern better than any other possible interpretation.

Indeed this is a major component of the pattern. If Snape is *not* Dumbledore's man, then I have misinterpreted the whole pattern of the series.

I may turn out to have been taking another scenic cruise down the Martian canals, but I *am* discerning a *pattern* here. And I see too many indications that the pattern really *is* there to be able to dismiss the "Snape is Dumbledore's man" component any more than I can dismiss all of the indications that Harry is the 6th Horcrux.

The most prominent indication of this pattern that I am seeing at the moment is that — based upon the last two books and their echoes and reflections of the first two books — I AM CONVINCED that we are being set up to watch Book 7 echo and reflect major elements, and indeed the primary thrust of PoA. And events over the course of HBP have conspired to put Snape into the position of stepping directly into the role previously played by Sirius Black. I mean, really, can anyone claim that Snape's position *right now* in the story arc, is significantly different from Black's position at the opening of PoA?

The "great revelation" of PoA was that — all previous indications notwithstanding — Sirius Black was NOT the traitor. He was NOT the enemy. He was trying to PROTECT Harry, not to kill him. The "traitor" was someone whom everyone had trusted and who was believed to have died at Black's hand.

I am confident that this pattern will repeat in Book 7.

Ergo: Snape is Dumbledore's man. Dumbledore is not gone. Dumbledore deliberately enabled the partial Prophecy to escape.

So, just for fun, let's *literally* bring back the Shack. This is a speculation, not an actual prediction, but I suppose something like it *could* happen.

Snape, who was in at the death of Lord Voldemort, and whose actions contributed to the final outcome, but probably ambiguously enough that it is still not clear whose side he was on, Disapparates from the scene of Voldemort's final defeat.

The trio follow. They find themselves in the Shack, which is outside the Apparition barriers of Hogwarts. They corner Snape and disarm him, they have him down.

Harry of course is shouting accusations of everything Snape ever did to fit up his parents', Dumbledore's murder, supposed actions undertaken during Book 7, what have you. Snape hears him out, very much playing the Sirius Black role, only perhaps with considerably less charm and rather more style. Harry is working himself up to kill him, as he had intended to kill Sirius, when Fawkes suddenly appears, gets in between them and won't budge.

And then Snape tells them that everything he did—

"Was done on my orders." Says Albus (ghostly or otherwise), from behind the trio.

Following this bombshell comes the big exposition that to deploy the Prophecy seemed the only way that they could have tricked Voldemort into setting up the conditions of his own destruction.

Because when the final reversal comes, I am convinced that Albus will be there to share in it. It will not be *all* about Snape, alone. And that is about the only way that Rowling will be able to keep Snape from walking away with the whole book.

It cannot be very often that one gets a Hero, *and* an anti-Hero, *and* a Villain, all in a series marketed to children. But we definitely seem to have one of each. And you have to sit on anti-Heroes, or they will run away with the whole show. Not many other character types have the authority to keep an anti-Hero like Snape under restraint. I'd say Albus is probably our best bet. Maybe our *only* bet. Harry certainly can't do it. He hasn't the presence.

And it will be Harry's choice as to how to take their information that finally "reveals" to us what *he* is.

Oh, yeah, Harry forgives the pair of them. Even if the decision to turn the Prophecy loose *was* stupid, and wrong, and unworthy and Albus and Severus both *admit* that it was stupid, and wrong and unworthy. By that time Harry will realize that the stakes were much higher than just himself and his parents. And that Sirius Black had managed to bolix up everyone's careful plans to protect them.

But about that death.

I've had over a year to think through the death of Albus Dumbledore and a couple of side issues have occurred to me regarding the established traditions pertaining to the deaths of great wizards as they are presented in literature and folklore.

I'm not sure that the traditions are something that we can afford to overlook.

Merlin, Gandalf, whoever (although those two are the ones most built to the established tradition, Tolkein was following a template far older than he was):

Their "official deaths" all seem to have something in common.

They don't leave bodies.

Usually nobody actually *sees* them die. Or, not and have them stay dead, anyway.

And they definitely don't leave tombs where, over the next couple of hundred years, somebody's bound to get the bright idea to break into it and steal the *bones*.

Instead, they usually just disappear.

Generally in some manner shrouded in Mystery.

Which makes Dumbledore's death — and even more to the point, his *funeral* — very, very unusual when regarded in a traditional context.

And even more convinces me that Albus just isn't *in* that white tomb.

Even if he *is* dead.

What strikes me as being most in character for the death, or perhaps I ought to say the *departure*, of a Great Wizard, would be for him to reappear briefly *after* the hero has completed his great task, and to take a highly visible part in mopping up the stray odds and ends and seeing to it that justice is done to all of the active participants —

[Which in this case is an *absolutely necessary* function if any kind of justice is to *be* done. If Snape and Albus have been in cahoots ever since before Harry was born, then Snape has *never* really acted independently, and he has nothing really to atone *for*, apart from a nasty disposition; and yet he has *always* been required to play the villain. Things cannot help but to look very black indeed for him without Albus to Explain It All. — It might also be nice for Harry to be able to actually make *use* of Sirius's house without having to bring any new friends in blindfolded every time they visit, since they cannot *see* the place, and for his kids to be able to find their way home unassisted.]

— and then to slip away quietly without fanfare. Typically in some mysterious manner leaving people to make up their own explanations and probably spin some "goofy legend" that if the need were ever great enough he might come back.

What Dumbledore actually got was your boilerplate Hero's send-off, or more accurately, the tribute to a great King.

You can just *about* rationalize this on the grounds that he *was* allegedly one of "yesterday's heroes", and he was very close to being the uncrowned King of wizarding Britain. But he wasn't serving the *function* of a "hero" in the story. *Or* that of a King. He was serving the *function* of the "wise old wizard".

So for all that his funeral was very moving, I'm not sure it really *fits*.

I mean, wouldn't you say that it was rather *overdone*?

What *would* fit the traditional template (*and* Rowling's established pattern) would be first; for Harry and his allies to settle Voldemort; and THEN Albus would make his final appearance, do his usual debriefing, make sure that no one is going to suffer for their actions in the war who doesn't *deserve* to, and then quietly slip away from the resulting celebration and step through the Veil.

I mean, we all *know* that eventually we are going to be getting back to that Veil.

Indeed, what would fit the template very well indeed, would be for Albus to make his rather subtle personal farewells to various individuals, in the course of circulating at some crowded, overblown Ministry wrap-up, and for Harry to notice after a while that he is no longer in sight, suddenly realize what Albus has done and race down into the Department of Mysteries too late to see anything but the Veil still fluttering in the breeze of his passing.

And if the pattern holds, it will be Snape who keeps him from following.

And it will be Hagrid who reminds him that he has friends to grieve if he should run off before his time.

The Usual Suspects

We have now reached the equivalent point that in a classic "puzzler" murder mystery would herald the signal for the entire cast of suspects to assemble in the library where the Great Detective would now proceed to Explain It All to them. During this exposition, the villain is invariably unmasked before all witnesses in a manner that Albus Dumbledore would most heartily endorse, and led off to justice in police custody. Indeed, this is a template so certain to have had Professor Dumbledore's approval that I am a bit astonished that Hercule was not among his string of primary and secondary names. (Although one is forced to admit that his individual style is more reminiscent of that of Miss Jane Marple.)

Unfortunately for the Harry Potter fandom, there is no Great Detective at hand, and even Albus Dumbledore is currently unavailable. Furthermore, we will not have the final set of clues in our hands until the release of Book 7, which is as yet unannounced, but generally anticipated to be unveiled at some point during the summer of 2007. The "mystery" is demonstrably not yet solved.

Still, having spent an entire collection individually weighing the evidence presented to us over the course of HARRY POTTER AND THE HALF-BLOOD PRINCE, *the natural progression is for us to now direct our attention ahead, to our expectations of the yet impenetrable mysteries of Book 7. What we confidently expect to see answered; what we hope to be able to expect to see answered; what we expect the answers to turn out to be.*

As with the LiveJournal "experience" in chapter 5, this is a community effort, undertaken by the cast of players. And, as is in keeping with such an inherently "staged" event as the "confrontation in the library," may we beg your indulgence for our failings, and hope that you have found, and will continue to find, our efforts both entertaining and edifying. — J. Odell

Brandy and Revelations in the Library

ELL, IT LOOKS AS THOUGH I rather anticipated the purpose of this particular chapter in the winding up of my main piece in the previous chapter, wherein I laid out my conviction that we were all being set up to watch some version of a redux of the events of Book 3, THE PRISONER OF AZKABAN, play out in Book 7. (An interpretation of the underlying pattern of the series that W. B. Harte has dubbed "the Unified Theory of Everything".) But, I think that after all I am not going to explore that issue very deeply here (it would take far too long). But it seems to me that we might reasonably take a closer look at the whole subject of "expectations" in itself.

Just what are we, the readers, *entitled* to feel that we may reasonably expect from the conclusion of a series as complex as that of The Adventure of Harry Potter and the Dark Lord?

We have manifestly arrived at the end of an era. The final action of the adventure will take place off Dumbledore's watch. At least officially. As I state throughout the Red Hen collection, Albus Dumbledore may indeed be most sincerely dead, but I suspect he isn't *gone*. One way or another I think he will make it to the last page and depart peacefully after the crisis is resolved.

Which makes me rather hopeful regarding the pattern that Rowling appears to have established for the last three books of her series, in which she repeats the themes and mimics the events of the first three books. The indications are that the events of Book 7 might be expected to reflect the events of Book 3. The real question is: how much can we depend upon this. Because it seems to me that the salient point of the conclusion of PoA is that nobody and nothing died of it. In fact, we do not know of a single death that took place during that entire year. This is unlikely to be the case with Book 7. However:

The final climax of PoA was not about the destruction of things but the saving of them.

Earlier in the book, Scabbers was believed to have been killed. But he wasn't. He faked it.

MUCH earlier in the story arc, Peter Pettigrew was believed to have been murdered. But he wasn't. He faked it.

The Fat Lady really *was* attacked, but she got away, unhurt.

Buckbeak was *condemned* and scheduled for execution, but he escaped.

And Harry's primary actions at the final show-down were to forgive the traitor and to save the innocent.

He braved the willow and followed the Grim to rescue Ron.

He couldn't bring himself to kill Crookshanks, even though that meant sparing Sirius Black, who he "hated more than Voldemort" by that time (is that an echo I hear?).

Query: just how much did Sirius Black owe the cosmic balance for his part in the werewolf caper? And to whom? For he wronged just about everyone involved in the matter except Pettigrew. Did he fully repay that cosmic debt? Did he repay it by spending 12 years in Azkaban, or did his debt require that additional year immured in the Black family hell and a quick trip through the Veil?

Harry deliberately and voluntarily spared Pettigrew. Who, by then, he *knew* had betrayed him and his parents to Lord Voldemort.

He then went on to make considerable effort to save Buckbeak AND Sirius Black.

And, in reward for this, he managed to connect with the one part of James Potter which still lived on within himself — which is the only part that still matters.

So how much of this can we expect to see transposed to Book 7?

Such as:

A MAJOR issue that I think is going to occupy the emotional payoff of Book 7 involves the fallout attendant upon Harry finally discovering, or figuring out, what was really going on concerning the death of Albus Dumbledore.

Because things are simply *not* as they seem related to that death, even if my own interpretation of the events turns out to be wrong. And, after my last round of dodging toppling dominoes, I think that Rowling is saving this bombshell up for the grand finale.

Rowling has been dropping anvil-sized hints for the past few years that there are some real horrors in store for Harry Potter. Claiming that *she* would not want to be him, since she knows what is going to happen to him. I do not think she was tossing out red herrings in those statements.

The fans, of course, have taken these statements and run with them, proposing all sorts of gaudy, but ultimately rather unimaginative scenarios involving Crucio, or disfigurement, or of having to see more people that matter to him die.

I do not say that none of these things will happen in Book 7. There is a better than average chance that Harry will catch another round of Crucio over the course of book 7. And a *much* better than average chance that he will have to see someone else (apart from Lord Voldemort) die in it.

But I really don't think that those are the horrors that Rowling has in mind. And I think Albus's death is intimately connected with the ones she does mean. And Albus's past *life*, and past *actions*, are even more relevant to them.

But, when you stop and think about it, she has given herself one monster of an agenda that needs to be met in the final book of this series. By this time there have been so many questions raised that merely to hunt down the Horcruxes, bring Lord Voldemort to bay and destroy him would probably leave the reader feeling curiously unsatisfied. I wouldn't be astonished to find that Book 7 turns out to be the longest book in the series, after all.

For example:

We all need to know what was going on with Albus's death. At least to the point of knowing whether Albus had deliberately *chosen* to die at that time in that manner. And, if so, *why*. Spelled out so there is no mistaking it.

We need to know why he trusted Snape.

We need to know just what part in the overall story arc Snape has played.

We want to know what that triumphant gleam Harry thought he saw in Albus's eye when he first told Albus about Voldemort having used his blood to create his simulacrum meant. According to Rowling, as recently as July 2005 that gleam is still "significant".

I do *have* an idea regarding that gleam. I suspect that the gleam may be related to the way that Voldemort attempted to possess Harry during the battle of the Atrium and couldn't, or not without agonizing pain to both of them. He certainly didn't expect *that*, and it wasn't *anything* he had planned.

And it was also pretty, blooming *strange*.

When you stop and consider it; Harry and Voldemort had just spent the whole of year 5 flitting in and out of each other's heads without sustaining anything more than a confusion over whose emotions were whose. What is more, there were occasions over the year when it read as if Harry was responding to something other than his own conscious prompting. It is difficult to believe that these occasions were prompted by Voldemort, since they were universally to Harry's benefit, but nothing related to any of this was causing Harry any appreciable physical *pain*, and it isn't likely that Voldemort was feeling negative effects from the connection either.

But as soon as Voldemort attempted to psychically and physically *possess* Harry — as he had possessed Quirrelll — the attempt threw them both into agony until Harry managed to heave Voldemort out of his mind with the thought of seeing Sirius again. (Or more probably with the fact that he started welcoming death. Voldemort has a horror of death.)

Something protected Harry from being vulnerable to possession by Lord Voldemort.

Was this due to the fact that Harry is probably harboring one of Tom Riddle's missing soul fragments?

Or is this the effect of their physically sharing blood?

Or is it a combination of the two?

Among the minor clankers and awkwardnesses peppered throughout the series, the climax of OotP was particularly confusingly handled. This is a direct result of the original authorial decision to tell the story as completely as possible from Harry's POV. In the climax of GoF Harry may not have known all of what was going on, but the only part of the action that he completely missed due to a Voldemort-induced headache was the murder of Cedric Diggory. (And it isn't clear why he should have, since it was Pettigrew who did the killing. There was no headache in play when Snape presumably killed Dumbledore.) The reader was able to get a direct line-of-sight on the rest of the proceedings.

With OotP, it seems that for the most significant part of the showdown we have to take Dumbledore's word on everything. At face value, too, since Harry was far too incapacitated to be aware of anything but the pain, the statements that Voldemort made through him and his own reasoning processes.

What *appears* to have been going on, is that by possessing the boy, Voldemort was trying to get Dumbledore to kill Harry rather than to do it himself.

Why not do it himself? Had he failed at it so often as to have become gun-shy? I'm not sure that really "reads".

But we have only Dumbledore's word for it that the attempt caused *Voldemort* agonizing pain. And, while I can't see any reason for him to be shaving the truth in this matter, I'm really no longer so inclined to accept Dumbledore's unsupported word for everything without question.

From Harry's POV, it was only the reflection that if he died NOW he will see Sirius again that threw Voldemort out of his head and made the pain stop. So was it the attachment to Sirius or the willing embracing of death that actually repelled Voldemort?

And, if the attempt at possession hurt so much, why didn't Voldemort withdraw, so he would at least have control of his own wand? If he was also immobilized with the pain from trying to possess Harry, why didn't Dumbledore or somebody attack the (now undefended) simulacrum? For that matter, what happens to the simulacrum when Voldemort is off in someone else's head? Was Dumbledore afraid that if the simulacrum was destroyed Voldemort *wouldn't* withdraw from Harry at all? Did Voldemort not withdraw from Harry because he was *stuck*? Is this due to Harry and the simulacrum sharing the same blood?

After all; on a computer you cannot replace a folder with a file. Or vice-versa. Or give them the same name.

Or was the gleam due to Dumbledore's realization that Voldemort had now introduced a paradox into the equation, in that by the protection that Albus had layered on top of Lily's, in which so long as Harry was a minor in company with persons related by blood to Lily Potter he was protected from Lord Voldemort, and that by using Harry's blood to create his simulacrum Lord Voldemort was now among such persons and, consequently, so long as Harry was a minor and in Lord Voldemort's company, Lord Voldemort would be unable to kill him?

But we are clearly going to have to wait a while before we know whether any of this is anywhere near the right track.

So, to continue with the shopping list:

We also still want to hear the *full* story of what went down in the werewolf caper. WHY did Sirius Black set Severus Snape up? And *how* did he do it?

And what happened *afterwards*?

sigh And, all right, all right, *did* Severus Snape have a crush on Lily Evans? Or she on him?

And just what part does Peter Pettigrew have to play in the *solution*? He's got to be significant to the resolution somehow, but how does *he* relate to the problem of the *Horcruxes*?

Speaking of which: what the hey is up with the fake one? What purpose did *that* serve?

And what is with the *Dementors*? They've got to be even more significant than Pettigrew! Particularly if I'm right about Book 7 reflecting Book 3.

And where's Malfoy gotten to? Are we going to have to be dodging him through the last book as well as the Death Eaters?

How long is it going to take the kids to realize that the 6th Horcrux *isn't* the snake?

And while we're at it: just how are you supposed to *destroy* a Horcrux without getting blasted by it? Or DO you just pitch it through the Veil?

Speaking of which: are we ever going to be filled in on why Sirius Black "had to" be killed *when* he was? That is what Rowling told us. Was this meta for reasons to do with the construction of the story? Or was there a reason yet to be served by it IN the story? (Wendy B. Harte may have nailed that one, I think.)

And that's just for starters.

Along about the year 2000 Rowling told us that what Harry's parents did was "important". No word on that since. What's the payoff there?

She said on her official site that the Lestranges and Barty Crouch were "sent" after the Longbottoms. Why? And by whom? Voldemort was gone by then.

And, for that matter, what about the puzzles that she went out of her way to suddenly *introduce* into the storyline over the course of HBP? They aren't in there by accident. Have we a right to expect some sort of closure on all of them? I make it at about four so far;

There's Montegue who couldn't pass his Apparition test, but still somehow managed to Apparate *into* Hogwarts from the cabinet. I've *no* idea of what *that's* about.

There's the dratted Potions book. Nothing about that book adds up. No matter what explanation you try to graft onto it there is always some piece that doesn't fit.

There's the stirring adventure of R.A.B. and the Dark Lord's Sea Cave. Nothing about that really fits either.

And of course there is the riddle of the Horcruxes. Or, conversely, the Horcruxes of the Riddle. Whatever. At least *that* puzzle we are virtually guaranteed an answer to. I'm not so sure of the others.

And, of course, we do all *feel* entitled to see how the bloody Prophecy plays out.

But of a rather more deeply overall thematic importance, there is the question of taking responsibility for one's own actions.

Harry has been allowed to skate through the first 6 books of the series without ever having to take full responsibility for the effects of any of his own actions. Whenever things go wrong, there have been a lot of other people who have been all too willing to share the responsibility with him, if not to take the responsibility *for* him. Eventually he is going to be unable to dodge that particular bullet. And Albus is no longer around to take that bullet for him. Even Harry realizes this by now.

And he *hasn't* learned his craft. He has sluffed along learning what interests him, or what *he* thinks is important. But he hasn't buckled down to learn what more experienced heads than his have told him that he needs to know.

He *is* probably going to end up learning a great many of Albus's secrets in the course of the final book. He is going to need to. He doesn't have the information he needs to carry this mission off yet.

Including just *why* Albus trusted Severus Snape.

And that is not likely to be a painless lesson, either.

I also suspect that Harry may have to decide whether the wizarding world is *worth* saving. But that suspicion may just be me being characteristically pessimistic, so don't place any great dependence on Rowling investing much in it.

And, of course, there will be a fine, old-fashioned, extended wrap-up at the end of the story to let us all know how everything (and everyone) turned out.

This wrap-up is the famous "last chapter" that Rowling has claimed to have already written as a promise to herself that she will eventually get there. Consequently, it will be the *previous* couple of hundred pages which will contain the run-up to the climax and the showdown with Lord Voldemort. The wrap-up isn't actually a part of the active *story*.

Regarding which: Rowling set off a little flurry of controversy with statements made in June of 2006 that she was going to have to rewrite this chapter a bit. One of the characters who she had originally intended to kill off got a reprieve. Two who had been expected to survive haven't. And, for all the storm of speculation this statement set running, I rather suspect that "*haven't*" may really be the correct term. That chapter was written before she started on the body of the work of writing the series, and it consequently reflects her master "plan" of over a decade ago. There has been a lot of water under the bridge in the last 10-12 years.

For that matter, there has been a lot of water under the bridge in the last 7 years. We've forgotten how quickly the first four books came out. Bang, bang, bang, bang. Four books in four years. And with the fourth one she hit a snag. She has stated in interviews since GoF came out that she fell into a major plot hole that opened up in the middle of the story, requiring her to rewrite nearly a third of the book to plug it.

She also tells us that after taking a year or so off to recoup from a case of incipient burnout, she subjected her master Plan to three months of intensive review to make sure that there were no more such pitfalls lurking for her in the rest of it. I can't answer for anyone else, but I certainly felt a distinct shift in OotP from the books that had preceded it. And, for that matter, HBP appears to have soundly ignored or dismissed just about every new issue that was raised over the course of OotP. I very much doubt that Rowling has only just made her decision regarding the deaths of those two characters who now won't be making it since she started writing Book 7. Those eventual deaths may already have been telegraphed over the course of the last two books that we've already got. They may have even already taken place. And we may have already watched the person who now *does* make it *get* that reprieve.

And at this point there is absolutely no way of telling whether any of our guesses are right.

Which is probably more than you needed to hear from me. With the cast disappearing in reverse order of appearance, we now will have a word from Swythyv, and then, for a treat, Daniela, Wendy, and John have put together a Tri-Theorist's Tournament for that edification and amusement that I mentioned in the intro.

BRAIN UNLIMBERED? Check!
Folded newspaper hat? Check!
Visual inspection of extremities? Check!

1. The Prophecy

In Book 7, we will finally hear the whole prophecy. The missing parts — and the person who tells it — will come as shock to Harry and likely upset his sense of himself.

One twist may be that Harry is not the One. Dumbledore told Harry that the keeper of the Hall had re-labeled the Orb, adding Harry's name to it because "it seemed plain." He also told Harry that only a person to whom a prophecy referred could take an Orb without suffering madness. Harry's behavior in HBP certainly does not rule out madness. ;D

The second twist will be who else knew. Dumbledore told Harry that the "only two people in the whole world" were "both standing in this smelly, spidery broom shed." He did *not* say "Just you and I, Harry."

Non-people: The portraits of Phineas Nigellus and Mrs. Black

Corporeal non-people: Kreacher. And technically, Crookshanks the cat.

People: Possibly Snape. Surely Regulus Black.

Regulus Black will turn out to have heard the prophecy made. I think that Dumbledore in the broom shed had recently learned about Regulus' survival, but I will be truly charmed to learn that he spied Regulus in there. Because Regulus *could* have been — by my reckoning he was spotted quite nearby afterwards. ;D

2. The Marauders and That Night at Godric's Hollow

In Book 7, we will finally learn what happened at Godric's Hollow. I doubt that it will reflect well on most of the "good guys."

We will learn that all four of the Marauders — and Lily too — were keeping bad company. Each of them had dangerous associates of whom the others would have disapproved had they known. In Lily's case, hers was protective. With the others, not so. In fact, we will learn that at least one (and probably all) of the Marauders was compromised dating back to the Werewolf Frolics at Hogwarts. "Compromised" is the key — not Evil Incarnate, but known and weakened in such ways that they could be taken or used.

And we'll learn that there were at least two more people in the room with Lily, Harry, and Voldemort that night: Peter Pettigrew and Regulus Black. I think Regulus Black was the voice heard in the house warning Lily to flee, while Pettigrew came in with Voldemort. Voldemort could neither see nor sense Regulus, but the others could.

After the deed was done Pettigrew and Regulus dueled. Pettigrew blew up the house, hit Regulus with a shape-change (likely got him while he saved the baby), and fled.

I think we'll learn that Hagrid saw Regulus in the wreckage guarding Harry. Hagrid didn't spare him any attention or mention him afterwards, because Regulus looked like a cat; and it happens that Hagrid doesn't like cats. They make him sneeze. ;D

3. The Horcrux Pursuit as Snipe Hunt

We — and Voldemort with us, from watching through Harry — might conclude from HBP that in forty years of trying Dumbledore had succeeded in identifying only four of six horcruxes. Of those four, Harry had destroyed the Diary by accident and Dumbledore had been seriously wounded destroying the Ring. They apparently had the Locket but lost it again through sheer incompetence, and had no idea where to find the Cup. Dumbledore managed to drink poison for a mere nyah-nyah note and died the same night, without even telling Harry how *not* to dispose of a horcrux.

If I were Voldemort, I'd be laughing. There's no credible threat.

And we'll learn that Dumbledore went to considerable trouble to give him that idea — because the horcruxes have already been rounded up, and most of them destroyed.

Going by history, R.A.B. was as effective as Dumbledore in the horcrux sweepstakes. And again, we were led to think that one was his bag limit. Who knows how many more he took? Figuring out Regulus Black will be the real quest of Book 7.

Harry may have a special ability to destroy horcruxes without taking personal damage, but I predict he'll end up a bit surplus to requirements in the project — with the exception of the one he's got stuck to his head. ;D

4. The Return of Regulus Black

Regulus should have been back by now: Book 7 will reveal how the Blacks protected him (not pretty), and see him saved by the back-up plan. Regulus seems like forethought personified. He and Hermione are going to be quite a team. ;D

Regulus is protected by a Fidelius charm, his secret keeper is protected at 12 Grimmauld Place, and Phineas Nigellus has been overseeing the situation. I think matters came to the boil when Phineas learned that Sirius was dead: he had to induce Dumbledore to act.

We'll learn that Dumbledore had to stage the "Who owns the house and elf?" rigmarole to conceal the fact that the house and Kreacher belonged to Regulus all along. Kreacher had been strictly bound to conceal this by acknowledging first Sirius and then Harry as his "masters." Which he did with murderously bad will — but complete fidelity. And I think we'll learn that Phineas told Dumbledore he'd need what was in the Cave.

I'm guessing that the note (and/or the locket it was in) will cue the secret keeper to give the bearers Regulus' secret, once they bring it to the Black house. That will render Regulus knowable — and fortunately, Hermione's seen the non-verbal spell needed to fix his remaining, furry little problem.

Regulus — and the Noble and Most Ancient House of Black — are going to owe Hermione *big time*. *Sniff* It's so romantic. ;D

5. The Potions Book

For Heaven's sake, Jo, put me out of my misery. :D

I predict that we'll find out that there *is* female handwriting in the book. And that "Property of the HBP" was only revealed because Hermione cast the Revelatio spell, and that Severus Snape did not inscribe it there.

I also think that Snape will turn out to have been afraid of where *else* Harry might have got Sectumsempra from, and that he actually calmed down once he satisfied himself that it was from that book.

Past that, I give up — I've got nothing. ;D

6. The Prank

In Book 7 we'll learn that there were more things going on and more people involved in The Prank, and that it had about as much to do with Lupin as did the children's trip out to the Shrieking Shack at the end of PoA. My best guesses:

Snape saw Lupin being led to the tree from the only place in Hogwarts that we were told *had* a line of sight to the tree: Gryffindor Tower. I think he was ransacking James and Sirius' dormitory. Sirius maliciously "mentioned" the willow tree protocol while Snape was concealed there in an altered form: animagus, maybe, or perhaps Polyjuiced into someone Sirius knew to be elsewhere, like Lupin.

Someone from Voldemort's camp was in the shack that night, desiring something to be brought out of Hogwarts. I'm guessing Lucius Malfoy and Bellatrix. I think that the Marauders and Snape had been contending for possession of whatever it was, but that the Marauders were drawn out by the promise of mischief and pranks while Snape's situation was more dire, like Draco Malfoy's task. I think it was the Diary.

Someone went down the tunnel in hot pursuit of a friend.

Someone went in hot pursuit of an enemy.

Someone was there in an altered form and was never detected.

Someone was rendered unconscious and missed critical events.

Someone was forced out of his animagus form and bound by his enemies.

At a point when it could all still have been sorted, Lupin transformed.

Sirius fought rear-guard during a retreat in disorder.

The desired thing ended up in possession of Voldemort's camp.

All will be revealed in Book 7, and I expect we'll learn that this incident was how James got scared straight, how Snape bonded with Dumbledore, and how Sirius learned nothing and wrecked his birthright. Voldemort had been after them all; he got a few footholds.

7. The "Fifth House," Lily's Fame and Warlocks

In Book 7 we will be shown a "fifth element": a sector of wizarding society that discards House affiliation and rises above blood status. It is the *merit* path in this closed society. Those who rise to the top in it may change their names, and become their own tradition.

There are witches and wizards, and Hogwarts School of Witchcraft and Wizardry… and then there are Warlocks. Dumbledore is a specimen. So is Voldemort. And so, I think, was Lily Potter. It will be revealed as rather like a Lodge, whose members may be identified by dress and hair — the reason that Molly was badgering Bill to cut his.

Warlocks deal in Sorcery, and from them arise Sorcerers. Albus Dumbledore is a "Grand Sorc." according to the Hogwarts letterhead, as well as Chief Warlock (*not* Chairman) of the Wizengamot. And as the US title clues us, Sorcery is Alchemy — which is Mysteries.

Voldemort wanted to be "the most powerful sorcerer." He was afraid of Dumbledore, and reluctant to kill Lily. In Book 7 we'll find out the framework of why that was.

These do as they darned well please, with Dark Arts or otherwise: they are the wizards' wizards. They can be very powerful (including socially or politically according to individual choice), but utterly eccentric. It is from them that advances in magic come. The wizarding world gives lip service to Wizarding Pride, but Warlocks can also be frightening and Not Quite Nice: they make ordinary folk feel a bit like they think Muggles ought to. Most comfortably viewed on Chocolate Frog Cards, is how I'd put it.

I predict we will learn that Lily was a rare genius, inducted right out of Hogwarts, and that she tackled some Mysteries. I suspect that Warlocks are like geeks, predominantly but not exclusively male, and that these rare female Alchemists can achieve some unusual results. If "the Potters" were known to wizarding society, the celebrity was *Lily's*. Book 7 is going to go rather hard on the illusion that the Marauders were hot stuff. ;D

I hope you've all enjoyed your trip on Flight of Fancy Airlines — guaranteed to lose your baggage, and always a departure point near you — you may now return your brain to it's upright and locked position. Thank you! ;D

GREAT EXPECTATIONS
BOOK 7 PREDICTIONS

"Ah, Harry, how often this happens, even between the best of friends" —
Dumbledore, HALF-BLOOD PRINCE Chapter 17

HOW IS IT that so many people can read the exact same source material and end up with completely different conclusions? Welcome to our own staff's Tri-Theorist Tournament. There will be three tasks that are meant to divine Jo's mind, tackle outstanding questions, and predict the ending of the series. Who will win eternal theorist glory?

TASK 1:

OUR FIRST TASK IS TO FORECAST WHO WILL LIVE OR DIE AT THE END OF BOOK 7?

(LIVE / DIE)	WENDY	DANIELA	JOHN
HARRY POTTER	LIVE	LIVE	LIVE
RON WEASLEY	LIVE	LIVE	DIE
HERMIONE GRANGER	LIVE	LIVE	LIVE
LORD VOLDEMORT	DIE	DIE	DIE
BELLATRIX LESTRANGE	DIE	DIE	DIE
PETER PETTIGREW	DIE	DIE	LIVE
REMUS LUPIN	LIVE	LIVE	LIVE
NYMPHADORA TONKS	LIVE	LIVE	DIE
MINERVA McGONAGALL	LIVE	LIVE	LIVE
GINNY WEASLEY	LIVE	LIVE	DIE
LUNA LOVEGOOD	LIVE	LIVE	LIVE

(LIVE / DIE)	WENDY	DANIELA	JOHN
NEVILLE LONGBOTTOM	LIVE	LIVE	LIVE
MOLLY WEASLEY	LIVE	LIVE	DIE
ARTHUR WEASLEY	LIVE	LIVE	DIE
FRED WEASLEY	LIVE	DIE	DIE
GEORGE WEASLEY	LIVE	DIE	DIE
PERCY WEASLEY	DIE	LIVE	DIE
BILL WEASLEY	LIVE	LIVE	DIE
FLEUR DELACOUR	LIVE	LIVE	DIE
SEVERUS SNAPE	LIVE	LIVE	DIE
DRACO MALFOY	DIE	DIE	DIE
LUCIUS MALFOY	LIVE	LIVE	DIE
NARCISSA MALFOY	DIE	DIE	DIE
RUBEUS HAGRID	LIVE	LIVE	LIVE
RUFUS SCRIMGEOUR	DIE	DIE	DIE

TASK 2:

THE SECOND TASK — MAKE 25 BEST GUESSES ON SERIES QUESTIONS:

1. Dumbledore: did he die at the end of Half-Blood Prince?

Wendy: Well, if Jo says he died, then he did. He was most likely Stoppered Death Dumbledore throughout HALF-BLOOD PRINCE, and this state was ended following the Tower tumble. However, I suggest that the benefit gained by having Death cool its heels in the Waiting Room must come at a huge price. I strongly suspect that there will be a Book 7 plot surprise regarding the exact parameters of Dumbledore's Stoppered Death situation.

Daniela: Yes — but we will hear him speak again. Perhaps the first time will be through his portrait. Then, perhaps Harry will see him in the Underworld (of the dead). Also, Dumbledore will need to appear publicly in some form after Voldemort is defeated. Otherwise, I find it difficult to explain Rowling's statement in the F.A.Q. section of her web site, in answer to the question of why Dumbledore did not have the whole school sing the Hogwarts song again after the first year: "Should Dumbledore ever suggest a rousing encore, you may assume that he is on top form once more." Still, I think Dumbledore died on the tower.

John: No, Dumbledore died well before the events on the Astronomy Tower. The death was staged between Slughorn and Snape to allow Snape to live as a deep plant among the Death Eaters. We'll have our "Dumbledore Denouement" at story's end, albeit with Slughorn revealing how he Polyjuiced the Headmaster's part with Severus through most of HALF-BLOOD PRINCE.

2. Will Hogwarts open up for Year 7?

Wendy: Yes, I think it will — with low but loyal attendance for at least part of the year.

Daniela: No — at least not for the fall and even winter terms; in the spring, things may look brighter. I think the school governors (or the Ministry, if it has the power) will override the professors' willingness to keep it open.

John: Yes, it will. There will be less disruption to the storyline than Harry says there will be. Something he learns on his trip to the Dursleys' house, the alchemical wedding, or his pilgrimage to Potter acres in Godric's Hollow will send him scurrying to Hogwarts for help, refuge, or as a Horcrux search location.

3. Who will be the D.A.D.A. teacher in Year 7?

Wendy: Perhaps Kingsley Shacklebolt — Harry admired him.

Daniela: Lupin needs a job and he was the best ever D.A.D.A. teacher. I hope he gets back his position at Hogwarts despite the prejudice (there will always be a Potions Master on hand to give him Wolfsbane).

John: Pulling a name from the hat, I get… "Nymphadora Tonks".

4. D.A.D.A. Teacher after the story ends?

Wendy: Harry Potter!

Daniela: Lupin again, if they find a cure for his little furry problem. Bill would be a cool teacher, too, especially if he wants to stay in Britain, close to Fleur. (One of the wolves!)

John: The curse on the position should be broken at the end of the novels. If the D.A.D.A. teacher survives, it should be theirs to accept or decline.

5. Snape: Good or Evil?

Wendy: It is abundantly clear to me: Dumbledore's man through and through!

Daniela: Almost evil. Slytherin but not Voldemort's man through and through. He uses any means to achieve his ends, including murder. He wants to defeat Voldemort, but in his own way. He was getting impatient with what Dumbledore wanted him to do (spy), and resented the fact that Dumbledore trusted Harry with the Horcruxes (which I am sure he figured out). He was also pressured into the murder by Narcissa, and perhaps he saw there was no way out of the Unbreakable Vow without losing his credibility and endangering his access to Voldemort's confidentiality. Did he do what is right or what is easy? (Is murder easy? But it is definitely not right!) I believe he betrayed Dumbledore in not sharing this information with him. His feelings for Dumbledore are mixed and troubled. I think he was feeling a bit competitive for Dumbledore's affections and also with Dumbledore himself in the fight against Voldemort; he thought the Headmaster underestimated or limited him in what he could bring to the table.

John: Severus Snape is the alchemical, Gryffindor/Slytherin Hermaphrodite of the series with the Slytherin front who transcends the oppressive metanarrative of the Founder's Myth. He is nobody's "man," certainly, but he was Dumbledore's trusted friend and equal in this respect. Dumbledore had the Gryffindor front and Slytherin back but was similarly an alchemical androgyny in whom the usual contraries have been resolved in love.

6. Snape's Boggart?

Wendy: Neville Longbottom — a weak and incompetent simpleton (from Snape's point of view, not ours)

Daniela: Good one, Wendy! My guesses are: first: James Potter; second: a girl laughing at him; third: a werewolf.

John: Tobias Snape, vampire, attacking a student, or mum (Filch, sans pasties).

7. Snape's Patronus?

Wendy: Spider! Levicorpus (the spell he invented) and spiders both hang upside down. His all black attire is reminiscent of a Black Widow spider (known for its toxic venom). He is likely referenced in the Goblet of Fire riddle (spy-d-er), and it is clear misdirection by Jo when secondary characters comment on Snape's bat-like appearance. Snape's hidey-hole residence is called "Spinners End", so what more do we need to make the call?

Daniela: I'd second the spider, but maybe Rowling wants to surprise us, and that is why she's not telling. So then it's not a spider, nor a bat. And Snape must think a lot of his own Patronus if he finds Tonks's wolf "weak." I'll second John's choice: a dragon.

John: I've always assumed it was something heroic and frightening on the order of a dragon, a hippogriff, or a griffin, at least a lion or an eagle. Best guess: Dragon.

8. What is the Ravenclaw or Gryffindor Horcrux?

Wendy: The Opal Necklace.

Daniela: The Mirror of Erised

John: Voldemort's Wand.

9. Where is the Hufflepuff cup?

Wendy: In the earth somewhere. Riddle Graveyard, perhaps. However, it seems like it would have been the Horcrux most likely to be at the bottom of the cave basin (i.e. a cup under liquid), but it doesn't seem to have played out that way.

Daniela: Gringotts! Voldemort must know an awful lot about Gringotts to have been able to advise Quirrelll to break into it!

John: Transfigured into the house cup Horcrux (Hogwarts Trophy Room).

10. Is Nagini the 6th Horcrux?

Wendy: Yes, plus Harry's scar. I agree with Daniela's theory.

Daniela: Harry's scar is the 6th Horcrux. Nagini is the 7th.

John: Scar, not Nagini.

11. Who is the Heir of Gryffindor?

Wendy: Albus Dumbledore

Daniela: Albus Dumbledore is Gryffindor's physical heir. Harry is Gryffindor's spiritual heir. I think Godric's Sword was placed in the Sorting Hat by Godric Gryffindor himself so that it could only be pulled out by his own true heir, determined not by blood but by the heart. This was Gryffindor's way of teaching that it is our heart that make us who we truly are. But Dumbledore has Gryffindor's blood running through his veins.

John: Harry Potter …well, on second thought, make that Severus Snape.

12. Is Neville under a memory charm?

Wendy: Yes, but from his well meaning relatives. Not from the Lestranges, his parents, or Voldemort.

Daniela: Yes, I think so, for witnessing his parents' torture. But if he did, why would the villains have left him alone and not tortured him, too? Unless they did… Another possibility is that the Longbottoms were tortured away from home, and in the meantime someone entered their house, who was seen by Neville. S/he did not want to be remembered, and put Neville under a memory charm. Who would this person be? Snape? Why would Snape prowl about the Longbottoms' house a year after Voldemort's fall when Snape was supposed to be on the good side? And why would he hate Neville's poor memory so much if he had something to do with it (unless he wanted to keep him insecure and forgetful)? Maybe he wanted to see one of the guys who fit the profile of the Prophecy for himself.

John: No opinion either way. I certainly will be disappointed if he is! So nice to have the stock "slow boy" from schoolboy fiction on hand.

13. Percy: Git or Good?

Wendy: Misguided Git, unfortunately. I believe he will be the sole Weasley to pay the ultimate price. His unquestioning faith in the Ministry over his family, along with his unwillingness to think for himself will be the causes of his sad downfall.

Daniela: Git with some trace of good. His girlfriend's name sounded good (Penelope Clearwater) so perhaps he'll show himself loyal to his family in the end. Unfortunately, I think it will take a death to bring Percy back around… If it's Fred and George (after doing something very heroic), hopefully Percy will give them a eulogy at their funeral.

John: His name, of course, suggests heroic greatness. I'll go with "good" here in the hope that Percy is an Order plant among the movers-and-shakers at the Ministry. Hard to imagine a Weasley really being a git… Remember him after the second Tri-Wizard Task?

14. Slughorn: Good or Evil or Both Sides?

Wendy: Good, but uncommitted until Chapter 22, "After the Burial". Throughout HALF-BLOOD PRINCE we view Slughorn from Harry's perspective, and he appears to be a slightly distasteful and transparent opportunist. Slughorn may be a social networker, but he took great pains to distance himself from the offspring of Death Eaters. Slughorn is a flawed man — a cowardly adult who had to work his loyalties out and rise to occasion.

Daniela: Good. He's too much into glamour and he hurts those he ignores, but his heart is more or less in the right place. The fact that he liked Lily says a lot. He was also ashamed of his memory, which is the reason he didn't share it at first. That he could feel such shame shows how good he is. And I am proud of him for finally showing the courage to share it.

John: I'm with Sally Gallo. Horace Slughorn/Goldin pulls off Staged Death on the Astronomy Tower. Not good or evil but "great."

15. Harry and Ginny: Happy Ever After?

Wendy: Yes!

Daniela: Yes!

John: Pass. I deliver all my packages by hand. No 'shipping.

16. Ron and Hermione: Happy Ever After?

Wendy: Yes, in a Molly and Arthur sort of way.

Daniela: Yes, a bit like Molly and Arthur, I agree.

John: As the quarrelling couple of alchemy, they'll always be paired. In the Rubedo, this couple usually dies after the alchemical marriage but, if Fleur and Bill play this part (as I think they are meant to), Ron and Hermione don't have to be paired in death.

17. What did Dudley see when he was attacked by the Dementors?

Wendy: That he had magical powers, and is therefore a freak in his parents' eyes. Alternatively, that he was an orphan, like Harry

Daniela: He remembered Hagrid giving him a pig tail. Come to think of it, that whole day was a nightmare for him.

John: My mother taught me never to crawl into small, closed spaces. Like Dudley's head. I'm not going in there.

18. Which Hogwarts' teacher is married?

Wendy: Albus Dumbledore — to the Trolley Witch who lives in Hogsmeade at Honeydukes Candy Store. Recall the passage connecting Honeydukes and Hogwarts. It is interesting to note that when you enter the tunnel from the Hogwarts side, you have to squeeze in. Maybe this keeps plump Mrs. Dumbledore from dropping in on her hubby at the office unexpectedly!

Daniela: They all seem like loners to me... Maybe Madam Sprout?

John: Filch and Pince, like Harry thought. Irma Pince = I'm a Prince, Eileen Prince and Tobias Snape/Filch, safely under wraps.

19. Who ends up a professor at Hogwarts after Book 7?

Wendy: Neville (Herbology) Harry (D.A.D.A.), Hermione (Headmistress of Hogwarts)

Daniela: Neville (Herbology). No one else (I think Rowling said just one would become a teacher). I see Hermione on the Wizengamot, becoming a big wig there and eventually helping rectify some laws (S.P.E.W.)… Ron will play keeper for the Chudley Cannons and help them win the league one year (but make them lose spectacularly the next). If Luna spends any more time with Trelawney she might become a Seer but perhaps she will continue her dad's work for the Quibbler. Harry and Ginny? They would make a cool team of Aurors, although they might not want to be connected with the Ministry. It would be nice to see both of them play Quidditch for the Cannons together with Ron while Hermione rolls her eyes and attends all their games (always taking the time, despite her Wizengamot career).

John: Neville, Herbology Professor and decorated hero of the Battle at King's Cross (Order of Merlin, first class, dragon rider cluster).

20. Who loved Snape?

Wendy: My wild guess as there is zero cannon: Florence, likely Florean Fortescue's daughter. Recall that Bertha Jorkins was spying on someone kissing Florence who threw a hex at her. It seems like something teenage Snape would do.

Daniela: If Rowling hadn't said "Who on earth would want Snape in love with them? That's a very horrible idea," I would second Florence. Maybe it was his mother who loved him.

John: I guess someone is obliged to say "Lily Evans." Shudder.

21. Who will develop magic late in life?

Wendy: Filch

Daniela: Filch. It would make him so happy (and maybe it will soften him up).

John: I'm voting for Dudders because of the conceptual struggle this would be for all three Dursleys. I'm rooting for Arabella Figg.

22. Will Peter Pettigrew repay his life debt to Harry?

Wendy: Yes, but unclear if it will be willingly, inadvertently, or under pressure to save his life. My guess would be that he will do so as a rat saving his own skin.

Daniela: Yes, if Snape keeps annoying him. Maybe he will help dig for Hufflepuff's cup at Gringotts and then crush it with the silver hand that Voldemort gave him.

John: Yes and no. He thinks he will be repaying Harry by striking Snape down when he thinks Harry is trapped by Severus, but this murder from the shadows will be the tragic ending of the books.

23. Location of Harry and Voldemort's last battle?

Wendy: At Hogwarts, the only place both Harry and Tom ever considered home. Hogwarts is also home to the Sword of Gryffindor, a proven snake slaying weapon.

Daniela: Wendy, I think you called it! Final showdown in the Chamber of Secrets. (And Harry will chop off Voldemort's head with Gryffindor's Sword.) Don't ask me why I kept seeing a forest!

John: We can bet it will be underground or have an element of burial or death about it like the battle-grounds of the first five books ("miles and miles beneath Hogwarts"). I'm guessing a return to the Chamber of Secrets for a mano-a-mano or a three ring circus at King's Cross Station.

24. Where was Voldemort "living" during Book 6?

Wendy: Somewhere in the Underworld. Like, some abandoned tunnel beneath the London Underground. Alternatively, in the back of Borgin and Burkes.

Daniela: Like Slughorn when he was in hiding, some (temporarily) uninhabited home.

John: I bet the Malfoys have some nice guest rooms.

25. Where are Snape and Draco in hiding when Book 7 opens?

Wendy: I'm just going to assume they joined Lord Voldemort in his lair directly after the tower scene. Doubtful Draco found it a fun vacation from school.

Daniela: Not the Malfoy mansion and not Spinner's End. Like Voldemort above, some (temporarily) uninhabited home.

John: I assume no one outside the Death Eaters knows about the apartments at Spinner's End. Snape didn't socialize or eat with anyone outside that circle.

BONUS QUESTION: Guess the title of Book 7

Wendy: Either "HARRY POTTER AND THE BLACK FAMILY CURSE", or "HARRY POTTER AND THE SWORD OF GRYFFINDOR"

Daniela: Ok, I think Wendy called it: "HARRY POTTER AND THE SWORD OF GRYFFINDOR." The Sword will be left to Harry by Dumbledore in a will, telling him that Harry is its rightful heir (because of his heart). Harry will chop off Voldemort's head with it. I think there may be other powers associated with the sword also, and that Harry may be able to use them unexpectedly on Voldemort. For example, Excalibur could emit lightning bursts when needed. It would be funny to see Voldemort looking silly with a wand, and Harry wielding the sword.

John: "HARRY POTTER AND THE ALCHEMIST'S CELL" (this is one of the few titles we know will *not* be the book 7 title because it is on the Warner Bros copyright list Ms. Rowling has said she will not be using – but I still love it)

TASK 3:

AND NOW WE COME TO THE 3RD AND FINAL TASK — TACKLE 10 BIG AND LARGELY UNKNOWABLE HARRY POTTER MYSTERIES:

1. What was behind Dumbledore's 'gleam of triumph'?

Wendy Explains: During the Riddle Graveyard scene, Voldemort re-pieced himself back together with his father's bone (his genetic body), Pettigrew's hand (to perhaps gain some Animagus powers), and Harry's blood (to get back some of his lost capabilities). In ORDER OF THE PHOENIX we found out that the Dark Lord could possess Nagini from afar, and Harry could go there as well. I think Dumbledore's gleam was a recognition that if Voldemort's body could be destroyed first, then he would very likely move to possess the snake Nagini. With some controlling combination of parseltongue and blood, Harry might be able to get Voldysnake into the Chamber of Secrets. I speculate that by using Harry's blood, Voldemort accidentally created this sort of vulnerability that Harry can exploit. Maybe we will hear Nagini say "thankssssssss" after she is set free.

Daniela Explains: If Harry will need to enter Voldemort's body in order to engage in soul to soul combat, perhaps the fact that his own blood is running through Voldemort's veins will help him, kind of like having an ally within the enemy walls. Or maybe, if Harry needs to die in order to destroy the Horcrux inside himself, the fact that his blood is running through Voldemort's veins will bring him back to life to finish off Voldemort.

John Explains: For Harry to defeat the Dark Lord, both must be Gryffindor/ Slytherin androgyns so Harry's pure heart will destroy Voldemort as he (and Snape) run a current of love through this conductor. Dumbledore's gleam of triumph was his delight in learning that his plan to make the "new, improved" Dark Lord, Heir of Slytherin, a Gryffindor in body (because of Harry's blood in the rebirthing bath) had paid off.

2. Is there any significance to the fact that Harry has his Mother's eyes?

Wendy Explains: I am going to be very controversial on this one and say: nothing magical. The green eyes are meant to link Harry with his mother. He may resemble his father physically, but all who meet Harry who also knew his parents, find themselves drawn deeply to a memory of Lily's goodness. Eyes are the mirror of the soul, and Harry's parents live inside him

Daniela Explains: All that we know so far about eyes and magic is that eye contact is often necessary for Legilimency (and the look of the basilisk can kill). Could it be that certain kinds of eyes are more powerful than others at types of magic that require eye contact? Harry does need to become a good Legilimens I think. Or perhaps Harry's eyes will be able to open something that only his mother could open.

John Explains: No plot significance except what Wendy shared.

3. What was the source of James' fortune?

Wendy Explains: I think James' family hunted the Demiguise and they created rare and costly Invisibility Cloaks. Only skilled wizards can capture the Demiguise which turns invisible when cornered. The fact that both Harry and James wear glasses and have quick Seeker reflexes is rather interesting. Harry's vision is a continuing theme throughout the septology. The Demiguise is covered with hair. JKR makes many mentions of Harry and James' thick heads of hair, which defy tidying or trimming. Invisibility Cloaks are, as Ron says " …really rare, and really valuable". So they sound expensive (a wealth generator) and hard to come by (worthy of being an heirloom) Dumbledore's presentation note to Harry reads like a family heirloom: Your father left this in my possession before he died. It is time it was returned to you. Use it well.

Daniela Explains: I don't know if we will find out. James basically inherited his family gold, and Rowling says he therefore did not need a job that brought him a lot of money (I wonder what "low-end" job he had? It's a big secret…). I suppose his ancestors could have been treasure hunters like Bill or merchants…

John Explains: Snape's comment to Lupin that the Marauder's Map must have come "directly from the Manufacturers" suggested to me that James and Sirius started a business, using Uncle Alphard's gold, creating and manufacturing magical jokes and trinkets like those sold in Hogsmeade at Fred and George's shop in Diagon Alley. The several links of James & Sirius with Fred & George in canon seem to support this possibility.

4. What was Lily's occupation?

Wendy Explains: She worked in the Department of Mysteries, specializing in Potion-related knowledge seeking

Daniela Explains: Considering the mystery in which Lily's occupation has been shrouded I wouldn't be surprised is she did work for the Department of Mysteries. Maybe she studied love! Another possibility, considering she was very good at Potions and Charms, is that she was a Healer, but she may not have considered that career adventurous enough.

John Explains: At her death, she was a devoted mum to Harry and thorn in Lord Voldemort's side as a member of the Order of the Phoenix. I have my doubts the times and her new family allowed for much of a career.

5. Who does Petunia's "awful boy" reference refer to?

Wendy Explains: I have gone back and forth between Snape and Pettigrew on this one. I don't think she means James. I pick Snape, but only as an admiring friend. Sorry folks, but I don't believe in a Snape/Lily romance. I think Snape and Lily were connected by their potions prowess, and perhaps Lily was friends with "Florence" (my theory of Snape's phantom love). Maybe Snape discovered that he enjoyed snogging his girlfriend, but he had more in common intellectually with her best friend, Lily (who was out of his league).

Daniela Explains: I don't know if Rowling would make such a mystery of it if it was one of the Marauders. I think she is staying mum over who else talked to Lily because it has shock value and opens up big questions. I think Snape qualifies as a shock factor, and he was certainly an "awful boy." If Snape went to talk to Lily before their fifth year (because he admired, say, her potions skills), and Lily rejected whatever invitation he was making, we can understand why he would angrily call her a "Mudblood" later. Since Voldemort came out in the open and began wreaking havoc in 1970, at the same time that Lily was starting school in 1971 (www.hp-lexicon.org), it is likely Snape was warning Lily about Voldemort and his agenda of killing Muggleborns and he tried to impress upon her the danger she was in and so on. His warning may have involved an unwelcome invitation that was an indirect test of how willing she would be to join Voldemort later (join my Dark Arts club in order to be safe) and I think Lily must have rebuffed him, causing him bitterness. Lily's attempt to "save" Snape later from James and company would have intensified Snape's annoyance.

John Explains: James Potter.

6. Is the shape of Harry's scar important?

Wendy Explains: Dumbledore did fall off the Lightning Struck Tower and Harry is marked with a Lightning Bolt, so those two elements of fate must connect somehow. I think it is a Horcrux which would explain why the Dementors are so attracted to him.

Daniela Explains: Rowling said the shape of the scar is not the most important thing about it. Perhaps that means the shape may simply be symbolic. I think the lightning looks a bit like a snake, indicating maybe that a piece of Voldemort's soul is lodged in the scar. The lightning could also stand for the "flashes" of insight that the scar gives Harry. And it could connect Harry symbolically to the gods (e.g. Zeus, who controls the lightning bolt), so that perhaps, like the immortal ones, he has a chance at surviving his own death in the seventh book.

John Explains: Ms. Rowling says "no." The shape is not the important thing, as Stan might say, "it's that it is a blooomin' Horcrux that matters, no?"

7. Was anyone else present in Godric's Hollow during the Potters' murder besides Voldemort?

Wendy Explains: Peter Pettigrew is the most likely suspect to be present. When Voldemort was short-circuited into Vapormort, Peter grabbed his master's wand and held onto it.

Daniela Explains: Yes, it's possible it was Peter Pettigrew. Voldemort may have wanted him nearby in case things went wrong. But when Peter saw Voldemort get blown to smithereens, it would seem that instead of sticking around to see if there was a Vapormort left, Peter took the wand and ran for it. That would explain how Voldemort got back his wand, if he could not hold a wand himself when he lost his body. But wouldn't Vapormort have seen Peter take the wand and tried to communicate with him?

John Explains: One more vote for Peter, if only to explain how the Wand Horcrux survived.

8. Will we find out what is behind the locked door at the Department of Mysteries?

Wendy Explains: I feel like Jo won't be able to pass revisiting this spot. It might be a back door to the Veil, or a room full of "Love".

Daniela Explains: The terrible and wonderful power of love. I don't know if that room will ever be unlocked. Perhaps Harry needs to open that room to rid himself of the piece of Voldemort's soul inside his scar. That piece of soul may not be able to survive in a room full of love. If Harry enters it, something else could probably happen there, too. He would probably get into contact with his loved ones and hear Phoenix song, too.

John Explains: Dumbledore says it is a room containing the power greater than nature, etc., that Harry has in abundance and with which he will defeat Voldemort. We know what that is so we don't to go there to find out what is there. I wouldn't be surprised, though, if the final scene with Snape, Dumbledore, Hagrid, and Harry (Pettigrew in the wings) takes place in the Veil amphitheatre.

9. Why did Lord Voldemort offer to let Lily live?

Wendy Explains: So he could imperius her and have her march into the Department of Mysteries to fetch the prophesy which might have dealt with her baby. He is far from being a nice guy, so I doubt he meant for her to go on her merry way. I do like Daniela's thought that due to his own issues, Voldemort wanted to test Lily and see if most mother's would make the same choice as his own, validating his theory that love isn't the most important thing

Daniela Explains: It may have something to do with Voldemort's issues with his own mother who didn't live for him. He may have wanted to prove that Lily didn't love Harry either, and would let him die. Perhaps such an action on Lily's part would have made Voldemort stronger. It is also possible Lily's job and her talent with charms may have had something to do with it, and that Voldemort hadn't given up on recruiting her. Or perhaps, if Snape had feelings for Lily, Voldemort saw in her a person through whom he could manipulate Snape.

John Explains: Perhaps as a sop to Pettigrew who asked for this favor after betraying the Potters. Voldemort didn't take this pledge very seriously, though, did he?

10. Make five Book 7 Plot Predictions:

Wendy:

1. We'll see Dumbledore's inherent good nature pay off in support of Harry's mission. We will likely see house elves (commanded by Miss S.P.E.W., Hermione?), some giants, centaurs, merpeople and other creatures co-operating as either spies or warriors in the battle against the forces of evil.

2. Voldemort will kill a significant supporter, and it will alienate much of his human base, leaving him to depend on Dementors, Giants, Inferi and other dark creatures who aren't so easy to control. I think he will kill Narcissa Malfoy, as Draco didn't succeed in the exact task assigned, Snape did it for him

3. Oh yes, we will return to the Chamber of Secrets!!! When Harry and Ginny exited it in Chamber of Secrets, the door re- sealed with an audible hiss. I assume that means the chamber can be opened again by a Parslemouth. I am rather certain that Voldemort left something interesting there in his Tom Riddle days, and this creates an excellent trap opportunity for Harry.

4. At Bill and Fleur's wedding Hagrid will be the one who tells Harry where to go in Godric's Hollow. Perhaps the trio will travel there on Sirius' motorcycle, which Hagrid likely still has.

5. The second to last chapter will be Harry looking into the Mirror of Erised, seeing himself, Ginny, their kids, and their whole extended family together. It will end with him looking at his desired reflection, which does not include the scar.

Daniela:

1. Draco, on a second assignment from Voldemort, will tail the trio, eventually becoming polyjuice Ron (while Ron is imprisoned), Harry's "best friend". He won't need long to find out what he needs, and then will have only one choice, unless he has no foresight. (Voldemort would murder him for his pains; he can't have Draco running around with information about his Horcruxes.) Thus Draco will unmask himself and join the trio in the fight against Voldemort, becoming a (double) spy even, the Snape of the new generation. Perhaps Draco will kill Harry (with Harry's consent?) in order to destroy the Horcrux, and will die in the attempt to finish off Voldemort himself (like a tragic Regulus of the new generation). Whether from Draco or otherwise, Voldemort will discover the Horcrux hunt, and the action will be brought to a huge crisis. Harry will need to move on the offense with his scar as the only tool left to track the Horcruxes and Voldemort. There will be a huge trap that Harry will walk into near the climax. Ron will be a hostage of Voldemort's. When Draco will take Harry and Hermione to Ron's prison, they will find out he has been taken by Voldemort. Ginny will join Harry in order to save her brother. None of them will die, except Draco, and his mother, having turned against Voldemort because of her son's death. Lucius will live on to reflect on his losses.

2. Off to Gringotts! This will be the most exciting part of the Horcrux hunt, and it's been set up ever since the beginning of the books: deep down huge caves with stalactites and stalagmites, underground ravines and an underground lake, labyrinthine tunnels descending at breakneck speed, dragons! Goblins, enchantments, treasure, and more! That's where it's at. There was a hint that Harry might come back: "Harry tried to remember, left, right, right, left, middle fork, right, left, but it was impossible" (PS/SS Ch 5 "Diagon Alley"). Bill could come in handy, and Hagrid, who wouldn't say no to a dragon. Can the trio enroll them?

3. Snape will do an immense good deed before the book's end (save Ron's life). If Rowling can work it in, perhaps Snape will go on trial, and Dumbledore in some form will witness for him. The victim will forgive the murderer. Snape will go free. I believe he will become a monk and break his own wand and reflect on the spiritual side of life.

4. Fred and George will devise a major weapon for the final battle to make up for the Peruvian darkness fiasco. They will do a very heroic deed in the seventh book, but they will die. There will be thousands of people at their funeral; Percy will give a eulogy to a standing ovation (which will stun him, never having been popular in his life); and people will bring all the funny objects that the two Weasleys have invented and set off hundreds of fireworks in a kind of kaleidoscopic display of contrasting emotions. A weeping and dazzled Molly will be comforted by Harry, who will speak to her about the spiritual world he saw while he was temporarily dead (he will have seen again his parents, Sirius, and Dumbledore).

5. There will be a major return to the roots, and a lot more history will be uncovered: about the Founders, Dumbledore, the Order, James, Lily, Sirius, the Blacks (as predicted by Wendy), Snape, the Malfoys. Harry will have learned from Dumbledore that he needs History. One professor will always be at Hogwarts: Professor Binns. The Room of Requirement could turn into a specialized library. The Cemetery at Godric's Hollow could have information on its tombs. Florean Fortescue may have information. Hagrid, too, about Harry's parents. Aberforth.

John:

1. The unknown Horcruxes are [1] the Mirror of Erised or Hufflepuff's cup transfigured into the house cup, [2] Harry's scar, and [3] Voldemort's wand. Voldemort tried to make his wand into a Horcrux after killing Lily; this caused two pieces of his soul to attach to the wand because of the two murders he had just committed. One of these soul fragments caused the wand to backfire during the failed AK and make Harry a Horcrux.

2. We will learn along the way to book's finish that Draco is a werewolf, Trelawney is Bellatrix, Pettigrew is Lupin, and that Snape and Slughorn have both played Dumbledore as Polyjuice stand-ins.

3. Harry seems to die in a beheading but escapes in a headless hat. Severus Snape sings away the scar in some sectumsempra surgery. Neville, Hagrid, and Luna are the great heroes of the last battle which I had hoped would feature Norbert the Norwegian Ridgeback (but how does he get into King's Cross Station?).

4. Fleur and Bill die but not before giving birth to a son, the orphan that is the Philosopher's Stone (and return to the beginning of the books, cycles complete). Expect the end to echo the beginning strongly; vanishing glass, Dumbledore, Hagrid, and McGonagall conferring, the Dursleys, maybe even a return trip to the

Hut-on-the-Rock, The Sea, in addition to the orphan child.

5. The three Hogswarts Hermaphrodites, Harry, Severus, and Tom "Twin" Riddle, meet in a death embrace; the Dark Lord is destroyed in a something like a love electrocution. Slughorn/Dumbledore explains all to Harry at story's end.

Well, when Book 7 is published, likely in the summer of 2007, we'll see which of these three Theorists will be judged Champion. You have read little consensus on nearly every prediction — simple and complex.

So, have we spoiled book 7 for you? Did we accurately divine the activites in book 6? There is no way of knowing at this point in time. Jo made one comment regarding Dumbledore in August 2006 causing us to frantically review the logic in our theories. The point of this exercise is to look at the clues, triangulate and research the data, develop a theory, and then see if it has a place with the "Unified Theory of Everything" (and perhaps have some intellectual fun). If we have it wrong, then so be it. The essays in this collection are meant to make you think about the Potterverse in a new light. If we manage to get something right… well, that is gravy.

There is a famous film called RASHOMON by Japanese director Akira Kurosawa. The movie is about uncovering the truth based on conflicting accounts of an event. Perceptions by the witnesses result in substantially different, but equally plausible interpretations. Is that what you have experienced here as well? All of us read the exact same words Jo wrote for HALF-BLOOD PRINCE, and we all ended up in different predictive places. This phenomenon likely says something about us as theorists, but it also says something about Jo's mystery writing abilities: they are highly effective. — W.B. Harte

Finis

About the Children's High-Level Group

The contributors to this collection are donating a portion of the profits from the sale of this book to Children's High Level Group (CHLG), a charity Ms. Rowling helped found in 2005. Two of us have ties to Romania and the others believe in the importance of the work CHLG is doing. Thank you for joining us in supporting their efforts to help children in Eastern Europe.

From their web site: http://www.chlg.info/content_pages/02.html

WHAT IS THE CHILDREN'S HIGH LEVEL GROUP?

The Children's High Level Group (CHLG) is a charity whose mission is to improve the well-being, health and protection of vulnerable children. We were founded by, amongst others, MEP Emma Nicholson and the author J K Rowling in 2005, who were very deeply moved by the poverty, sickness and maltreatment of children and decided to act.

WHY IS THE CHILDREN'S VOICE CAMPAIGN CENTRED ON EASTERN EUROPE?

Initially we have focused our activities in Eastern Europe where practices such as the caging of children and infants remain a matter of concern. CHLG is targeting a number of countries where it can make a difference for children across a range of issues. These countries include Bulgaria, Czech Republic, Moldova, Slovakia, Romania and the Ukraine. One of our principal aims is to ensure that the common minimum United Nations standards of child care and protection are observed everywhere in Eastern Europe. By countries that are members of the European Union and those that are not.

CAN THE CHILDREN'S VOICE CAMPAIGN REALLY MAKE A DIFFERENCE?

We target the highest ranking officials and decision makers within the government of these countries to effect change. We have found that these are the people most effective at bringing about an immediate change to the way childcare operates in these countries.

All of the countries where we currently operate are signatories to the UN Convention on the right of the child and we work with these countries to enable them to meet their obligations under the Convention.

Romania is an example of a European country that is attempting to improve conditions of the children in its care. Around 22,000 Romanian children have been returned to family-based care in the past four years, with over half of this number returning to their parents or relatives. A change in the law in Romania means it is now not possible to institutionalise children under two years old.

There is still a great deal of work to be done in countries like Romania, but the changes that have already taken in place, in a relatively short space of time, give us hope, and provide inspiration for neighbouring countries where the maltreatment of children is still taking place.

The layout and design of this book was produced by Joyce Odell of Red Hen Publications, utilizing graphics resources from Dynamic Graphics/Liquid Library, The Pepin Press, and the incomparable Marwan Aridi.

It should be noted that inspiration for the design of this book has been provided by the classic board game of CLUE™ from Parker Brothers.

The text has been set in the ITC Bailey Sans family, from Bitstream, with a number of custom modifications. Title and Initals are set in Pablo from Letraset. URLs are set in OCR A & OCR B. P22's DaVinci Forward has also been used in this project, as has been Cassady & Greene's Black Knight. Additional decorative elements have been provided by Letraset's PF Household Items, Bil's DECOrations and BelfryBats Demo.

http://www.redhen-publications.com

Printed in the United States
66819LVS00005B/172-177

9 780972 322119